THE BOYS FROM BAGHDAD

Dedicated to the 300 or more
(the number is still rising) private-military contractors,
who, for money and adventure, have lost their lives in Iraq,
including Akihiko Saito – *Legio Patria Nostra*.

THE
BOYS
FROM
BAGHDAD.

From the Foreign Legion to the Killing Fields of Iraq

SIMON LOW

MAINSTREAM
PUBLISHING

EDINBURGH AND LONDON

First published in Great Britain in 2007 by
MAINSTREAM PUBLISHING COMPANY
(EDINBURGH) LTD
7 Albany Street
Edinburgh EH1 3UG

ISBN 9781845962838

This book is a work of non-fiction based on the life,
experiences and recollections of the author. In some cases
names of people have been changed to protect the privacy
of others. The author has stated to the publishers that, except
in such minor respects, the contents of this book are true.

A catalogue record for this book is available
from the British Library

Typeset in Sabon and Frutiger

Printed and bound in Great Britain by
William Clowes Ltd, Beccles, Suffolk

ACKNOWLEDGEMENTS

This book would never have happened if Geds had not persuaded me to get my act together and write about my experiences in 'burning Baghdad', as he so aptly put it. Cheers, mate, and thanks for the loan of the laptop.

As in all walks of life, having true friends, be it on the end of a telephone or when together, makes life good, even when things get a little heavy, so thanks Geds and Sarah, Al and Sharon, and Dave and Zoe – you all kept me believing.

A special thanks for the endless cups of tea made by Ruth, who also managed to sit and listen to me spouting off every line of this book, over and over, again and again, time after time, change after change, with grace and selflessness – she put me to shame on several occasions.

Finally, to my editors J.P. and Paul M., who calmly put it all together – thank you.

'Run for your life from any man who tells you that
money is evil.'
Ayn Rand

'A viler evil than to murder a man is to sell him suicide as
an act of virtue.'
Ayn Rand

'Nothing in life is so exhilarating as to be shot at
without result.'
Winston Churchill

'Dogs that are fierce in the woods are quiet at home.'
Anonymous

CONTENTS

PROLOGUE   9

1   HAVE GUNS, WILL TRAVEL   11
2   ANBAR PROVINCE AMBUSH   32
3   THE ROAD TO SAMARA   57
4   GSXR600 MEETS HILTON PARK LANE   77
5   BACK TO BAGHDAD   150
6   OUT ON THE TILES   186
7   TIKRIT NEXT STOP   197
8   KIRKUK FOR CHRISTMAS   209
9   THE VORTEX   263

EPILOGUE   276
WHERE ARE THEY NOW?   279
GLOSSARY   282

PROLOGUE

The distance left to Ar Ramadi was down to about 100 kilometres. If we continued to make good time, we'd be safe and sound in less than two hours. This meant a shower and a shave, chicken and chips, and only the occasional mortar lobbed into the base at night to dodge. The lead elements of the convoy were now about 250 metres up ahead, and my vehicle had just passed under one of the many desolate bridges that spanned the road. Suddenly, Allah gave out an almighty roar. From the left-hand rear window he had begun firing his Kalashnikov on full automatic. I sprang left, looking out of the driver's window, and saw several prone figures positioned 300 metres or so out in the sand. 'This is it, this is it,' raced through my mind. At the same time, I registered that Allah was still firing and that Abid One (we had another Iraqi called Abid, hence the number) had tensed right up, his knuckles glowing white with the grip he now had on the steering wheel as the spine-chilling cracks of incoming rounds reverberated loudly through the desert air.

Instinctively, I pushed my Kalashnikov behind Abid One, and with the barrel out of the window cocked the weapon and let rip with long bursts. Taking this action seemed to distance me from the frenzy of what was happening, making the scene almost surreal. I could clearly see men crouched and firing, and I tried to creep rounds onto them through the clouds of sand that my preceding bullets had kicked up.

All of a sudden, my weapon stopped. 'Fuck me! Fuck me! Mag change! Mag change!' Fumbling as I tried to get a magazine out of my chest webbing, fear was now getting a grip on me, and I was starting to panic. Glimpsing Allah, I realised with alarm that he had stopped firing and was also frantically trying to change mags.

Suddenly, I was thrown sideways from the impact of a massive barrage of rounds whacking into our vehicle. Abid One froze, and I felt the vehicle begin to decelerate. The realisation was instant: along an insignificant stretch of black-top road, lost in a wilderness of rock and sand deep in the notorious Anbar Province in Western Iraq, my 42 years on this planet were about to end. 'I'm going to die. Fuck me, I'm going to die . . .'

1

HAVE GUNS, WILL TRAVEL

I poured a dab of milk into my tea and stirred, clinking the spoon twice on the side of the cup, then sat down on the folding bed. 'Good boy,' I said, fondling Spinney's ears as he nuzzled affectionately against me. He, not surprisingly, was tired too. Even a boisterous three-year-old lurcher addicted to the chase needs a kip now and again. Through the caravan window I could see the dawn light was beginning to break over the moors. It had been a good night, and our patience had paid off. Two rabbits for the pot tomorrow.

After a year as my constant companion on Bodmin, Spinney and I were now completely in tune. After sunset, he and I would sit together, Spinney winding the breeze, both of us anticipating those ideal conditions for lamping when the leaves gently rustle and a soft drizzle falls. As soon as I put on my wax jacket, which I only used for hunting, he'd know the game was afoot and start wailing with uncontrollable excitement. Once out in the fields, though, he was all poacher, following my pace loyally and obediently for however long it took. Our bond had formed through a mutual love of wild and windy nights: nights out where we shouldn't be; nights abroad while other men slept.

Turning on the radio, there was more news about Iraq. Violent fanatics and suicide bombers were now streaming into the country by the thousand, hell-bent on blowing themselves, the infidels and anyone who sided with them to kingdom come. I decided to ring Jock tomorrow. What was I saying? It was tomorrow.

The Great Western train crept quietly into Paddington Station and came to a gentle halt. After the farewells to my mum and sister Sophie, I'd been glad of the swift, smooth journey up from Plymouth. Spinney, of course, had been hard to leave, but I wasn't going to be away for ever. If anything did happen to me, I knew he'd be safe and happy enough with Sophie and her husband Michael. Jock, my ex-Legionnaire mate already in Baghdad to set up a convoy team for Armor Group, had seemed delighted to get my phone call, or at the very least had told me to get my arse up to the office because he wanted me out there pronto. I didn't need telling twice.

Armor Group's offices were located just behind Victoria Station, not far from Buckingham Palace, and as it was a fine May day I decided to exit the tube at Green Park and enjoy a walk. I had been engaged by Armor Group (formerly Defence Systems Limited, and known to all and sundry as DSL) several times on and off since leaving the Legion in 1998. A lot of my mates had worked for them, too, and it was always fairly easy to pick up casual assignments overseas, either for a short-term daily rate or on year-long contracts. The lifestyle suited me. My seven years in the British Army, even the following ten in the Foreign Legion, seemed almost boringly predictable compared to life as a private-security contractor. You never knew what was around the corner and could to a large extent choose when and where you worked.

On arriving at the office entrance, I pressed the intercom, and when a female voice answered, I said, 'Simon Low to see Lucy.' I then took the lift to the fifth floor. The lady on the front desk was, as usual, pleased to see me and asked how I was. She then gave me a visitor's pass and said with a smile, 'You know where you're going!' Yes, I knew where I was going. In the main office, with its tall windows overlooking some famous London landmarks, several nice girls sat typing. One said, 'Lucy's round at the hotel in Buckingham Gate giving a presentation.'

I went round to the hotel and walked in on Lucy – a mature Miss Moneypenny type – in the middle of presenting a slide show to 20 or more suited and booted ex-regular soldiers in serried ranks of plastic conference chairs. 'Gentlemen, this is Simon Low,' said Lucy. The guys watching the slide show swivelled round to scrutinise me. 'Simon has worked for us for many years and tomorrow will be deploying for Iraq.' Embarrassed at being stuck on a pedestal, I simply said hi, desperately wanting to slide into the nearest available chair and play the grey man. Instead, I forced myself nonchalantly to the second row from the front as the next colourful image of a Baghdad street clicked up. Discussing the current situation for private-military contractors (PMC), it emerged that some operatives were being ambushed three times a day.

When the presentation was over, I grabbed a cup of coffee from a thermo-pot on the white crisply laundered tablecloth and had a chat with Lucy, catching up on the news of my old colleagues. Though informal, she maintained an air of consummate professionalism, keeping our conversation on a need-to-know basis, and asked me what I'd been up to since last working for Armor. After I had finished my coffee, I returned to the office, where I signed the service agreement and picked up my air tickets. I didn't read the agreement.

The money was of no great importance; I just wanted to get over there and into some action. That stuff about three ambushes a day had been music to my ears. The Armor girls all wished me safe and well, and I said my farewells. After that, it was round to Harley Street for my pre-deployment medical. Usually, I'd use my own doctor in the West Country, but there wasn't time.

That night, I took the tube to my younger sister Rachel's flat in Epping, where I spent most of the night watching telly. I was already missing Spinney, and I realised, with a sharp pang of loneliness, that my separation from him was my only regret about going. The next day, I went to Oxford Street and Covent Garden to do some shopping for lightweight shirts and trousers, a digital camera, some sunscreen, and lipsalve. Then I had a pizza and a couple of beers before heading to Heathrow for the 2200 BA flight to Kuwait. From there I was escorted to the US airbase and transferred to a Hercules. An hour and forty minutes later, the Hercules touched down at Baghdad International Airport (BIAP). Jock, a Burger King meal in one hand and an AK-47 in the other, was on the tarmac waiting for me.

The outfit Jock had got me into was the Armor Group Iraq Convoy Team, contracted to the US Army J4 Logistics Unit based in Baghdad. J4's official name for us was the now standard private-military contractors – only in layman's language were we hired guns, or what used to be called mercenaries. Since the invasion, the Americans had set up numerous military forward operational posts across Iraq, many of them separated by hundreds of miles of desert. These outposts required regular supplies of military and other equipment, most of which had to be transported across country by lorry. With the number of armed elements in the country who objected to the US presence growing, these clusters of heavily laden, slow-moving civilian vehicles regularly plying out from Baghdad and into the wilderness were becoming increasingly prone to attack. Our job was to ride alongside and defend them.

Our team consisted of me, a pool of 18 or so Iraqis and Dave. Dave, like me, had served ten years in the Foreign Legion, attaining the rank of sergeant, and was, to put it bluntly, 'mustard'. Of Irish descent, he was a hard and serious man who didn't take kindly to fools. He saved several lives while we were out there, not only by his actions during ambushes, but also because he took a stand and refused certain missions. If something sounded dodgy, Dave wasn't afraid to say no, even to the highest-ranking officers in J4.

Back then there was a lot of off-the-cuff, fastball stuff – 2004 being early days for the distribution of logistics throughout Iraq – but since it was our lives in danger out on the road, certain regulations (regs) still had to be respected. Fastballs were OK as long as drills remained in place. Some golden rules had to be observed no matter what; in particular that all military vehicles on the transporters must be kept covered over at all times and that there should be no more than ten articulated lorries in a convoy. Most of the dilapidated Iraqi articulated lorries (artics) could reach speeds of no more than 60 kilometres per hour, and our pace was obviously dictated by the slowest. A 'safe' speed for us would have been 120 kilometres per hour all the way! Also, we only had four escort vehicles, and so we most definitely did not want any fastballs to unknown forward operational bases (FOBs), especially up north, Mosul way!

There was so much gear to be transported that quite often on arrival at the Abu Ghraib distribution warehouse, the REMFs (rear-echelon mother fuckers) would try to palm us off with as much as they could get away with, to whatever destination. They once tried to send us to some unknown FOB located north-west of Mosul. Dave, being the convoy team leader, flatly refused the mission, arguing that we would do it but needed to have more information first, such as definite final-destination grids. We also wanted rendezvous points (RVs) en route and up-to-date intelligence on the specific area. Word-of-mouth directions like 'just turn left after Mosul', 'bear right at the first fork', etc., were a recipe for disaster and in no way acceptable. We would have been as well stopping to ask the way from a group of intense-looking bearded gentlemen positioned on high ground. When these not-unreasonable conditions couldn't be met, if my memory serves me well, Dave's words to the REMFs were, 'You can fuck right off.'

On one occasion when Dave refused a mission, the bod at the warehouse proceeded to call the colonel in charge of J4, who demanded in person that Dave execute the mission. He didn't. This was a brave decision on Dave's part, as Armor Group Iraq was paid a hefty sum for the contract, and to lose it would be, to say the least, major. Finally, a team from Custer Battles (another private-security company) agreed to take it on. Their team leader was killed just after midday. He was 25 years old. Dave, what can I say? Thanks, mate. Mind you, your vehicle would probably have been first up in smoke!

The 18 or so Iraqis on our team were all supposed to be ex-special forces and to have fought in the infamous Iran–Iraq War. Well, a couple most definitely had, but the others just made up the numbers. These Iraqis had been recruited by Armor Group staff at our Baghdad HQ, and with several contracts to fulfil throughout Iraq, plus all the other private-security companies hiring, CVs and interviews weren't exactly top priority. As regards their service history, there was also a problem with what was meant by 'special forces', and the Iraqis just seemed to back up each other's stories.

There seemed no way of checking them out, though we did get rid of a few guys who were clearly downright dangerous when it came to weapons handling and negligent discharges. When hiring Iraqis, it seemed to be a case of putting bums on seats, regardless of the candidate's experience. It was, therefore, of the utmost importance for Dave and me to space out our Iraqi recruits along the convoy, as it would seriously weaken our capability to react in a firefight if any team members didn't pull their weight! Language was also a problem, as only a handful spoke English, and out of that handful only two were of a standard to translate: Ahmed and Mohammed.

Ahmed's English was perfect, and he became Dave's right-hand Iraqi and driver. Having a driver that spoke English was a bonus; that he was a good driver was even better. Ahmed was about forty-five and a family man with two children. He was soft spoken, very polite and always well turned out. He had done his national service and could handle a gun, but I always felt sorry for him, because it was plain to see that he was an ordinary, peace-loving, wanna-bring-my-kids-up family man. However, since the American-led invasion, Baghdad was a dog-eat-dog place, employment was very hard to come by and there was definitely no help from the almost non-existent government. This meant Ahmed had no choice but to leave his family for a job that would take him to some of the most dangerous places on earth for a monthly salary of $500. Nevertheless, he was to react well, even after being wounded.

Mohammed's English was not as good as Ahmed's, though still adequate. Unlike Ahmed, Mohammed had been a career soldier in Saddam Hussein's so-called elite presidential guard. He often boasted that he had taken care of an American tank somewhere near Al Hillah. I very much doubted this, as even though he followed orders in our subsequent firefights, his demeanour was that of someone on the verge of a trembling, pop-eyed panic attack. I didn't like or trust the man, or his brother Abid Two. The pair of them sported full beards, and both were devout Muslims – it was Abid Two who seemed to be in charge of all the Iraqis during their prayer sessions. I always kept a good eye on them, especially before setting off on a mission, watching for any sign of betrayal.

When on a mission, Mohammed was vehicle two's commander, so at least it had someone on board who could understand the radio messages and even possibly react to them. The driver for my vehicle was Abid One: no beard, no English, but he could drive fairly well. He was about 35, single and, before the first ambush, good at his job. My gunner was called Allah, who, along with his AK-47, carried the belt-fed PKM machine gun. For me, Allah was the best of the bunch, an ex-Iraqi para who most definitely had seen active service in the Iran–Iraq War. He had two words of English: 'good', always said twice in a high-pitched voice, and 'no good', said twice in a very low voice, followed by two tuts while he simultaneously waved his index finger in front of his face. I trusted implicitly his judgement about suspect cars and occupants and would respond swiftly. Allah was my right-hand man – someone I knew wouldn't let me down, nor I he, if I could help it.

Attacks from the insurgents came in many forms, including remotely detonated bombs (IEDs), mortars, mines, suicide bombers with explosives strapped to them and car bombs (VBIEDs). The last could either be parked on the roadside or driven at you by a suicide bomber. Then there was good old small-arms fire, or, in some cases, not-so-small-arms fire. These attacks were not weekly occurrences but happened on a several-times-a-day basis. The world's media report regularly on the numbers of US and British military killed and wounded in Iraq, but there is also a high attrition rate within the private-security sector that doesn't always make the news. Armor Group, during my fifteen months with them in Iraq, lost five PMCs, and that's not counting the Iraqis. (Since I left, they have continued to lose men.) Five may not sound a big deal, but as a percentage of the men on the ground for Armor Group Iraq I think it equates to something like one in every twenty-five. Some of the other private-security firms' attrition rates were higher. Hart, a British company based in Cyprus, lost all bar one of a twelve-man convoy team in a single ambush. One of those killed was an ex-Legionnaire I'd served alongside, a Japanese man called Saito, who had more than 20 years' service under his belt. Saito was a very professional soldier, but the insurgents were fast stepping up their levels of violence, catching a lot of security companies with their trousers down on the logistics side, notably regarding the calibre of their personnel (both Iraqi and expat), weapons and vehicles. This is no reflection on the bods on the ground (although the abilities of some were highly questionable), but rather on individuals higher up the food chain. I know that viewpoint is going to rattle a lot of influential cages, including at Armor Group, but we could have been better equipped, to say the least. For instance, after our third ambush, Dave and I were at our wits' end, shitting it and demanding that we be given better armoured vehicles (ours were soft skinned) with mounted guns on the back and to have only expat private-security boys, i.e. men who'd go bang-bang in ambushes, something a lot of the Iraqis had difficulty with.

The firm's falling behind the game had a lot to do with the bottom line. An Iraqi earns less in a month than we were earning in a day. And an armoured vehicle needs a lot more Co-op stamps to buy than a non-armoured one. This was all pretty understandable, because Armor was in Iraq for financial gain, just as I was. But even given the firm's profit agenda, an element of false economy was surely emerging. At that point, we in convoy alone had already lost five vehicles in three ambushes, not to mention the fact that several of our men had been wounded.

The firm's stance on this, or at least what filtered down to little old Dave and me, was that Armor Group did not want to be seen as a private-military company. Fucking hell, Dave! There's me and you trotting back and forth from Baghdad to Fallujah, Ar Ramadi, Najaf and Mosul, and although we haven't got Red Cross parcels, we'll tell the insurgents not to shoot cos we don't belong to one of those horrible private-military companies! Or worse still, imagine this one in my local rag: 'Simon Low was killed in Iraq whilst en route to Fallujah. He worked for Armor Group, which is not a private-military company'.

I can just see all the head-sheds breathing a big sigh of relief at the non-association. Who gives a toss if Armor is or is not a private-military company? It's all very ambiguous, but Armor Group is, in fact, a security company that has armed contractors in Iraq, along with many others. Dave and I thought about making a couple of placards up and in good old American style marching in a little circle around the Armor Group HQ in Baghdad chanting, 'We want big guns. When do we want 'em? Right now! We want armoured vehicles. When do we want 'em? Right now!' In the end, we settled for, 'Right, that's the last fucking ambush I'm gonna do for you until our terms are met.' And we promptly sat in the villa getting paid, just running up and down to the BIAP to pick up and drop off bods. I say just. The stretch of road from our villa to the airport was officially the most dangerous highway on the planet, and many US soldiers and private-security operatives met their maker there.

There is video footage of a team working for another private-security company on the BIAP road. Whilst waiting for the US Military to clear an IED further up ahead, they position their three unmarked cars in a sterile zone (clear of all other traffic) between the US Military in front and the waiting Baghdad traffic stopped behind. The footage of the attack was filmed from a camera strapped to the dashboard of the third vehicle. For a few seconds, all is quiet, then the thwacking sound of incoming rounds can be heard and clouds of dust are kicked up around the two vehicles positioned approximately 30 metres in front. The gunfire (which sounded heavy, like 12.7-mm rounds) was concentrated and accurate, killing three of the team. Sam, a former marine, can be seen reacting swiftly, along with the others, doing their best to control a bad situation. I only watched the video once, as it made my blood boil, giving me an intense craving to hunt down and massacre those fucking insurgents, strictly in accordance with the Geneva Convention, of course. But forget all this palaver for the moment.

On most missions, the vehicle under my command was the last of the four and the very last one in the entire convoy, fulfilling the CAT (counter-attack team) role. Our weaponry wasn't really all that spectacular; mind you, there wasn't much we could have done with anything big, as our four convoy vehicles were five-door silver Mitsubishi Pajeros. Every man carried a 9-mm pistol, and along with this the drivers each had a Heckler & Koch MP5. Every other man had an AK-47, and my vehicle also had the PKM. I made sure my AK-47 was of Eastern-bloc manufacture and not some crappy Iraqi copy. Mine was Hungarian and well put together. However, just as most train drivers are not train spotters, I am not a weapons anorak. The stock-in-trade of a soldier is not armaments, per se, but the weapon-handling drills: stoppages, magazine changes, firing, stripping and assembling. I'm always wary of someone who goes into mind-boggling detail about the specifications of the latest must-have piece of Gucci hardware – shouldn't they be in a workshop somewhere mending the bloody things? Dave and I used to enjoy winding these types up sometimes, and if we found ourselves in earshot of some fierce-looking security operative, who for some reason felt the need to wear full kit, armour and weapons when eating in the American chow halls, we'd start spouting off verbal diarrhoea about some fictional new weapon we'd just thought up.

My main responsibility, as the name CAT suggests, was to counter any attack. My vehicle would bring up the rear, and depending on whether we were in town or country, all other traffic had to be either kept well back behind us or filtered passed the convoy in a controlled manner. I was also to cover any vehicles coming from the other direction that Dave, signalling over the radio from his position up front, thought looked suss. Such vehicles included Mercedes, BMWs and 4x4s moving at a rapid rate of knots. Why? It was a common tactic for insurgents, especially in the Mosul area, to get towards the end of a convoy and then let rip with AK-47s, PKMs or whatever arms they had. With the speed afforded by their vehicles, they could reap their carnage and be long gone before you even realised what the fucking hell was happening or that your oppo was dead! This scenario occurred with one of our Armor Group teams on another contract up in Mosul, killing one expat security operative. His brother was in the same vehicle. So, if Dave signalled that an oncoming vehicle was suss, I would tell my driver to position our Mitsubishi so that we were clearly visible and get Allah to aim his weapon out of the driver's-side window. This left any potential attacker in no doubt about our firepower and readiness to use it. Very much a case of 'You really want some of this?' Not very hearts and minds, of course. Fucking right it wasn't! Hearts and minds was for uniformed armies, paid by their governments to rid the world of evil dictators hoarding weapons of mass destruction, and those who'd like to teach the world to sing in perfect harmony. I mean, do you really think that when answering the call for 'ex-military types for interesting work in Iraq', the desire to win hearts and minds was what got the boys on the phone? There might have been some crusaders out there, but what I wanted was adventure – got guns, will travel, and, fuck me, my bank manager's gonna want to be my best mate! Fuck the family driving too fast in the opposite direction. That kind of drill kept *my* heart and mind in one piece.

Who knows how many of those fast-moving vehicles carried insurgents? There were many other situations in which we used drills that were not strictly, or even remotely, politically correct. But I had reached the conclusion whilst fighting in Africa with the Foreign Legion that it was better to be on the 10 o'clock news (in those days it was the 9 o'clock news) as a suspected war criminal than simply as another military fatality. That might sound very OTT, but there is a memorable lesson to be learned from the story of some Belgian peacekeepers in Rwanda, whose mission was to ensure the safety of a female Burundi politician. They found themselves surrounded by a group of the opposing faction, who demanded the politician be handed over to them. The officer in charge on the ground relayed the situation back to his HQ, who ordered him to comply and surrender the woman. She was promptly executed on the spot. Her executioners then asked for the peacekeepers' weapons. Again, the officer consulted HQ, who once more instructed him to comply. This time, however, they were not killed, at least not straight away. First, they had their Achilles tendons severed before being slaughtered one by one. This version of events was relayed to me by an officer from Luxembourg, who had done the Belgian Staff College, when he was attending a course with the Foreign Legion. Events like this underline the need for decisions to be made on the ground. My life and the lives of my men are my top priority, regardless of any mandate or politically correct agenda. This, I hasten to add, would never knowingly manifest itself in the cold-blooded murder of anyone.

The Geneva Convention, I believe, states that women and children should never be used as cover. Well, when the convoy approached known hot spots for IEDs or small-arms attacks, we would let a volume of cars build up behind us for a few miles, whenever the traffic situation allowed it. Then, just before we got to the point of potential attack, we'd wave the tailback through en masse. This meant that when the head of the convoy hit the danger area, there was already a nose-to-tail stream of traffic to our right or left and stretching well ahead and behind. Whether it was left or right was dictated by the relative ambush potential of the terrain on either flank; or else it was just a 50–50 chance. There would be all sorts of people in such a stream of vehicles: women, children, bakers, bus drivers, yet-to-be-born-again suicide bombers and insurgents dicking (sussing out you and your drills) our tactics on their days off. 'Yeah, mate, it's the other convoys that go through in a sterile zone that you want, not us.'

On one occasion, when our vehicles were low on juice, we were obliged to look for a civilian petrol station. Orders were issued over the radio to stop at the first place we came to and then form up in all-round defence while we commandeered the pumps. One of the consequences of the occupation of Iraq was a crippling shortage of petrol, resulting in lines of volatile pissed-off civilians queuing for days while slowly inching their cars forward. Often a family would take it in turns to sit in the queue while the others went home to eat, sleep or go about their business. Anyway, having found a station, we debussed in seconds, commandeered the pumps and took up all-round defensive positions. Why all this pomp and ceremony among a bunch of civilians? Because, like all terrorists, insurgents in Iraq are capable of mounting a reactive operation within minutes, especially when the locals are armed with mobiles and sat phones, ready to give a quiet and deadly tip-off. As the vehicles were being refuelled, I positioned myself with my back to the rear wall of the petrol station. Crouched in the nearest car and staring up at me wide-eyed were two innocent-looking young children: sandbags mark two; they don't stack as well as the mark ones, but . . .

Dave paid the cashier for the petrol, and we roared off never to darken their doorstep again. Obviously, to avoid a recurrence of this, our administration had to be better. To run dry once was acceptable, twice a crime. It wasn't a good idea to carry cans of reserve petrol on the escort vehicles, offering an easy bullseye to the insurgents, so we would strap a few cans to the backs of the lorries instead.

One of the biggest liabilities that we faced was the poor soldiering quality of our Iraqi colleagues. However, we hoped that some intense training back in the Green Zone would sort the problem out. At that time, the Green Zone housed the Coalition Provisional Authority (CPA) – about to make way on 30 June that year for the Iraqi Interim Government, ha-ha – in the grounds of Saddam's palace. Near the palace, Saddam had built a large ceremonial square, the 'Butcher's' very own Horse Guards Parade. At its entrance were two fifty-feet long crossed swords. There was also a memorial from the Iran–Iraq War, a kind of sculpture made from hundreds of soldiers' helmets melded together. This ceremonial square now made an ideal training ground, being large enough for the dry drills required to bring those that needed it up to scratch. Unfortunately, the place soon resembled a council swimming baths at half-term – fucking crowded! And because it was just me and Dave on convoy, and there was no other team with whom to alternate the missions, it meant that we were unable to spend much time training our boys.

We would deploy on a mission, be it a one or four-day job, then return to Baghdad to refuel and sort out any material or equipment shortfalls, meanwhile reading the updated int-reps (intelligence reports) before redeploying the next day. This regime continued relentlessly for three months, but we weren't complaining; in fact, we were loving it. Just me, Dave and our Iraqis, trekking like latter-day Lawrences of Arabia all over this much-talked-about country, to which the eyes and ears of the world were tuned – it was the stuff of folklore and a privilege.

This, of course, was before we started getting targeted on a regular basis. I suppose we were both a bit naive up until then. Death and destruction, we soon realised, were constant, not only in Baghdad, but also in many parts of the north and west of Iraq. Our training was on-the-job, and we were fucking lucky if we could learn by our mistakes. As the old saying on the firing range goes, 'Targets will fall when hit.' Simplicity. If you're not happy, fill yer boots. Welcome to convoy.

There we were, working non-stop, just the two of us, while other Armor contracts had up to twelve expats on one project. VIP had about a dozen, but in the first three months that I was in Iraq they only ever had one bigwig to protect. Convoy smelled of death. If the other lads had their way, we would have walked around ringing a bell shouting, 'Convoy, convoy, unclean, unclean...' Even our villa was far away from the others. Each project team had its own accommodation, none of which were in secured areas. A little reminder of this fact occurred one morning. The majority of bombs that target buildings in Baghdad go off at around 0800. At that hour, we would usually be doing final checks on weapons and equipment before deploying on a mission. We learned that it was more prudent to wait for this moment and thus allow any IEDs to wreak their carnage before we set out. Part of our SOPs (standard operating procedures) was to lie up on the roof of the villa just before leaving and survey the immediate and far-reaching areas of Baghdad, using a tried-and-tested method of observation: presence of abnormal; absence of normal. As we watched, bombs would often go off, sometimes in the distance, sometimes just a bit too close by. Then there would be the chatter of answering small arms. These observations would determine the route we would take to any of our various pick-up points in Baghdad, such as the Abu Ghraib warehouse or the police academy. One morning, there was an almighty explosion, which shattered all the glass in the villa and threw up clouds of thick choking dust everywhere. It took a few seconds for me to realise that the intended target was not us but a Kurdish centre about 100 metres north of us, which was completely obliterated. Later that day, after we'd deployed, a forearm was found by our cleaner in the grounds of the villa. You can imagine the scene: 'Who left this lying about? I'm sick and tired of picking up bloody arms after people!'

The Armor Group HQ villa had a much narrower escape one morning when a suicide car bomber detonated just outside, killing an Iraqi minister and demolishing nigh on one side of the offices, which luckily weren't occupied, as the lazy bastards hadn't yet started work bashing the keys on their typewriters. I am not going to reveal the specific districts our villas are located in, since, to my knowledge, they are still operational. However, they are all in downtown

Baghdad, which is, in some ways, much less of a target than the Green Zone and Camp Victory, which are magnets for mortars. (Camp Victory is a US military base, covering some five square miles and incorporating Baghdad International Airport.) One unlucky individual met his maker whilst taking a shower in Camp Victory. That mortar, from manufacture to impact, must, as the cliché goes, have had the guy's name on it.

Prior to all deployments from our villa, the two static Iraqi guards that remained behind to secure the villa would be tasked to take up positions 30 metres either side on the residential street outside. Those Iraqis not deploying would take up fire positions on the villa roof, with one or two of them always slightly visible. Our neighbours were just everyday Iraqi families who were well aware of our presence, which meant the bad guys also knew we were there.

The SOP from on high – in fact, from our in-country boss at the time – was that all movement in and out of the villa was to be as discreet as possible. That is all very well if your daily routines are of a fairly casual and unpredictable nature, like those of the HQ staff. We in convoy, however, usually left the villa within the same one-hour window every time we deployed. We could either turn left or right, and at one end of the road was a fairly major highway that could easily serve as a fire base, with good means of exfiltration after the shoot – 'Shoot and scoot'. Again, we had to mount a strong 'you want some of this' visible deterrent, as it's not the shoot that seals your fate, it's the recce or dicking beforehand!

To reinforce the cover, my team would deploy first and secure the relevant junction, picking up our position once the other vehicles had passed. Also, the routes in and out would be checked by our Iraqis beforehand on their way to the villa. None of this was watertight, but our reckoning was that if other teams weren't doing this from their villas, they would be the ones targeted. A case of, 'It's them you want, mate, not us.' I'm a great believer in that.

Once on the main roads of downtown Baghdad, it was heads-up time, and we were all switched on for possible dangers: faces at windows, people on roofs, occupied vehicles and unusually parked cars, such as BMWs, Mercedes or 4x4s with blacked-out windows, positioned up ahead or following at a discreet distance. Then there were the suicide car bombers; the intelligence we received on these was fairly general: for example, to be on the lookout for a make and colour of car believed to have been fitted and ready to blow.

From leaving one location to arriving at the next, there was never a dull moment, and the safest way to drive was fucking fast. The only thing to stop for was any scared US squaddie holding up a clenched fist, as they shoot first and don't ask questions after. The Italian team that extradited a kidnapped journalist found this out to their detriment. One of the security team sent to pick up the journalist after her ordeal was shot dead by a US soldier manning a checkpoint. As the team's vehicle approached, for reasons best known to the Americans manning it, shots were fired by at least one soldier, killing one of the security contractors and wounding the journalist. The Italians stated afterwards that the brave actions of the killed security contractor, who threw himself in front of the journalist to shield her from the hail of bullets, saved her life and prevented a perverse ending to her hostage drama.

The flow of traffic around Baghdad has been seriously affected by the concrete blast walls that have been erected around sensitive sites, by the closure of main highways wherever they overlook US bases and by temporary diversions due to suspect or confirmed IEDs. The net result is gridlock. The Iraqis are quite resilient and adapt by using every available bit of hard standing or pavement and driving their cars up and down the same side of the road. You just have to go with it, forcing other cars off the road if need be in order to make any progress. All this whilst maintaining all-round observation. It is just one of several hardships endured by the locals on a daily basis and definitely doesn't help the so-called 'rebuilding Iraq' idea. We would clear a path by pointing our guns at all and sundry – not for the hell of it, but through sheer survival instinct and the imperative to keep moving. Teams were regularly targeted by insurgents on the Baghdad roads, and our aim was not to get into any scraps with them but to make ourselves as difficult to ambush as possible – a tactic known as hard-targeting. In theatres like Northern Ireland, hard-targeting would include squaddies being covered whilst moving fast over open ground, junctions or high and exposed areas. We just mutated this into hard-targeting in vehicles. It was not a hearts-and-minds winner with the Baghdad populace, but given the level of threat, fuck their bleeding hearts.

Not once whilst deploying on Baghdad streets did we get involved in a contact (firefight) with insurgents, though several other teams did. Our driving at times did border on the reckless, and this could have done for us on many occasions. There was a fine line between trying to get our Iraqi drivers good at fast, evasive driving, while, at the same time, getting them to stop short of the 'I'm a fucking nutter, foot to the floor, wind in your hair and hang on' school of motoring. My driver, Abid One, managed to succeed in putting the shits up me right from the start, but it didn't have anything to do with his driving. It was because of the ritual that he used to perform before getting under way, reciting some sort of mantra in a whispered mumble, accompanied by his right hand touching his forehead and then the vehicle. Afterwards, his whole demeanour would change, and he would become bright and perky again, ready for whatever the day would bring. Another cue for the ritual would be anytime we passed a burial ground or bombed-out vehicle. Nice touch that, Abid – lest we forget, or but for the grace of Allah, etc. Then again, none of us really knew what was out there waiting for us.

2

ANBAR PROVINCE AMBUSH

Anbar Province is situated west of Baghdad and is a stronghold of the Sunni Arab peoples. Located within Anbar lies what has become the most infamous place in American military history since Vietnam's Hue – Fallujah.

Fallujah might be described as a satellite town of Baghdad. Taking the main highway out of the capital, the last complex of buildings on the right is the scandalous Abu Ghraib Prison. Drive for another 45 minutes and Fallujah starts springing up about 100 metres away to the left of the highway, with a long line of villas in a perpetual state of semi-construction running parallel to the road for several kilometres. Some of these dwellings are inhabited, others have a look of abandonment. Perhaps there is a shortage of good builders – or live ones since the US Marines paid a visit.

Heading deeper into Fallujah, the buildings remain low-level but are more densely packed and dotted with frequent minarets. Off in the distance is the town centre, where clusters of larger buildings protrude into the desert sky. From the way our Iraqis said the word 'Fallujah', it was clear that they had a kind of admiration for the fighters and people of this town, whom, it has to be said, had put up fierce resistance to the best troops America has on offer – not once but on several occasions. And in the incident which provoked America's equally ignominious and unforgiving response, the Fallujans also showed the world their utter contempt for human decency, even in a time of war.

Not long after the ground war was declared officially over by George W. Bush, private-security companies began to establish footholds in and around Baghdad. The smell of money was irresistible, and SOPs were gonna be issued just as soon as! However, four fortune hunters got more than they bargained for in the great Iraq gold rush. The men were private-military contractors hired by the US firm Blackwater on a mission that would take them through Fallujah. The Blackwater four were swiftly set up, misguided by the Iraqi Police straight into a killing ground. It was a well-laid ambush, but the death of their prey wasn't enough for the murderers. The bodies of the hated invaders were stripped and dragged through the streets of Fallujah by a jubilant mob of all ages, then hung from a bridge and set alight. All's not always fair in love and war. A convoy team from Hart, diverted from the main drag, also met their ends, all bar one man, in the Anbar Province.

So that's Fallujah. An hour's drive further west along the same highway is Ar Ramadi, another stronghold of Sunni Arab resistance. And after Ar Ramadi you get the distinct impression you've dropped off the arse end of the world, as we were to find out . . .

As usual, there was gridlock in front of Abu Ghraib Prison on the highway leading west out of Baghdad. The prison was a veritable magnet for insurgents, who if not setting off an IED, would be attacking the building with firearms, letting their comrades held within know they were not forgotten.

It was 11 July 2004, at around 0900, and our armed convoy team of me, Dave, ten Iraqis and four Mitsubishi Pajeros were with cautious aggression forcing our way through the several rows of static civilian vehicles. Ahmed was doing a good job squeezing his lead Pajero forward, whilst Salah, the gunner, was gesticulating from the rear as only an Iraqi can, ordering the already frustrated locals to inch their vehicles back, forward or in any fucking direction out of the way! Any form of protest, be it an eyebrow raised too quickly or, worse, the insult of a right hand waved at head height with the thumb touching the tips of all four fingers simultaneously, would be met with increased arm movement and verbal abuse from Salah. It worked.

Dave, I knew, would be looking ahead to see what the hold-up was. He was also giving me the necessary heads-up on any suss vehicles and Iraqis over the radio. One was coming through: 'White people carrier, my immediate right, all bearded males, no weapons seen.'

I clocked the said vehicle, acknowledging eyes-on by clicking my radio talk button twice. The questionable vehicle's side sliding door was open, and inside I saw 12 bearded males all wearing traditional dish-dash. The car was crammed in among the traffic, waiting like the rest of the jam for the road block to be lifted. The men paid scant attention to us but were definitely suss, as apart from the beards they were all in their 20s and heading in the direction of Fallujah. I got Allah's attention, pointed at the men and said, 'Chouff, chouff (look). He was already aware of their presence and acknowledged with a waving index finger and a 'No good, no good, tut tut tut tut'.

Dave's voice came over the radio: 'IED up ahead, US bomb disposal are *in situ*, go firm, eyes up, wait out.' I acknowledged with two clicks, vehicles two and three doing likewise. We had now managed to position ourselves more or less at the front of the hold-up but reassuringly with enough saloon cars around us not to stick out like the sore thumbs our silver Pajeros were in a land that had never seen the likes of them before the invasion. I started to scan the vehicles and surrounding area for anyone paying particular attention to us. I then did a cursory panoramic of the surrounding terrain – clear. I ran my eyes over the terrain in more detail – clear.

'Controlled explosion in five,' said Dave. Click-click. Click-click. Click-click. Dave had liaised with the US element, which not only kept us in the picture, but they now knew we were there. No nasty blue on blue (friendly fire). There was a boom and a small mushroom cloud of smoke, confirmation of Dave's message. Instantly, all the civilian vehicles burst into life as the Iraqis, by now well accustomed to these drills, got set for the off.

'Let's go,' said Dave. Click-click. Click-click. Click-click. That was us clear of Abu Ghraib – next stop the border!

Our mission from J4 was to escort a total of 35 vehicles on transporters from the Jordanian border to FOB Ar Ramadi, from where they would be delivered to the Iraqi Border Patrol Force. As always, when the Iraqi transporters were empty, they would run alone to the pick-up point. This was by mutual consent with their drivers: we much preferred to travel at high speed, as opposed to the top speed of 60 kilometres per hour that could be reached by the decrepit rust-bucket transporters owned and driven by Iraqi entrepreneurs; and they didn't like us escorting them unnecessarily and making them legitimate targets for the insurgents. So, until there were any goods on board, we went our separate ways.

Articulated transporters, like everything in Iraq, were in short supply, the Americans having already commandeered a great many to add to the huge number brought in from Turkey and elsewhere. These made up convoys of one hundred-plus vehicles bringing in logistics from Turkey down to the main distribution centres in Baghdad, or up from Kuwait, escorted by about ten US military Humvees per convoy. That's when we came into the picture, escorting the goods on from Baghdad and distributing them throughout Iraq.

These large convoys bringing goods into the country – which were often several miles long – were easy meat for the insurgents, who took advantage of the thin-on-the-ground escort parties. The ambushers would lie in wait or prowl along the main north-to-south highway, and when a sizeable gap occured, swiftly intercept, killing or capturing one or more of the unfortunate drivers. Killing, I think, is the better option – for the driver, that is, since insurgent hospitality could well include the non-optional extra of a Baghdad haircut. (Gives a whole new meaning to the phrase 'Off the ears, sir?', and you definitely won't need 'something for the weekend'.)

Vehicle shortages meant that private-security convoy escorts got all the shit that was left over. And there was no vetting in place for the Iraqi drivers, who were all in possession of Thuraya sat phones and hailed from all over Iraq, including places such as Fallujah and Ar Ramadi, and were therefore not to be trusted in the slightest. Breakdowns were also common. With no reserve truck *in situ*, vehicles were often just left stranded, even in dodgy areas. The local police were informed and sometimes managed to get the truck and goods to a safe haven, but a lot of the time both ended up in smoke.

We had arranged for our four transporters to RV at the border crossing with Jordan some three hundred kilometres from Baghdad. After the hold-up at Abu Ghraib, we made swift progress, passing Fallujah some 30 minutes later without further incident. Dave was a bit concerned about us being the only vehicles on the road, but this was due to our swift restart from Abu Ghraib. And as the day was to prove, in that region of Iraq, unlike when travelling north, people, cars and settlements were all very thin on the ground. Also, it was hardly surprising that we had an incident-free run to and past Fallujah, as the US Marines were dug in all along the highway from Baghdad. Any sense of security once past Fallujah, though, was false, cos the US forces ain't there no more!

With Fallujah in the rear-view mirror, I started to get a really lonely feeling. Dave, I knew, was as well. It was good just to hear his voice on the radio. There was still occasional traffic that required our attention, and the empty terrain forward, left and right demanded constant surveillance. From the daily intelligence briefing sheets, we were well aware of the kind of incidents that took place on the highway. In fact, I had an excited yet scary feeling of serious trouble awaiting us. This sense of foreboding intensified after passing Ar Ramadi, as any US presence that had been there before was clearly now well and truly gone. At that time, there was no US movement in the area by road – we never saw any, that's for sure. American troops were airlifted in and out by helicopter, just as British soldiers were in Northern Ireland's bandit country. Even in Saddam's time, and with good reason, this place had the reputation of being a lawless wilderness. On the up side, the road was in good order. We also knew that there was one if not two petrol stations en route, which Dave and I would mark on each of our GPS systems. On this trip, a fuel stop was essential, as the number of vehicles to be loaded onto the transporters would require two journeys from the border to Ar Ramadi, taking two days and without the possibility of refuelling at an FOB. Although there was a station at the border crossing, it could not be relied on to have either petrol or diesel. So, not only were we driving on one of the most desolate and dangerous stretches of road we could find, but we were going to do it twice in quick succession. If they didn't hit us on the first run, our sheer audacity in turning round and doing it all over again would surely be a red rag to any insurgents!

Progress was swift, and the terrain around seemed empty. Dave signalled on the radio that we were fast approaching escarpments to the left and right, with the road forming a gorge through the middle. From about 50 metres away on each side, the escarpments rose steeply to about 150 metres in height and ran parallel for about 400 metres along. It was a perfect spot for a killing zone. Our tactic for obstacles of this nature was for the last two vehicles – my own and number three – to slow right down so as not to enter the suspected ambush area at the same time as vehicles one and two. By keeping separate, we would then act as a slow-rolling fire base should one and two come under attack. On reaching relative safety on the other side, vehicles one and two would then cover us through the zone.

All eyes were scanning the tops of the two escarpments for any sign of movement, form or shine. All seemed clear. I depressed the radio talk button and said, 'Covering. Go, go, go.' I received a click-click in response. The two lead vehicles snarled, lurched forward and then raced off through the gorge.

It was at such times that our vehicles seemed utterly inappropriate for the job – Chelsea tractors with shooters stuck out of the windows! Something like an effective deterrent in this situation would be large pick-up trucks with mounted guns scanning the ridge lines – one for the wish list, which I couldn't wait to write, because it would mean that I was safely back in the villa!

No one spoke as we made our way through the gorge. All eyes were on the escarpments, all reflexes ready to open up. The radio hissed into life: 'Through, clear, covering. Go, go, go.'

With my heart pounding, I gave Dave the two-clicks acknowledgment and ordered Abid One to drive: 'Go, go, go.' Engines growled and we were off, vehicle three leading, guns out on either side maintaining cover. Several seconds later, we were on the other side.

'Fucking hell, Dave,' I said, my voice jovial with nervous relief. 'We've got that three more times.'

'One at a time, Simon,' replied Dave, matter-of-factly, his Irish drawl seeming more pronounced.

We reached the border crossing early that afternoon and reported to the US Marine unit based in a secured zone. They were expecting us, which made a nice change, and reluctantly showed us to an open area where we could get our heads down for the night. The reluctance concerned our Iraqis, whom the Americans were not happy about allowing within their base. This was to become a growing problem for us.

The empty transporters had not yet shown up, which was expected, as we knew the Iraqi drivers would stop to eat and swill sweet tea at every opportunity. They finally arrived late in the afternoon and, being denied access to the base, parked up for the night on the border approach road. It transpired that they hadn't just been filling up on tea en route, but had also managed to refuel the transporters at the unreliable border filling station. There was nothing left to do now but wait and mull over the job in hand.

That night, I had a fitful sleep and found myself wide awake at three in the morning, lying on my back gazing up at the pin-sharp stars dotting the sky. Despite the sombre atmosphere among the team and the scary mission ahead, it was one of those moments that heighten my appreciation of the adventurous life I am fortunate enough to lead – me, an insignificant product of Camberwell Green, south London, and Dog Kennel Hill Primary School. My mind filled with distant memories of nights spent beneath other foreign skies, many moons ago – French Guiana, Congo, Chad. The sheer enormity of life's eternal conundrums, the elusive, beguiling 'what the fuck's it all aboutness', sent me into a deep reverie. How many people, hundreds and thousands of years ago, had done just this, gazing up at the universe wondering, 'Why am I here, at this particular point in the history of the world, an infinitesimal speck on the map, doing what I'm doing?'

'What the fuck's that?' My thoughts were shattered as the ceremonious wailing of the tape-recorded call for prayer from the minaret, considerately located right next to the base, slapped me out of my trance. Maybe I was actually asleep. I certainly didn't notice Abid Two or the others getting up and preparing for prayer. Dave was awake too, lighting his first of several cigarettes. Lying like me, facing the night sky, he quipped that he was getting rather partial to this form of wake-up call. 'Yes, Dave, the soldiers here must just love it!' Of course, I'd often faced Mecca myself as a kid, although that was the bingo hall in the Walworth Road. At least they had a live caller summoning the faithful, usually some check-suited, florid-faced refugee from Butlins. 'Eyes down, ladies. And now, on his own, number one!' Lighting up a fag, I drew comfort from the meditative trail of exhaled smoke and wondered what Spinney was up to . . .

Later that morning, 'shit, showered and shaved', we had time on our hands before any move could be made, so we carried out a thorough check of materials and equipment. Magazines were emptied, rounds counted, cleaned and 'rebombed', weapons cleaned, radios checked, and chest webbing firmly secured to our black body armour, which was tried on for manageability. The imperative criterion for the body armour was ease of access to the six upside-down magazines slipped into the black canvas pouches. The drivers were then sent off to 'first parade' the vehicles, and once our checks were completed we sauntered over to charge them with our packs, taking extreme care when placing them not to obscure sight or hamper movement within the cramped passenger space. Having access to both sides and the rear of the vehicle, for firing and instant debussing, was a categorical, life-saving must!

With all personnel briefed, and all weapons, equipment and vehicles in a state of readiness, the only thing missing was the US captain from J4 and the pick-up vehicles that were to be transported. On every convoy we escorted, a US military soldier accompanied the goods, enabling our access at the given destination and taking responsibility for signing off the delivery. For this trip, we were informed that Captain Lang was to be our military presence. The captain had been on a two-week swan to Amman, where he had procured the pick-up vehicles. J4 had given us his personal body armour and helmet, as he hadn't taken them to Jordan with him, but the powers that be in the US military decreed that for some jobsworth reason we could not take Captain Lang's M16 rifle. This was inexcusable, denying the captain the means to defend himself and us some valuable firepower.

Captain Lang arrived with the pick-up trucks on Jordanian transporters just after 1000, having, of course, sailed through border control – well, in Iraq, America Rules OK . . . The first thing we noticed about the pick-ups was that Captain Lang had not wasted any time preparing them for their new role. Painted in large black letters on the side of each and every vehicle were the words 'BORDER PATROL' in both English and Arabic. Great, now every self-respecting smuggler/ insurgent on our route would know we were assisting the authorities. Carrying this lot for all to see, we'd be breaking one of the golden rules!

The Jordanian transporters came in and unloaded, and our Iraqi transporters, after being thoroughly searched by the US military, were let on the base to load up. This all took several sun-scorching hours. Then came a bit of a bombshell, figuratively speaking; after all the shenanigans, it turned out we could only load the bottom rung of the transporters, as putting the pick-ups on the top rung took them way over the maximum headroom for some of the bridges we had to pass under. And since taking detours was not advisable, the upshot was that to get all the pick-ups delivered, we were now faced with three convoy runs – five more escarpment cannonballs. 'One at a time, eh, Dave!' It was starting to look as if we could do with Captain Lang's missing M16!

'Hey, sir,' I joked in a deathly voice. 'When the shit hits the fan, just take the nearest dead man's AK.'

Not to be outdone, he countered, 'I'll kill him to get it!'

Without his weapon, he was not a happy bunny, but in true officer style he didn't let it show, although I suspected, as the Americans say, that 'someone's ass was gonna fry' over the matter. The captain was a reservist who'd been called up, like so many of the specialist soldiers we encountered. He was a family man who owned his own company back in the States and was rumoured to be a millionaire. He was the sort who never shirked responsibility and, in fact, was the only officer that went out on the road. Like the majority of Americans in Iraq, he was a real-live nephew of Uncle Sam. He believed staunchly in the crusade. I didn't in the slightest. For me, America and Britain were the hot knife and Iraq the tub of cheap old margarine. But it was a good tub for me to ply my trade in.

Formed up and ready to roll, we checked the radios: 'All vehicles, this is vehicle one radio check, over.'

'Vehicle two, OK.'

'Vehicle three, OK.'

'Vehicle four, OK.'

'OK, eyes up, let's go.'

It was 1445 on 12 July 2004 as we left the base and trundled slowly out onto the highway to Ar Ramadi. Dave's and Mohammed's vehicles were up front, and my one, along with the one commanded by a young but reliable Iraqi called Hassam, closed the march, the transporters firmly sandwiched in between us. It took a few hundred metres for us to establish the correct distances between the vehicles. Once this was achieved, I informed Dave: 'OK, mate, that's us.' He responded with a click-click. Dave then ordered Ahmed to accelerate, pushing up the speed of the convoy. I radioed Dave again: 'That's about as fast as truck three can go.' Click-click. Dave held the speed.

We didn't like the American military presence accompanying us to get involved on the radio. We had our job to do, and they had theirs. Captain Lang, in vehicle two, was 'along for the ride' only.

We progressed steadily, passing our first RV – the intersection with the road going north to Syria – without incident. As there were no bases en route, we had pinpointed a series of prominent landmarks, and if we were lost or separated for any reason, we would regroup at the nearest of these. Though concentrating my eyes on the immediate terrain, a constant nagging vision of the upcoming escarpment was ever present in my mind. I just wanted to get there and deal with what or whoever might be waiting for us. I didn't have long to wait. Dave's dry Irish voice ominously announced, 'Escarpment visible, one kilometre ahead.' This was the signal for my vehicle to race ahead, stopping some 300 metres from the mouth of the gorge. I would then scan the ridge lines with binoculars. Click-click.

Abid One didn't need any orders, just a confirmatory nod of my head. With the pedal to the floor, we tore past the transporters, leaving Hassam in vehicle three to secure the rear of the convoy. I stared ahead of me, giving Dave the thumbs-up as we overtook him, preoccupied by the responsibility of the task ahead. Dave slowed the convoy to a crawl. 'Right, Simon,' I thought. 'Presence of the abnormal, absence of the normal.' Like abnormal hordes of fucking blood-lusting, desert-dwelling insurgents – or would that be normal here?

Approaching the gorge, everything seemed as it should. Motioning Abid One to start slowing down, Allah and I prepared to debus. 'Stop,' I shouted, jumping smartly out and using the vehicle for what protection it would afford. I then trained my binoculars on the escarpments, peering intently for so much as a gnat lifting his leg to fart. Allah was also out like greased lightning, a remarkable feat given his portly build, and lying in the prone position alongside the vehicle to give cover with the PKM. Abid One remained in the vehicle with engine running, ready to move. It was slick but passed without remark, as there were more important things to do than give out compliments.

A cursory sweep of the escarpments revealed nothing. I then swung the binoculars back again, moving more slowly and focusing on each section of the terrain, examining the rocks, the details, the silent shadows. Now and again, I dropped the binoculars and used my naked eyes – peripheral vision sees things binoculars miss. Rising like translucent silk, the heat haze performed its shimmering, deceptive dance. Nothing else. I moved the binoculars down to the black road at the bottom of the gorge and the terrain immediately to its left and right, looking for any suggestion of an IED, any marker for the initiation of fire or of detonation. Insurgents used animal carcasses, old drums and even hollow concrete blocks to hide IEDs. But there was nothing there either, only the same ever-receding haze.

'Dave, it's clear,' I said. Click-click.

I swapped the binoculars for my Kalashnikov and faced the escarpment, scanning continuously. Dave and his entourage rolled forward, passed us and proceeded into the mouth of the gorge. As they did so, Allah and I piled back into the Mitsubishi, and along with Hassam's vehicle took up the rear again, remaining one bound (about three hundred metres) behind the convoy, hopefully making anyone hidden out there think twice. It seemed an eternity before Dave announced, 'Clear of obstacle.' Click-click.

Knowing we were through, the fear gone for the moment, I could taste its flavour, feel the rush. And there were four more passes to come . . .

'OK, lads, well done, but it's not over yet. Stay alert.' Dave liked to keep everyone on their toes. All vehicle commanders acknowledged with a double click.

It was back to steady movement along the sticky, black tarmac road, with the windows rolled down and only the hot desert air for a fan. I guzzled down some cold water from the cooler box, doused my face and threw a bit down the back of my neck, then passed the bottle to Allah, who in turn offered it to Abid One. Refreshed, we settled into convoy mode: watching and scanning. Nothing but an undulating desert of sand and rock stretched out ahead of us. Every so often, there was a bridge spanning the road met by dust tracks on either side, a means of crossing for shy locals.

At the rate we were progressing, we were due to make it to the FOB at Ar Ramadi in good time. Since leaving the border, we'd passed very few vehicles in either direction, so the sudden appearance in the rear-view mirror of a large

Mercedes and a Toyota Land Cruiser, both new models and running together, made us sit up and take notice. It was clear that both vehicles were rapidly catching us up, and Allah's ominous chants of 'no good, no good, tut tut tut tut' were also coming on too fast for my liking. Nervous and annoyed, I snapped, 'All right, mate. Just shut the fuck up and cover them with the PKM.' The Mercedes was now nudging very close, the Toyota still tight behind it. Allah swung the PKM effortlessly onto the packs in the back, splayed the bipod, rammed the butt into his shoulder and aimed the gun at the two fast-approaching vehicles, pulling the cocking lever back hard then forcing it all the way forward.

'Dave, we've got two fast-approaching vehicles rear – one Mercedes, one Toyota Land Cruiser – pax not known. Hassam, block, block.' Dave acknowledged, and Hassam moved into the inside lane just ahead of me, forming a rolling block, leaving a clear space to my right so the suss vehicles could be called forward. 'Nice one, mate,' I thought. Although only moving at 60 kilometres per hour, we always ran the convoy in the left-hand overtaking lane, so any vehicles we let pass would have to go by on the gun side, not the driver's.

With my binoculars trained on the vehicles, I could so far only see a driver in each. 'Dave,' I said, 'looks like one pax in each. I'm gonna call one forward at a time for a rolling search.' Click-click.

The two vehicles had now slowed their advance and were maintaining pace at about 100 metres behind. I levered half of my body out of the window and with exaggerated gestures pointed my finger at the Mercedes then at the space to my immediate right – I repeated this instruction another two times. The Mercedes got the message and started to advance, but with the 4x4 following. Not wanting both unknown vehicles approaching so close together, I stuck my top half out the window again and pointing at the 4x4 clenched my fist several times. This had the effect of stopping both vehicles advancing. Good, they were following my orders. I then pointed for the Mercedes to move in again. This time the 4x4 remained firmly behind, while the Mercedes crept up to the rolling garage to my right, watched by several visible weapon barrels. Pulling level, the driver turned his face and gave an 'I really hate you but . . .' kind of smile. Abid One, being well rehearsed, nudged slowly over to the Mercedes, which edged evasively off to the right. I gesticulated at the driver that we were going to take a look, pointing to my eye then his vehicle. Abid One closed in, and I had a good look into the car. Just the one middle-aged driver – clear. Satisfied, I motioned him to drop back then called the 4x4 forward, which Allah was still covering. The 4x4 driver was another smiling nice guy. Again, I could see nothing else inside the vehicle.

'Dave, that's the two cleared,' I said.

'Send them through, Simon,' he replied. Click-click.

Hassam returned to his usual position, while the two vehicles were waved on. Once they had passed, he tagged in behind to push them through the convoy.

Allah was looking at me. 'No good, no good,' he said.

I relayed Allah's message: 'Dave, they're dickers, mate – sure of it.'

'OK, everyone, heads up, let's get this done,' he replied. But I could hear the apprehension in his voice. Weapons that had been cocked (one up the spout) when the Mercedes and 4x4 were spotted were 'made safe', and with a heightened sense of alertness, cranked further by the fact that dusk would soon be upon us, we made our way closer to a little bit of America and safety.

My weapon state when not in a contact or suspicious incident was always made safe. That is, with a magazine engaged and the safety lever on automatic but no round in the chamber. To have one up the spout and the safety off is unprofessional madness, but it was a habit some expat security guys were prone to. Where they picked it up from, God only knows, and in a cramped vehicle it can mean murder, or at best suicide. To start putting rounds down, all I had to do was cock the weapon and it would burst into fully automatic life. The difference in having one up the spout and the safety applied was that when flicking to automatic, single shot could be selected by life-endangering default. Instead of firing at a rapid rate, you'd only get one highly ineffective round down. Not good when the objective is to get the insurgents heads firmly up their mates' arses so you can flee the killing zone to regroup and react. By virtue of a simple mistake, you'd be staying in the killing zone for the rest of your life, i.e. not long.

There were about two more hours to go – a further one hundred kilometres and we'd be winding down in the US Marine base at Ar Ramadi. Then, just as we passed under another bridge spanning the highway, I heard Allah shouting. He suddenly swung into action and fired his AK-47 on full automatic out of the rear left-hand window. 'Fucking hell,' I thought. 'This is it. Here we go!' Though Abid One couldn't see Allah directly behind him, he too knew that we were suddenly deep in the shit and in the killing zone of an ambush, for he had tensed right up, staring dead ahead, his knuckles turning white as they locked onto the steering wheel.

I looked frantically past Abid One and through his open window, where I could see prone figures some 300 metres out in the sand. In the split second of taking all this in, I realised that the dry cracking noises reverberating all around me were incoming rounds, bullets that could splatter my innards all over the inside of the Mitsubishi. Instantly, my arse cheeks and stomach buzzed with raw, uncontrollable fear, making me squirm. I felt an overwhelming urge to dive into a ball in the footwell of the vehicle. Fighting the impulse, I forced myself forward, ramming the barrel of my AK-47 behind the head of Abid One and out through the window, at the same time ripping back the cocking lever. I squeezed the trigger, letting loose with a long burst on full automatic. The roar of the weapon and the vicious vibrations through my arms as the rounds spewed out calmed me down. From a state of panic and a desire to run away, I now felt a strange, perverse enjoyment of the situation take hold of me.

Shortening the automatic bursts, I tried to creep rounds onto the insurgents, marking my aim by the sand clouds kicked up from the impact of my preceding fire. I was now definitely loving it, distanced from the terrifying reality by my total concentration on trying to kill the bastards. Then it all changed, as my weapon stopped without warning. So too did my body – in the sudden absence of the noise and power of the gun, I was completely unable to function again. The incoming rounds continued, but with my own weapon silenced, fear rushed in to fill the vacuum and panic flooded my thoughts.

Allah had also stopped firing and was grunting and groaning, fumbling with his webbing as he tried to get another full mag on his Kalashnikov. Abid One was now rocking backwards and forwards, still super-glued to the steering wheel, although his foot had come off the accelerator, and the vehicle, instead of accelerating hard out of the killing zone, was slowing down. My mind was now racing. 'Fucking hell,' I thought. 'I'm gonna die, I'm gonna die.' A barrage of rounds whacked into the vehicle, shaking it from side to side. I tensed up anticipating the next one, the one that would rip into me.

Adrenalin kicked in. I smacked Abid One round the side

of his head and screamed at the top of my voice, 'Fucking driiive, driiive.' We quickly picked up speed, but I was starting to lose it again: 'I'm gonna die. Shit, shit.' Then as Allah resumed firing, it somehow got me going. I got my weapon back out of the window and fired, action distracting me from my fear, helping me to stay in control. Suddenly, we lurched over to the right. Abid One had wrenched the wheel to dodge some hurtling shape. I saw that it was Hassam's vehicle, which was rolling over and over again. It must have taken a direct hit from a rocket-propelled grenade (RPG). Survival instincts didn't allow me to dwell on the probable implications of this. Only the blank, meaningless thought 'they're dead' flashed through my mind and out the other side. It was then swiftly followed by 'I want to live'. I yelled at Abid One: 'Keep going!'

We must have travelled another 200 metres before it dawned on me that we were no longer being targeted. I shouted at Abid One to stop. In a split second of artificial normality, I half expected him to say, 'Make up your bloody mind!' We debussed, and I flattened myself in a prone position, facing back towards the ambush point. 'I'm alive,' I thought. It was the first really coherent one I'd had since seeing Allah blasting off several moments earlier. The mental rush was staunched as Allah came to the rescue again, opening up with the PKM. The insurgents, now some five hundred metres further back along the road, were returning fire from around two white pick-up trucks.

Spurred into life, I shouted over the radio, 'Dave, come back. Hassam's vehicle is down.'

In a calm voice, Dave replied, 'Ahmed is hit, and the vehicle is in a bad way.'

I wasn't aware of much more of the conversation, my attention being focused on the two white pick-ups that had been in dead ground (that which was obscured by the undulating terrain). They were now legging it away. Somehow I had to fight the panic and all-round disorder, and try to regroup our band of Iraqis into an effective force. We had to get Hassam, Awls and Wissam out of the overturned vehicle.

Allah was still pounding away, even though the insurgents were at least 700 metres distant. I looked up and saw Captain Lang by his vehicle about 100 metres away. I shouted at him to get it turned round and follow me back for Hassam, Awls and Wissam. It was then that I saw Captain Lang's driver, another Mohammed, running up the highway towards me and firing his MP5 single shot wildly up into the air. I jumped to my feet and raced over to him, at the same time screaming at Abid One to bring our vehicle around ready to go back for Hassam and the others. Drawing level with Mohammed, I snatched away his weapon and shook him hard, shouting at him to get a grip. I was still shaking the living fucking daylights out of him when Captain Lang screeched up to us in his vehicle. I applied the safety to Mohammed's weapon and handed it to Captain Lang, who then pushed him into the driving seat. I threw myself into our Mitsubishi and shouted at Allah to come and get in. Once again, Allah's agility belied his build, as he sprang up from the ground and, crouching low and effortlessly carrying the PKM, sprinted towards me and dived onto the rear seat. 'Go!' I ordered. With the doors flapping open, we accelerated at speed back towards our wounded colleagues, closely followed by Captain Lang's vehicle. The insurgents seemed to have beaten a full retreat. Looking at Hassam's upturned Pajero, I could see no movement and prepared myself for the worst. Stopping short, I debussed and told Captain Lang to get everyone down to cover the danger area. Dave's vehicle was already heading our way. It was listing badly to one side and making a horrendous squealing noise. Two of the tyres had been shot out. With everyone covering me, I ran to the edge of the road and down the two-metre drop towards where the upturned vehicle lay, all the while steeling myself for the unpleasant sight of bits of brain all over the place. I saw Awls the fat driver and Hassam. They were out of the vehicle and conscious but clearly in severe pain. 'Hassam, Awls,' I shouted. They both looked up at me. 'Good, they're OK. Leave 'em,' I thought. Dave then joined me. I looked at him and smiled. 'Fucking hell, Dave,' was all I could say.

He swiftly replied, 'Come on, come on, let's get them out of here and fuck off.' I crawled in through the upturned vehicle and found Wissam. He looked unconscious or dead. There was blood on his head and face, but apart from a gash on his forehead he seemed to be in one piece. I grabbed hold of his body armour at the shoulders and dragged his limp body out of the vehicle. I checked his pulse, which was very weak. His breathing was also shallow. Closer inspection revealed a gunshot wound to his right forearm. We all carried an abundance of first field dressings, so I quickly applied one to his forearm and one to the gash on his head, which looked to have been caused when the vehicle rolled over. Dave, meanwhile, had got Hassam and Awls carried up to the vehicles. They both appeared to have broken bones.

With the wounded all accounted for and up in the two serviceable vehicles, Dave and I returned to the wreck for the men's weapons and packs. Dave put a burst of rounds into the vehicle's radio, and we beat a hasty retreat back up to the road. Dave's limping vehicle was going nowhere, so we cross loaded its material and shot up its radio, too. I then did a quick headcount. There were thirteen of us crammed into two Pajeros. The wounded were slung in the rear vehicle, apart from Ahmed, who had received a gunshot wound to his left thigh and was placed in the first. It turned out that, during the ambush, he'd carried on driving and then taken the vehicle back in to help recover the other wounded. The transporters, miraculously unscathed, had stopped along with Dave's vehicle. Having only two escort vehicles now, we sandwiched the whole lot between us. My vehicle carried me, Abid One (who was driving), Dave, Captain Lang, Allah and Ahmed, leaving the other seven in the second vehicle.

Throughout the remainder of the journey, we tried to call the incident in using the emergency numbers on our sat phones but without success. Each time we dialled, a recorded message by a cheery, black-sounding, southern American female voice greeted us: 'This service is temporarily out of action.' There wasn't even a press one for blah-blah, two for whatever or three to hear the options again! Mind you, if it had been a British Army number, we'd probably have been routed to an Indian call centre. Ere, lads, anyone interested in some home insurance? 'Anytink else I can help you with, sir? Many thank you for calling, sir . . .'

We reached the US Marine Corps base at Ar Ramadi at 2150, where all the wounded were taken straight to Aid Station Charlie for treatment – Awls and Hassam for suspected broken bones and minor cuts and bruises. Luckily, Ahmed's wound turned out to be a non-serious, though nasty-looking, burned gouge along the back of his thigh. Wissam, who was now conscious, was whisked into a field operating room and expertly plugged and drugged. Meanwhile, Dave contacted our HQ in Baghdad and informed them of events. From what I could hear, Nigel the chief clerk seemed genuinely concerned, despite his professional reaction to our report. The rest of us were to be put up that night by the resident US Marine Corps unit, whose colonel, unable to locate a key for the transit accommodation, solved the problem Dirty Harry style. His name, Colonel Bolt, and his demeanour, were both straight out of a Hollywood film. Standing at 6 ft 5 in., wearing faded combat fatigues and chewing on a fat cigar, Colonel Bolt personally kicked the door in for us – sorted, as Grant Mitchell might say. The colonel didn't even remove the cigar from his mouth during the manoeuvre. This all-American, gung-ho-ness was no act, though, and he wasn't in the least trying to impress. What you saw was what you got with Colonel Bolt, and I was struck by his natural air – that of a born soldier. He was definitely in the right place.

We stepped past the smashed-in door and were all given beds in the large dormitory, including Captain Lang. The mood was very subdued. Our Iraqis sat in two groups, talking quietly amongst themselves and occasionally glancing towards me, Dave and Captain Lang as we installed ourselves at the far end of the room. There wasn't much conversation between Dave and me, just the odd word on what was to be done in the morning: sorting equipment, cleaning weapons, refuelling the two remaining vehicles and getting the show back on the road. But one thought was uppermost in my mind: that this stuff had very quickly become very real, and that I could have been killed just a few hours before. Me, Simon Low. After seven years in the British Army and ten in the Legion, this in itself was nothing new, of course. What was different was this whole Iraq fiasco. If I had died that day, I wouldn't have been joining the ranks of the glorious dead of the infamous Foreign Legion, having fallen in some long-to-be-celebrated battle. Not that that would change the fact I was dead. But to die for some private-security firm, whose motives were money and not a lot else, wasn't exactly inspiring. Would any observer or historian, even in the unlikely event that my death was noticed, talk about my commitment to duty or the *esprit de corps* within our little team? Did we have such a thing? Did I? As a hired gun plying my trade in the cheap old tub of margarine of Iraq, they'd say I deserved all I got, and they would probably be right. There'd be no corner of this foreign field that was forever Camberwell, mate.

As I settled down for the night, the same thought kept returning: a few hours before, a group of unknown assailants – insurgents, the enemy, call them what you will – along an insignificant stretch of black-top road, lost in a wilderness of rock and sand, deep in the notorious Anbar Province in Western Iraq, had tried to end my 42 years on this planet. Dead but not dishonoured, they used to say. And what would be on my tombstone?

I also relived my part in the ambush, mentally beating myself up about the fear I'd let surface while trying to change magazines. Far worse was the impulse I'd had to run away, even though I knew that Hassam's vehicle had been severely hit. I hadn't run, of course, but I couldn't deny having considered the option. It was an uncomfortable admission. Not a recipe for a good night's kip.

The next morning, Dave gave me the 'good' news that Armor Group HQ in Baghdad was mobilising three teams from another contract in Baghdad, who would bring us out two new vehicles and replacements for our wounded. We could then continue with our mission. Dave informed the remaining Iraqis, adding that if any or all of them wanted to quit, he fully understood and wouldn't hold it against them. No one moved – they were all staying. Mind you, if I could have had my way, quite a few of them would have been unceremoniously fucked off.

Privately, Dave also gave me the option to bail out. 'Nah, mate,' I said. 'I'm staying. I mean, what else is there to do? Money could be better, though.' During the sleepless night, I'd reached the conclusion I would soldier on. It was what I'd done for 17 years. The fear and possibility of death made the job what it was: bloody exciting.

After Dave's announcement, however, there followed better

news from Captain Lang. Having disappeared shortly after waking, he now returned to inform us that the mission had been cancelled. The remaining vehicles at the border were to be distributed directly to the police there. Despite my overnight decision, I seriously thought about becoming a born-again Christian when I heard this but thought it best to keep God keen for the foreseeable future. Apparently, the captain had communicated with his superiors in Baghdad and persuaded them to do the 'right thing', whatever that meant. He had been with us the night before and had witnessed Colonel Bolt's astonishment at how we had escorted the convoy from the border. The colonel had remarked that if they, a heavily armed unit of marines, were given an equivalent mission, they would only consider it with air cover from a helicopter gun ship. Mine had not been the only raised eyebrows!

Once the teams from Baghdad arrived, commanded by Sam, we all returned to Baghdad, taking our wounded with us. Wissam, after a few more visits to the American military hospital in the Green Zone, was back on convoy some six weeks later. Hassam and Awls's bruised and battered bodies were back on duty after a fortnight. Astonishingly, neither had suffered any broken bones as first suspected. Ahmed, faithful as ever, was on convoy again a couple of days following our return to Baghdad. If I was to tell you that Dave and I were personally commended for our actions by David Petraeus, a three-star American general, in Baghdad, you'd never believe me, so I won't.

3

THE ROAD TO SAMARA

Me and my big mouth! Leave? Who wanted it when you could be dodging bullets and killing insurgents? I did. On 19 July 2004, seven days after the ambush in the Anbar Province, I was sunning myself on the roof terrace of the villa in Baghdad, with a bottle of cold sparkling mineral water for refreshment and a PKM belt-fed machine gun and AK-47 for comfort. The sun was clearly the boss up in the cloudless blue Baghdad morning sky, turning my already browning face a few shades darker. At the same time the next day, I would be on a Hercules C130 plane, well on my way to a plush hotel in Kuwait for a night's stopover before a BA flight to Heathrow and three weeks of well-earned paid leave. Earlier that morning, Dave, my replacement – a noisy giant of a man called Jed – and the Iraqis had departed for the Abu Ghraib warehouse, scheduled for a three- or four-day mission to Mosul. By the time they got there, I'd be home in Plymouth with the family and Spinney.

Meanwhile, I wasn't up on the roof just to improve my suntan. It was also the place where I felt safest for the 24 hours I'd be spending alone in the villa. Strictly speaking, I wasn't alone; there were the two local armed Iraqi guards down in the front garden and, of course, the cleaner Emina, busy looking busy as she moved the dirt around the courtyard. From the roof terrace, I was afforded good all-round sight and sound observation. Sitting inside glued to Sky News, I could end up making the news.

The two guards below, along with most Iraqis in my eyes, could not be trusted. This is not racism. Iraq is a lawless state run by well-armed criminal and terrorist gangs. The Americans only come out of their bases to patrol, when some of them get killed by bombs or bullets. The lucky ones who make it back to base get their chance to die for their country the next day. While the tree of liberty gets watered with the blood of patriots, the gangs continue to run the show, bribes and threats are the norm and murderous insurgents inevitably infiltrate the swarm of private-security companies, ours being no exception. Forget or ignore this at your peril!

Feeling decidedly edgy, the 24 hours ahead of me were going to be long and lonely. But any of al-Zarqawi's mates who wanted to dress me in an orange jumpsuit would first have to dodge a couple of thousand PKM rounds pinging all over the neighbourhood. An equally vital defence was a casual but regular glance down into the front walled garden for the presence of the two guards. If they mysteriously went missing, I could expect visitors.

My mobile phone sprang into life. Dave's name lit up on the display. Concerned, I hit the answer button. 'Hello, mate. What's up?'

Dave's voice was measured and stoic: 'I'm at the Abu Ghraib distribution warehouse, and our Iraqis are refusing to do the mission. They're saying they don't want to wear helmets, so I've told them to leave all their weapons and equipment and go. So, Simon, can you get the Iraqi team from VIP contract on standby and ready to deploy so they can collect our vehicles and return them to the villa?'

I felt annoyed at the mutineers. At the same time, it was a relief to know I wouldn't now be alone in the villa overnight. 'OK, Dave, I'll give you the heads-up when it's all set up.'

Dave replied, 'I've given them time to think it over, but it's a dodgy mission, and I'm sure they're just looking for a way out. Once they've downed tools and left, I'll call you. Just get VIP and yourself on standby.'

'Okey-dokey, mate. Better off without the fucking wankers.'

The helmets had always been an issue, but they were now supposed to be worn at all times whilst we were on the ground. Judging by some of these guys' actions in the recent ambush, I would have thought they'd gladly wear anything that might save their precious skins. Selecting 'menu' on my mobile, I scrolled down and stopped at Simon A. over at VIP contract. Yet another bloody Simon! Just like London buses, coming along in twos, ha-ha. Thumbing the small green 'phone' button, I placed the mobile to my ear. Nearly too many rings later, I was greeted with, 'Hello, Simon.'

'Hello, Simon,' I parroted, before explaining the situation regarding the helmets and Dave fucking-off the awkward squad. No problem. Simon A. confirmed he'd send three vehicles and his 'VIP Team' Iraqis over to me at 'Convoy Villa' for retrieval of our vehicles.

Hanging up, I walked to the edge of the roof terrace and looked down into the garden. The two guards were still sitting on the grubby white plastic chairs and chewing gum. Their weapons were leaned against the wall. 'Oi, you two! Get those AKs in your dirty mitts, NOW!' I ordered. Jumping up, plastic chairs skating across the floor, they bumped into each other in their haste to grab their weapons, repeating, 'Sorry, mister Simon. Sorry, sorry, mister Simon.' I stared down upon them for a few exaggerated seconds then gesticulated and pointed two fingers at my eyes. In remonstrative tones, I said, '*Chouff, chouff* – look.' I then swung my own AK-47 off my shoulder, slapped and grasped the stock and cried, 'Yeah, understand? Hold the fucking thing!' With bags of head-nodding, the pair assumed something resembling vigilance.

Next, I surveyed the road and approaches, where all seemed normal: no unknown vehicles parked, nor absence of the normal. On the street, a small Arab boy who lived opposite was kicking his football around as usual. I knew he was expendable to the insurgents if the infidels were to be blown to kingdom come. At least he hadn't seen anything to make him run indoors shouting, 'Mum, Mum, al-Zarqawi's outside with a nasty-looking bunch of bearded men with big guns!'

'OK, son. Go on up to your bedroom and play on your abacus for a while.'

I was just about to ring Dave with a sit-rep (situation report) when he rang me again. 'Hello, Dave,' I said. 'VIP are on their way over to me now.'

'Good. Our boys have just walked out of the main gate, so get over here asap and we'll return to the villa. The job's going ahead tomorrow. I'll explain when I see you.'

Dave had not been idle during the mutiny. He'd been on to HQ, and the head-sheds at Armor had arranged for the VIP-contract Iraqis to fill the void. This showed the difference between a professional outfit and a purely money-making one. The former would have called the job off, whereas our bosses just got more bums to fill the empty seats. Armor was coining a daily five-figure sum on convoy and wanted all their lemons in a row for the jackpot to keep paying out. We boys weren't complaining, either. My personal wedge was now a cool $135,000 a year, and my reasoning had always been, 'You want it? You do it!' We were normal men in abnormal circumstances, paid to be shot at and to shoot back – we took the money, the bullets and the self-righteous stick from the holier-than-thou how-could-you brigade who sat on the moral high ground. Mercenary might be an embarrassing term in the military world, but that's what we were: from the head-sheds in London to the boys on the ground. Dress us up as romantic soldiers of fortune, with a heroic lineage from the nobility of the Middle Ages, or post-fucking-modern, euphemised PMCs, but it wouldn't alter the facts: we worked for large sums of money to possibly be killed and, if necessary, kill others. Enough said.

VIP arrived, and we promptly left for the Abu Ghraib distribution centre, with me in charge. Once there, we linked up with Dave and shunted the vehicles abandoned by the Iraqis back to the villa. Dave was most definitely not a happy bunny, and not surprisingly. With me going on leave and most of our team of Iraqis gone, there remained only Ahmed and Salah – they'd steadfastly refused to join the mutineers – who were practised in convoy drills. The rest, the VIP bunch, were 90 per cent clueless as to our ways. There was also the language problem and the Iraqi factor: bottle, or lack of it! Dave wasn't trying to make out that he was even a slightly happy bunny: 'Simon, I don't like the feel of this one. Our boys have walked, the VIP lot ain't up to par on our drills – in fact, they don't even fucking know our drills! – plus you're not going to be there and the final destination up at Mosul is dodgy to say the least. We're gonna get ambushed, that's for sure.'

'Dave,' I replied, 'I can't go on leave now.' His ominous words had left me no choice. As he started to protest, I continued: 'Listen, how can I go on leave tomorrow knowing that you're doing a job up to Mosul on your Jack Jones? Nah, mate, I couldn't live with myself if something was to happen. And more to the point, I'd want you to stay if I was in that predicament, so I'm on the job.'

He looked thoughtful for a moment then briskly said, 'Thanks, Simon. Right, get those VIP prima donnas in here and let's try and get some drills into them.' There was no more to be said. I would swap my place on the Hercules 130 for the front passenger seat of a pick-up en route for Mosul. As for leave, my family and friends would all still be there, and so would Spinney. Here, boy! Well, soon . . .

The two Pajeros we'd lost in the ambush had been replaced by a pair of week-old twin-cab Nissan pick-ups. They were soft-skinned and had no gun mounts on the back. Generally referred to as 'fucking melon carriers', they were a type of vehicle commonplace on Iraqi roads, transporting everything from fruit to goats. So, hey, maybe we would blend in a bit better. The only snag, though, would be the conspicuous articulated lorries interspersed among them all the way up to Mosul.

With no weapon mounts, we set about adapting the back trays of the pick-ups as best we could to allow one standing man to fire a gun resting on sandbags placed across the roof of the cab. It wouldn't be that effective, and would afford little protection for the firer, but it was better than sitting on the cramped back seat and trying to shoot.

Simon A. had volunteered his services to replace Jed, who had to return to his regular contract, as a mission had come up. Another expat wasn't to be sniffed at, especially one of Simon's calibre. A serious stickler, his attention to detail went hand in hand with vast experience gained from his time spent on the security circuit and ten years previous to that in the Royal Marines. I was pleased he was with us and up for it, as I haven't yet met a Royal Marine who was a bad soldier. I suppose they're all still in the corps!

The date of 20 July 2004 was another that was to firmly

etch itself into my memory. At the Abu Ghraib distribution centre, we discovered that the logistics sergeant who was coming along for the ride was already well known to us. He was, basically, on another planet – planet 'World Wrestling Federation and Harley Davidson', his two, and probably only, abiding passions. Dave and I thought it best that Simon A. get to know Harley man so assigned him a seat in Simon's vehicle. ''Ere, Simon,' I said as we prepared to deploy. 'Do you know anything about wrestling or Harleys?'

Screwing his eyes up, Simon A. replied, 'What you on about?'

'Nothing, mate. Forget it.' Smirking, I walked off.

The goods for escort on this mission were medicines – stowed in three twenty-feet containers, each on a flatbed rigid lorry – to be delivered to FOB Diamondback in Mosul. With only three lorries to shepherd, it was decided that Dave would lead, and I would follow immediately behind. The three lorries would come next, and the VIP escort vehicles would bring up the rear, with Simon A. closing the march in the CAT role. Simon had already done a couple of convoys, one with me a few months earlier to Basra, so he had a good working knowledge of our drills.

Dave and I were both pleased to be supporting each other up front. He knew I wouldn't leave him, and I vice versa. A big fear for both of us was being taken prisoner or, if killed, having our bodies taken. We received daily int-reps, some of which were written by other convoy teams describing their ambushes and subsequent reactions. One was so frightening – not the ambush but the team's actions – that we pinned it to our board in the office, lest we forget! That this team had driven into an ambush wasn't the remarkable bit – that is what happens when an ambush is well laid. You hear so much bollocks about 'once in an ambush, look for the enemy and fire well-aimed shots' – it's laughable. When an ambush is sprung, you're in their killing zone. So, rule number one: get the fuck out of it. The tried-and-tested method for this is to stick lots of guns out of your vehicle's windows and make as many empty cases as your magazines allow, an ideal piece of kit being a drum mag, which holds 75 AK-47 rounds. Meanwhile, your well-drilled driver keeps moving fast, if possible in control of both himself and the vehicle. Rule number two: once clear, regroup and react, either by turning the ambush back on the insurgents through establishing a fire base and returning for the wounded or, if you're all through, by carrying on in a controlled and organised manner, ready to react to the next ambush waiting for you further down the candy-striped road! Discipline in carrying out drills is what is required. A good soldier is always thinking 'what if this happens or that happens' and is running potential scenarios through his mind like a film – preferably not a Hollywood production, because the good guys always win in those.

Whilst the team were in the killing zone, a vehicle was taken out – quite a normal occurrence. The others carried on fighting through – nothing wrong there, either. Here's where it starts to stink. According to the team leader writing the report, once through, they regrouped some five kilometres further on. Now that smacks of wild, undisciplined panic. But the report did say that they stopped on high ground, giving good observation, and, wait for it, it gets better, one of the Iraqis that had been in the immobilised vehicle then reappeared in a taxi, which he had managed to flag down after running from the ambush. Unfortunately, the South African expat commanding the immobilised vehicle was killed, and the insurgents were able to drive up to the vehicle and take his body, which, like all the bodies they get their vile hands on, disappeared. In the Foreign Legion, you abide by a code of honour, one tenet of which is that you never abandon your wounded, dead or weapons.

Dave, after the final briefing in front of the lined-up convoy, gave the order to mount up. A radio check was done, followed by the order to depart. Simon A.'s vehicle and the third escort vehicle were up front at that stage, and they exited the base first to secure the junction. The convoy could then roll straight onto the expressway. Once this manoeuvre was completed, Simon and the third escort vehicle closed the rear.

No matter how many times I exited the base, I was always struck by the frenzied pace of Baghdad life. Inside the high walls, we were cocooned in a haven, which on occasion took incoming mortars but on the whole was a relaxing place to wait around in while the convoy base-staff got their artics and other shit together. However, the instant I left the base, I was always greeted by a constant fanfare of car horns from an endless stream of traffic, obeying no lane discipline. Many of the cars in the city had holed exhausts, and they loudly farted their way along, emitting acrid grey and black fumes. Then there were the men and boys milling about in their traditional white dish-dash robes, and the not so fortunate in rags wandering dangerously close to the speeding traffic. Endless hawkers lined the roadsides, selling everything from plastic containers of petrol to large fish, freshly caught from the Tigris and mounted high on sticks. Everyone was selling something, grafting at something or busily doing nothing in Baghdad.

Because there were only three non-articulated lorries on the trip, progress was a little more rapid than usual. The art was to keep them in close formation through the Baghdad streets, which became dual carriageway further north. Along with the problem of negotiating the manic traffic was the ever-present threat of sudden attack. Bridges had to be checked and double-checked by observation. Ramps leading off the expressway were always a danger, as a vehicle could engage you with automatic fire and then disappear into the rushing traffic. Flat-roofed villas were also a good fire base from which to attack slow-moving convoys. Then there was the danger of IEDs placed at the side of the road or in large potholes. Vehicle-borne suicide bombers – eager to plough into your side and blow you both up, while 40-odd virgins waited impatiently in paradise for the fat middle-aged balding bastard responsible for the carnage to ascend and claim his divine reward – were also becoming more frequent at that time.

So, our eyes and senses, against all the traffic distractions, worked non-stop from the second we departed the base. Each vehicle was responsible for a primary-observation sector: front, front-right, front-left, right, left, rear, etc. As well as this primary sector, we were all expected to make general secondary observations all round. Directly in front of me, Dave, who was heading into the unknown first, would be concerned with what was immediately ahead, while I took on both of our right and left. These sectors were not hard and fast but gave a working structure to the drill. The durations were split 70–30 between your primary- and secondary-observation zones. All of this was then backed up by constant radio chatter: 'Bridge up ahead'; 'Bridge, check. Bridge, clear'; 'Three pax on rooftop my three o'clock, two hundred metres'. Using the clock method for designating a suspect location, person or vehicle is highly effective – so long as you have visual with the reporting vehicle!

Moving through Taji, a suburb just north of Baghdad, the congestion on the main highway started to ease up a bit. Selfishly, I breathed a big sigh of relief, because controlling the flow of traffic at the rear of the convoy on this mission was Simon A.'s headache. I was sitting pretty in number two vehicle, the best position in my view. As I saw it, my main aim was to react instantly to any contact. If that should be an IED hitting the lead vehicle, the scenario in my head was to drive straight up, cross load all personnel in with me and accelerate out of the immediate area. If we took small-arms fire, or worse, were caught in an ambush, the film getting repeat showings in my brain featured the VIP Iraqi and me firing our Kalashnikovs on full automatic from the windows of our vehicle, which is being driven rapidly and under control through the killing zone. I had honed my part in this film through previous hands-on experience and visualised myself dropping a mag off my Kalash, grabbing another and snapping it home, arming and continuing to fire like there *was* a tomorrow, my future life being definitely part of the script.

On our right-hand side going through Taji was Camp Cooke. One of the entrances to this vast US base was closed following several vehicular suicide bombings, and large concrete blast walls now ran the length of the highway.

Apparently, some vehicle-borne suicide bombers leave their base rather as a taxi does when it goes out for hire, moving between areas where the prime customers hang out – Iraqi officials, police, US military, private-security vehicles and so on down the food chain. In Taji, when there are no punters for their one-way-fare offers, the local kamikaze drivers presumably just shrug their shoulders and sign off at Camp Cooke. In fact, a number of suicide bombings in Iraq do occur in the old yellow-and-orange taxis. So, if a cabbie ignores you when you try to flag him down in Baghdad, he could just be on his way home, but it's also possible he's got those celestial virgins topping his to-do list. I wonder what happens to the ex-virgins?

Simon A. was doing a good job checking and filtering the traffic, and the convoy was making excellent headway. At this rate, we'd have to park up and wait for lunch at FOB Speicher in Tikrit, whereas normally we'd be there just as grub was served. The radio hissed into life. It was Dave:

'Speicher in thirty minutes – cheeseburgers on the menu – but before that we've got to deal with the Samara bypass in three kilometres.'

Samara was a town that had gone quietly unnoticed as a hot seat of insurgency, yet it supposedly hosted foreign fighters from as far afield as Chechnya and Bradford, and the Samara bypass was a notorious flashpoint for attacks, bombs and ambushes. On the roadside, it wasn't unusual to see still-smouldering vehicle carcasses – just as I was getting an appetite for those juicy chargrilled burgers . . .

I took a sideways glance at my replacement driver Adel, a young, hook-nosed, lanky, skin-and-bone Arab. We hadn't communicated much for the simple reason we spoke precious little of each other's language, but scrutinising him I now felt it was time to say something. With theatrical actions and exaggerated emphasis, I said, 'Ambush. Bang-bang, you drive. You drive, OK. You drive, OK?'

'Yez, yez, no problem, me good, no problem,' Adel enthusiastically replied.

'Yeah, we'll fucking see,' I thought.

With the Samara bypass fast approaching, I would have forgiven Allah anything to have him at my side right then. The Iraqi sitting behind me was so young I doubted if he even remembered Saddam Hussein's reign.

We'd decided before leaving not to put anyone out on the exposed back through Baghdad; only after our stop at Tikrit would we man the rear. However, if the vehicle had been properly fitted with gun mounts and armour plating, a gunner would have been in place from the start.

My vehicle was 50 metres behind Dave's. I could clearly see his black-helmeted head turning left and right, continually observing the surroundings. Our speed was up to a breathtaking sixty kilometres per hour, the first of our three lorries was right up behind me and the bridge on the bypass was now only about four hundred metres away. Before that, at roughly three hundred metres, was the ramp off to Samara, whose golden-roofed mosque shimmered some two kilometres to the north-east. Dave came on the radio: 'Three pax, my one o'clock at two hundred metres, standing in front of a dark saloon car, no weapons seen. A further two vehicles parked fifty metres past the three pax, no pax visible.'

I acknowledged by double clicking the talk button and locked my eyes onto the people up ahead. Three Arab males, 30ish, dressed in shabby Western clothing were standing in front of a parked saloon car. They were highway side, next to the driver's door. I glanced further up the highway to the other two parked cars, one a black jeep, but couldn't see anyone standing around. Something wasn't right. The three men by the car were looking our way but not at us, and at no time did any of them glance at Dave's vehicle approaching them. I pointed the men out to Adel and the gunner sitting in the back, then quickly scanned the immediate area – nothing. It definitely wasn't right. I armed my Kalashnikov and stared at the middle of the three men. He had glanced at Dave's vehicle just as it had gone past him then looked quickly back down towards the rear of the convoy. I was now level with the men, who stood just three metres to my right. As we passed, the middle one looked at me, then threw open the door of the parked vehicle and pulled out a Kalashnikov AK-47. I shouted out, mainly for myself, 'He's got a fucking gun!' and positioned myself to engage him. Having driven past, this now meant turning sideways and firing my Kalashnikov with my right arm holding the grip slightly above my head. I let go a long burst and saw one of the men fall back against the car. Other shots were also being fired. I continued firing, though the angle of sight now made it nigh on impossible for me to hit the insurgents.

Slipping back into the vehicle, I saw that my stomach and thighs were covered in blood. I shouted, 'I'm hit!' but strangely felt no pain. Breathing heavily, I dropped the mag off my weapon, letting it fall to the floor, and snatched a full one from the map-pouch on the door. Blood seemed to be everywhere. As I armed the weapon, it ejected a round, meaning I hadn't finished the first mag, but I wasn't counting, that's for sure.

Adel was hunched over the steering wheel, in control, driving us out of there. 'Adel,' I thought. 'I love you.' The minor relief was short-lived, for up ahead was an image to chill the blood. We were fast approaching the other two parked cars, from which protruded a porcupine-like cluster of gun barrels. As we drew rapidly closer, the menacing sight took on a bizarre quality, for despite the weapons remaining resolutely pointed in our direction, there was neither hide nor hair of an insurgent to be seen taking aim. They must have all been ducking down shitting it! I let rip with my Kalashnikov at the vehicles, firing continuously for as long as the angle allowed. We careered past, Adel taking us towards the bridge bypass. I changed mags again, though we were now on the bridge and clear of the attackers.

A quick examination revealed the source of my bleeding: a deep two-inch-long gash on my left hand just below the little finger on the outer edge. The stock of my Kalashnikov had also taken two rounds, one on each side. Tearing a field dressing taped to my chest webbing's left shoulder strap, I ripped it open with my teeth and wrapped the bandage hastily around my wounded left hand, then used my right hand and mouth to tie the cloth straps and secure it in place.

The radio crackled; it was Dave: 'Simon, did you take any hits?'

I was now approaching his vehicle, which had stopped some 200 metres onto the bridge. He and his Iraqis were out on the ground in fire positions, facing back towards the ambush. 'Yeah,' I replied, 'my vehicle has taken a few rounds, and I've got a slight wound to my hand, but, apart from that, we're all OK.'

'Right, get yourself up here.'

At that moment, Simon A. shouted over the radio, 'Come back, come back. My vehicle has been hit and immobilised, and the US sergeant has been hit.'

'OK, mate, we're coming,' I immediately replied, but Simon's voice continued, so I doubted that he'd heard my message. Rather than try again, I reached to the floor and grabbed another weapon, one that we'd recently acquired. It was a type of AK-47 but with the addition of a longer barrel, a bipod and shoulder butt. I jumped out of the vehicle and ordered Adel to turn about, ready to retrace. I then leaped onto the open back of the pick-up, armed the weapon with a thirty-five-round banana mag and positioned its bipods on the three sandbags secured to the cab roof. I then banged on the roof with my bandaged hand, blood still managing to find its way everywhere, and shouted to Adel, 'Go, go!'

While we were turning around, Dave ordered the three lorries and the third escort vehicle to continue another two hundred metres down the road; the escort vehicle was then to secure its position and await further orders. Meanwhile, we sped back towards the ambush. I could hear the deep rhythmic reports of gunfire growing louder by the second as we approached. Dave's vehicle now came along the right side of mine and we advanced in line. Being the only one out on the back, I started to feel very exposed and vulnerable, and the realisation of what was taking place started to hit home. I could clearly see Simon A.'s vehicle, some 75 metres up ahead; his men were all posted out and firing towards the ambush. Seeing one of the insurgent's vehicles still in place, I started pouring rounds into it. However, with my own vehicle being driven none too smoothly, it was hard to get concentrated, effective fire down. With the 35 rounds quickly gone, I changed mags again, and while doing so saw that the black jeep was on the move, trying to accelerate down the off ramp and onto the approach road to Samara. Once there, it would be able to hide safely within the traffic that had stalled during the firefight.

Excitedly, I screamed at Adel to stop, which he promptly did, although in the process he also hit Dave's vehicle, which in turn came to a standstill. Now level with Simon A.'s men, I jumped off the back of the pick-up and ran to the side railings of the bridge for a clear shot and a solid fire base from which to take on the jeep. Some of our Iraqis were shouting wildly and pointing at the escaping jeep – it was turning into a turkey shoot. My blood was pumping, and I couldn't get to the railings quickly enough. Once there, I tried to calm myself down, but there was now only about 15 metres between the escaping insurgents and the civilian traffic. I sighted and squeezed the trigger. All of us were now lined up along the bridge railings, and dust kicked up all around the tinted windows of the jeep as it took several of our incoming rounds.

'Stop firing, stop firing. Fucking stop firing, now!' The gunfire ceased on Dave's command. The madness of extreme violence, with all its noise and destruction, faded, leaving only the faint sound of distant car horns and our own hard breathing. The black jeep had made it behind the line of civilian vehicles and was soon completely out of sight. It had taken several hits, and I could only hope that there'd be a lot of families wailing that night in Samara. As for the other two cars, one had disappeared across country, leaving the second one *in situ*, though anybody inside was no longer of this world.

I stayed kneeling against the railings, slowly getting my

breath back. The quietness seemed excessive. Dave ordered us to 'make safe' – in this case, an unload followed by a load. We were ready for further action, but no one was handling a weapon with one up the spout. We then carried out what we would call in the Foreign Legion a PAM – a Personnel Armament Material check. The US sergeant, still in the back of the vehicle, had taken a round that had entered via the door and travelled through his body armour and into his mid-back region. He was conscious but obviously a bit shocked, as he was no longer talking about wrestling or Harleys! It was soon discovered that the bullet had not in fact lodged in his back; it was more of a flesh wound, as the round had exited the other end of the body armour. A field dressing was applied, and we gave him lots of reassurance about how light the injury was in order to stave off major shock. Simon A. had several facial cuts from getting his windows shot out, and along with the small gash on my left hand that was the extent of our injuries.

As for the vehicles, Simon A.'s had been well and truly hit, with all bar one of the tyres shot out and bullet holes puncturing the bodywork in several places. Its mechanical fluids were all over the pitted tarmac road. My vehicle had taken six rounds, plus the two that had hit my Kalashnikov. On the insurgent side of things, I was sure I'd accounted for at least one. Simon A. had also taken at least one out, and we reckoned that the total killed was five. Just as we were about to send a team out for a sweep, a US military patrol arrived, so we left the task to them. They confirmed afterwards that there were five insurgents dead, which for some unexplained reason was later amended to three. Whoever said that truth was the first casualty of war obviously meant adding up. EuroNews also put out a broadcast that a firefight had taken place in Samara between US forces and insurgents, resulting in the deaths of five insurgents.

The arithmetically challenged US patrol escorted us to their base some five kilometres away, dragging the shot-up vehicle behind one of their Humvees. In the first-aid station, I received five stitches, and the Harley-loving US sergeant was flown to the military base at Balad. We met up with him a month or so later, and he was very tearful, thanking us for saving his life. As with all wounded US military personnel, he received a Purple Heart but wasn't at all boastful. Still fucking harping on about wrestling and Harleys, though!

The mission having been aborted, we returned to Baghdad one US sergeant light but with all the lorries and medical supplies intact. That evening, as the 'high' feeling from being in combat evaporated, I hit a real low. Gone was the exhilaration and energy, and I was filled instead with a deep gut-wrenching sense of impending doom. All I could see was the hard, evil face of the insurgent who, just before pulling out his Kalashnikov, had looked me square in the face. His eyes now took on a devilish quality in my imagination, the black burning pupils expressing sheer demonic hatred. Then I would see the array of guns pointing at me from the other two vehicles. I kept thinking, 'What if they had opened up?' I had always pooh-poohed any ideas about post-traumatic stress disorder, and I wasn't inclined to start believing in it now. But something had happened to me. A few hours before, I had been as high as a kite, relishing the thrill of the kill and that glorious, out-of-this-world, mind-blowing, adrenalin-rushing, take-life-by-the-fucking-throat-and-love-every-minute-of-it YES of being a soldier. Suddenly, that feeling had completely dropped out of the soles of my feet.

My brain just wouldn't switch off! I had to control myself, but panic was welling up inside me, and I had butterflies in my stomach with razorblades strapped to their wings – I could feel them cutting me up inside. And all the time I could see those guns opening fire on me as I stared back at them – a rabbit in the fucking headlights of death. I was scared – very scared – not only because of the day's events but because I knew that even then I wouldn't be quitting. I wanted to and yet I didn't. Looking back now, I can only reason that it was my 17 years as a soldier that stopped me from walking there and then. If I had, my career would have been a sham. The expression to lose one's bottle springs to mind. Losing your bottle happens before or after the event, when you imagine things going wrong or remember the things you did do wrong, all of them seeming inevitable, unavoidable and unforgivable. I spent many lonely hours after the Samara incident torturing myself about how different the outcome could have been. At the thought of death – or worse, the instantly sweat-inducing and very real possibility of capture, my pulse would quicken – I'd suffer uncontrollable bursts of adrenalin rushing through me and smashing into the tips of my fingers. The insurgents had been that close; a few well-placed shots and the vehicle could have been stopped. Wounded and unable to defend myself, I'd have been grabbed, slung into a stinking, suffocating car boot and driven away to a slow, humiliating and painful death, my tortured, broken features seen by millions on TV. How would my family ever be able to forgive me for the complete helplessness they would experience throughout the whole ordeal? My mum – my God, she'd be utterly destroyed. She didn't even know I was in Iraq.

The father of the first American hostage to be beheaded said that it felt like the insides of his stomach had been ripped out. Although his son is now dead, he and his family relive the death every second of their lives.

It might sound strange, but I suppose I've always been a bit sensitive. I can't abide to watch any form of cruelty on TV – things like mob violence, beheadings, or any sort of sadism or vindictive behaviour where pain is deliberately inflicted by one human being on another. The sight of it makes me instantly aggressive. At least that's the physical manifestation, but inwardly I'm distressed, and it takes me days to get the images out of my head. I once saw footage of a blindfolded Iranian woman being publicly stoned to death – shame on them.

The next day, after ten weeks in Iraq, I was finally due to take my first leave. There was just one snag to enjoying it, though: I simply didn't want to be at home, seeing people in that normal, relatively safe civilian world. How cosily seductive it ought to be: to take a shower whenever I wanted, go out for meals, laze in bed, take Spinney for a walk, stroll through the shops with more than enough money to buy whatever took my fancy and to be where the ebb and flow of normal life was a thing to savour. You'd think. The excited anticipation of leave with loads of dosh in my pocket was now well and truly lost. Instead, my mood was one of continual anxiety, punctuated with periodic bursts of uncontrollable angst and morbid premonitions. Mentally, I was running wildly out of control, worried about where this might all lead, and I did not want to be left alone with my imagination.

Meanwhile, I put on a brave front, especially when meeting up with some of the Armor Group office wallahs. But Dave knew my real fears. We were both very frank with one another, and with the unprofessional head-sheds' idea of back-up – or lack of it – he could understand only too well where I was coming from. As we would often say in the Foreign Legion, there was a *'Sacré Bande de Connards'* – (loosely translated as 'Right Bunch of Tossers') running the show. Worse was to come. Enough for now, I'll turn the tap off. The constant dripping is getting on my tits.

4

GSXR600 MEETS HILTON PARK LANE

Leave? Leave it out! I was definitely not going to have a relaxing time, not with the state my mind was in, convinced as I was that I would be killed when I returned to Iraq. This being the case, I devised what psychobabblers call a coping strategy; in other words, I decided to 'fuck it all'. Usually when I was on leave, I would put away most of the money I had earned overseas so that banks and investment companies could profit from it, but this time I would profit. How? By spending it – all of it!

On arrival at Kuwait airport via the RAF Hercules flight from Baghdad, I was met by the Armor Group rep, whose mission was to pick up the lads coming out of Iraq and whisk them off without delay to obscene luxury. This meant an opulent and extravagantly furnished five-star Kuwaiti hotel. In the space of 90 minutes, I'd gone from the grinding heat and dust of the most dangerous city in the world to a place of affluent, air-conditioned comfort, where, gliding past massive bowls of gleaming fruit, polished marble and beautiful women, silent elevators carry you effortlessly to umpteenth-floor rooms straight from the pages of *Fortune* magazine. Here, at the click of a button, you could enjoy satellite TV or summon bowing concierges to fetch you any kind of sumptuous food. Or you could just lie back on the spotless linen, gaze at the artwork and listen to the silence. The hotel was, in short, ghastly.

Being plunged into such total peace and tranquillity only intensified my anxiety, the quiet giving added space for my mind to dwell on the recent events and dark thoughts playing in my head. I was thousands of pounds better off and had a contract for one year with a private-security company, but I also knew that the firm could sack me for having my eyes too close together if it wanted to. The contract wasn't really worth anything, and I could quite easily walk away from the job and never go back. And although my 17 years' soldiering and pride in my profession baulked at the thought, the fear now hitting me so hard was only worsened by the knowledge that there was a get-out clause. If I weakened and jacked, I would have to live with my conscience. Yes, I could justify it by saying that it was only a security-company job, that I was doing it for the money and that my life was more valuable than either, but for me that wasn't a valid argument. If I did return to Iraq after this leave, I knew I'd be facing up to the biggest fear yet experienced in my life. Maybe then, after going back and soldiering on, I could walk away with peace of mind.

All this rationalising about why I was so full of angst didn't alter the fact that I was bloody scared and looked set to remain so for the rest of my leave. The thought of something bad happening is always worse than when it actually does. 'The only thing we have to fear is fear itself,' Franklin D. Roosevelt once said. I wonder if he ever faced an evil-eyed bastard with an AK on the road to Samara. I was now facing three weeks of agonising anticipation and the dread of what was to come – the only cure was a return to action. The sooner I got back on that horse the better.

The hotel room exuded its deafening silence. Adding insult to injury, there was no fucking beer, Kuwait being a strictly Muslim country. Thank goodness I had an endless supply of coffee and fags – what a combination! Hurray for cigarettes – pure comfort food. The warnings on the packets had ceased to have any effect on me, my over-fertile imagination having more important matters to dwell on: ambushes with narrow escapes and future ambushes without narrow escapes. This was how I was to spend my first night's leave, sitting up alone in the hotel room, smoking and drinking good strong coffee, my brain on auto rewind, going over and over the same thoughts again and again and again.

The BA flight to Heathrow found me sitting between a British police officer and a former guardsman. The policeman, on a six-month posting to the British Embassy in Baghdad, had been on the same Hercules as me the previous day. The ex-guardsman, a monster of a man, was now working for Olive, one of the many private-security firms on the bandwagon. He too was off on leave after a stint down in Umm Qasr, where he'd been opening and closing a gate. Mind you, not all of Olive's contracts were that safe; they also had their share of casualties. Sean, an ex-Legionnaire and good friend of mine, was with them in Baghdad when he was blown up by a vehicle-borne suicide bomber. He suffered a severed ear and several deep cuts from flying lumps of metal and glass. He was lucky, as two of his oppos were killed, along with the electronics engineer they were escorting. Sean did return to Iraq after his wounds healed, but a few more close calls persuaded him to call it a day. He's now working in pastures green – well, sandy.

The ex-guardsman sat glued to the tiny television screen on the headrest in front of him, shut off from all conversation by the plastic headset stretched across his enormous head. I chatted on and off with the policeman, getting the impression that he was not at all comfortable with life in Baghdad. He was also able to shed light on an incident that had occurred on our flight out of Baghdad the previous day. The Hercules C130 had just begun to level out after take-off when it fired off two lots of chaff. The two loud explosions that this caused shook everyone, including the usual pretenders to deep sleep, into an immediate state of alert; we all expected a missile to slam into us any second. The startled flight crew had anxiously scanned the portholes. Nothing further happened and no explanation was made. Everyone settled themselves back down to getting cramp again.

The policeman now told me that on touching down in Kuwait he'd phoned his embassy in Baghdad, who confirmed that a surface-to-air missile (SAM) had been fired at us. Aircraft landing and taking off from BIAP are regularly engaged with missiles. Some have had narrow escapes, like the DHL cargo plane that was hit on a wing yet still managed to land. On another Hercules C130 flight from Iraq, an Australian lost his life, hit by small arms fire just after take-off. A round hit the belly of the plane directly beneath him and entered his body through his backside, running riot before lodging further up inside him. Apparently, he had died instantly with no visible signs of bleeding and so was assumed to be asleep for the remainder of the flight. It was only when trying to rouse him on touchdown with the usual shake and ear-bashing – ''Ere, mate, wake up or you'll be back up in Baghdad before you know it' – that anyone realised he was dead. After this, an SOP was issued that body armour and helmets should be worn while over Iraqi airspace. And there were a lot of people who subsequently sat on their body armour when flying! After the SAM that was fired at our plane that day, another RAF Hercules was hit while on the approach to landing north of Baghdad at Balad, killing everyone on board.

Further conversation with the police officer revealed something else we had in common. After he had enquired about my bandaged hand, I told him about the ambush and subsequent firefight on the Samara bypass. His expression changed abruptly at the mention of Samara. It transpired he had taken part in a meeting with the Samara police force a few days prior to the ambush. Along with a delegation of high-ranking officials from the British and American embassies, he had flown up to liaise with the Iraqi security forces in Samara. The mission was to ascertain why the Iraqi authorities had lost their grip on the town. Without going into great detail, he told me that there were large numbers of foreign fighters and criminal elements installed in Samara, who now had the place effectively under their control. He added that a military assault was planned to win back the town. I asked casually, with my fingers firmly crossed, if this assault was scheduled to take place within the next three weeks. His answer was no. Shit – fucking lazy bastards! Still, something to look forward to on my return – a nice day out along the Samara bypass.

At Heathrow, I went straight to the bar and ordered a long-awaited pint of lager, then another one. I felt happy sitting there, watching the world go by. As the lager started taking effect, my mind began to let go of all the doom and gloom. Seeing the holidaymakers and folk just milling around was pleasant. The ebb and flow of normal life seemed to be doing it for me, after all – for now, at least. My plan was to have a couple of quiet beers, followed by about 20 noisy ones!

I woke up the next morning in a small, nondescript hotel somewhere in London. 'Three fucking weeks to spend all your dosh, Simon,' I thought, 'and you end up in this shit hole.' Amateur! The following night I booked into the Hilton on Park Lane. I still managed to wake up alone and with a hangover, though it was a much better class of hangover. I looked at my wounded hand, which had been gradually swelling up and was now almost double its former size. It throbbed constantly, and when I put it under running water the tightly stretched yellow flesh spat and boiled. I had to get it looked at.

I left London and flew down to Plymouth in style, if you call a Dash 8 serving Ginsters pies at exorbitant prices style. On board, a glamorous, shapely, big-lipped, 30-something stewardess turned her large dark eyes towards me and asked if I wanted a Cornish pasty. What could I say? 'Nah thanks, luv, they give me almighty wind'? I refrained, and trying to get into her good books, I bought two. If it didn't work, I could always show her my gammy hand.

Meanwhile, I had to see a woman about a dog. My sister Sophie, to be precise, and her husband Michael, a serving captain in the Royal Marines, having worked his way up from the ranks during 20 years' service. Sophie is a solicitor and her daughter Alice, my niece, is reading medicine at university. Alice has also represented England at the Commonwealth Games in a combat sport, so she'll have no trouble defending the NHS! I was looking forward to seeing them all and, after ten long weeks, the inevitably rumbustious greeting from Spinney.

For some reason, Sophie had insisted on picking me up from Plymouth Airport. I thought this strange, as I'd always made my own way to her home before. I hadn't really told her much about events in Iraq over the phone. Perhaps given the news flow, she thought I needed looking after. Oh, well, a lift is a lift.

My mum also lived in Plymouth, having moved down from

Aberdeen some 17 years earlier to help look after Alice when she was little. Before departing for Iraq, I'd been living fairly close by to them all, in the caravan on Bodmin. That year on the moors with Spinney had been a great time. For a start, there were no ever-increasing council, water and electricity bills to pay, and the thrill of living 'while others sleep' made me feel privileged. Most of my lamping had been on ground on which I had no permission to hunt, but this only added to the thrill. My poaching was not blind or random, though, as I would always do a recce the morning before. I looked first of all for signs of rabbit – such as rabbits still in the field, or the openings to several warrens on the earthy banks. If I could 'walk up' the field, I could tell whether the warrens were inhabited by looking for fresh, worn earth in the entrances or droppings nearby. Areas of lighter grass often meant rabbits had been bounding around. The old rabbit catchers, or warreners, would place their snares according to these signs.

I never took Spinney with me on these recces, as any landowner observing me would be only too well aware of my intentions. Some of them can be nasty bastards, either lying in wait for you with some local muscle, or setting traps to harm the fast-running dog. So, I always did my best to look like a rambler rambling! Ensuring Spinney wouldn't get harmed during the actual hunt was also of paramount importance, and I would search for any old machinery hidden in high grass or fencing. Just strands of wire, even telegraph poles, have done for lurchers in full flight. If I saw any of these potential hazards, I would rule out that location. Any given night of poaching would consist of going to at least two locations with several fields each. If on arrival one of these was suspect for any reason, I would move straight on to the second location. A golden rule of poaching is never to return and hunt up the same location in a season. There are plenty of fields – you just have to be prepared to travel.

I should explain that lamping involves using a torch beam to follow a rabbit during its bid to escape one of the fastest animals on earth – a lurcher. Depending on size, lurchers can also be used to run down and kill hare, fox and deer. A lurcher is a cross between a greyhound or whippet and either a terrier (such as a Bedlington) or collie. A good master can bring on his lurcher to catch the rabbit alive and retrieve it to hand unbruised.

The fact that I was poaching meant I couldn't use just any old lamp. A wide-beamed, million-candle-power job, lighting up Farmer Giles's field like a Rolling Stones concert, would be slightly conspicuous – a bit like the squaddie wearing all the latest must-have Gucci kit with a really wicked camouflaged face but whose watch double-beeps every hour on the hour! So, not wishing to draw any attention to my nocturnal activities, I used a narrower-beamed, though still quite powerful, torch. It takes a bit of getting used to trying to stay on the jinking prey but practice always makes perfect.

I was usually only out for two rabbits, maybe three if someone had put in an order. Ideal conditions were a fresh wind, causing any leaves on the swaying branches to rustle a little, married with a light, steady rain. This all helped to camouflage any noise I made, ensuring that the rabbit's ears remained firmly down, concentrating solely on eating, well away from their earth-bank holes. A bit of rain can also keep your insomniac farmer indoors next to his Rayburn.

Yes, it was by far and away the most fulfilling year of my life – one man and his dog. Henry David Thoreau, a philosopher-type, once said something like, 'A man's riches may be measured by the things he can do without.' I'd been well flush. Maybe I would be again. I knew Spinney would be up for it.

What Sophie hadn't told me was that I would have to wait for her for a while outside Plymouth Airport. I took the opportunity to light up, instantly bonding with two other smokers through our mutual leper status. As always, I managed to steer the conversation on to the best lurcher in the South West and how privileged they were, as Spinney would no doubt be turning up any minute in my sister's car. Spotting Sophie's metallic-orange Focus, I prepared for 'mad dog going nuts' time. I thought Spinney would by now be trying to jump through the windscreen, but all I could see was Sophie. Pulling up next to me, she leaned over and opened the door.

'Hello, where's Spinney?' I said.

'He's dead,' she replied.

I could see the anguish in her face. I slumped into the passenger seat, crammed my black bergen between my legs and buried my head in it. 'Just drive, Sophie.' We travelled in silence for about 30 seconds before I spoke again. 'How?'

'He was hit by a car while Michael was walking him. He's in bits.'

'Who? The dog or Michael?' I just couldn't resist it. The air cleared instantly.

Well, what now? I was deeply cut up about losing Spinney. But it had happened three weeks ago, and Sophie and Michael had been suffering all that time. Not only had a cracking little Bedlington cross-whippet, whom they adored, been killed, but for 21 days and nights they'd carried the agonising burden of how they were going to tell me! Michael was taking it bad, feeling he was to blame. I assured him he wasn't – it was part and parcel of keeping dogs. Anyway, if I hadn't gone off to Iraq, Spinney would have been with me, so maybe I was to blame. But ultimately no one was at fault for his untimely death, which was simply a matter of fate.

What next? A bloody tax bill, that's what, waiting for me on Sophie and Michael's kitchen table. On opening the scary buff envelope, I launched into a rant about how unfair it all was – there were people trying to kill me in Iraq, my dog was dead and now the tax man wanted my dough. Sophie just cracked up laughing. I looked at her dumbfounded. Still roaring, she said it would make a terrific country-and western song. She was right, it would. Brilliant. The only thing to do was laugh.

The following morning, my hand was no better. In fact, it was getting steadily worse, so I took myself along to A & E at Derriford Hospital in Plymouth. The nurses there did a great job, cleaning out the infected wound and using tape rather than stitches to hold the damaged skin together. I was in and out in an hour. Don't slag off the NHS. It might be on the ropes, but Derriford wasn't letting on. The X-rays didn't show any nasty foreign bodies and the infection was only local. Asking how I sustained the injury, a nurse did give an 'oh-yeah' look when I mentioned Iraq and said it looked more like I'd been glassed in a pub. Ah, so that's why they call it a 'local' infection.

What I fancied next, more than anything, was a bit of the old open road, and I reckoned if I could put on my old motorcycle gloves, I would buy a bike to go with them. Try as I might, though, my swollen hand would not squeeze into a Kevlar glove, so I bought a bigger pair and a matching bike – a three-year-old Suzuki GSXR600. Why buy a new one? It only had to last me three weeks.

I returned to London and booked into the now familiar Hilton with the GSXR600 locked safely in the underground car park behind the hotel. I then called up an old girlfriend, Megan, and arranged to meet her that night in Covent Garden at Rules Restaurant. Enter Rules and you enter 'Old England', dining amid richly sombre decor, while

Victorian grandees gaze down from gilt-framed oils and the unbelievably mouth-watering aroma of fine food fills the room. The Olde English Fayre is gob-smackingly good, and that evening was no exception. I did get on my moral high horse with Megan, telling her not to order the foie gras because the method of production is unbelievably cruel to the goose, and recommended the Morecambe Bay potted shrimps instead. Don't mention the cockle pickers.

Exquisite as Rules' grub is, they're missing a trick. They should open early morning for the best dish of all: yer full English, mate. You can just see the building lads in their mud-crusty strides, yellow fluorescent jackets, boots and hard hats, trooping in mob-handed for egg, bacon, sausage, fried slice, bubble, beans and a large mug of tea. With page three and the Pirelli calendar Sellotaped over the smudges. What would John Betjeman say!

After a few more days in London, the vibrant buzz became an annoying hum, and the Hilton Hotel was just a big building with attitude. As for Megan, well, old flames burn out. What more can you say? The effects of normality had now come full circle. Surrounded by people going about their everyday lives and having a good time was making me feel even more of an outcast, knowing that for me this kind of life was only temporary and that I would soon be back in the bedlam of Iraq with its everyday death and mutilation. The Hilton was a case of been there, done that – another box to tick on the list of things to do before departing this world. If I had a few seconds to spare as my life's blood trickled out in an acrid-smelling pool over a rubbish-strewn, pot-holed Iraqi road, at least I'd be safe in the knowledge I had stayed a couple of nights at the Hilton.

The two most important things for me in life are friends and family, and with this in mind I rang my good friend and former comrade Geds, who was still in the Foreign Legion and at that time the *adjudant unite* – company sergeant-major (CSM) – of the first combat company of 2REP (*Régiment Etranger des Parachutistes*), the Foreign Legion's parachute regiment. Geds was pleased to hear from me and could think of nothing better than us having a couple of 'quiet' beers together on a sun-soaked bar terrace in Calvi, tourist hot spot and home of 2REP on the island of Corsica.

Geds and I had first met in French Guiana when both of us were on a two-year posting to the Legion regiment 3REI (*Régiment Etranger D'Infanterie*). That was back in 1990 when I was a legionnaire first class and Geds was a *caporal*. We found we had a lot in common: beer, whores, more beer, more whores, and we were both from London. I had arrived in Guiana from a spell in a Legion prison due to an unlawful period of absence from the parachute regiment, Geds from the cavalry. After our two years of patrolling the rain forests, Geds did his jumps course and has since been with the parachute regiment, where he is now one of the most experienced free-fall jumpers in the Legion. I returned to the basic-training regiment in Castelnaudary as a sergeant taking new recruits through their paces. Two years later, I was posted to 2REI, the infantry regiment, in Nîmes. Mine and Geds' paths often crossed, most notably during what was to be my last year in the Legion, in Congo-Brazzaville (Republic of Congo) in 1997. As I often tell Geds, it was my company, the fourth, who came to sort out those nasty Congolese rebels for them . . .

The first Company of 2REP, along with Geds, then a sergeant, and its CEA (support company) had been deployed to the capital city Brazzaville in the expectation that French refugees would soon be pouring over the river from neighbouring Kinshasa, where violent rebel forces, hell-bent on overthrowing the government of the Democratic Republic of Congo (formally Zaire), were fast approaching.

But before the refugees could get their shit together and flee to safety, the local militias in and around Brazzaville had already got the tantalising smell of death and disorder in their nostrils. Wanting a piece of this sub-human excitement for themselves, they had promptly started attacking each other and, of course, innocent civilians. Though the names of these militia groups bordered on the comic – the Ninjas, the Zulus and the Cobras – their fighting, true to most African power struggles, was fierce, brutal and uncompromising. They even had the audacity to ambush the two Foreign Legion companies in the city streets of Brazzaville, killing two legionnaires. This was a big mistake, in retaliation for which 20-odd rebels met their deaths.

As a result of that incident, reinforcements were deployed to the country, me among them. My company, the fourth of the second foreign infantry regiment, was then serving in Chad, just a few hours' flight on a Transall C160 (like a Hercules but smaller) away. Within a day of the ambush, we were on Congolese soil and swiftly established a defensive position at the then abandoned Aero Club adjacent to the main airport, ready to evacuate the refugees and expats from both Kinshasa and now Brazzaville. Our mission was not only to secure the airstrip but to send sorties into Brazzaville to round up the expats, most of them stranded in their villas and hiding from the murderous rebels, who had even attacked the local zoo, shooting the Belgian keeper in the thigh. Fortunately, he managed to crawl away and hide under his desk. When we reached him, he refused to leave his gorillas, knowing that the Congolese would have no compunction about killing and eating them. So, we got the gorillas into portable cages and took them off to the airport.

Sitting there in the Aero Club, the animals became a must-see attraction, though they were a really rather sad sight in the unfamiliar surroundings. Like the human refugees, the gorillas had also witnessed cruel indiscriminate slaughter, the rebels having killed one of the babies when they ransacked the zoo, and they were now looking very subdued and nervous. Thinking they must be hungry, I went and got hold of some bananas to offer them a snack. The biggest one couldn't resist these, and when I tentatively pushed the bunch through the bars, a hairy if hesitant outstretched arm came forward to take them, his enormous hand making the bananas look tiny. Then, to my joy and amazement, he began to share them with the others, who delicately peeled and ate them. Wow. Humbled, I thought to myself, 'What must they think of us humans?' If we can't, as the Bible says, turn our swords to ploughshares, bananas might do as well. 'Watch out, he's got a gun. Nah, he's all right, it's a bunch of bananas!' A plane arrived soon after, and our furry friends, along with their loyal, courageous keeper, were flown up country to Pointe-Noire to sit out the troubles.

Sadly, not all the evacuations ended on a happy note. I can't remember which of us noticed it first, but a lot of the European women we saw had cut their hair, and that of their daughters', short. They told us it was to make them look like men so they wouldn't be raped. Some had already suffered this fate at the hands of the marauding, heavily armed gangs, who were frequently stoned on drugs. As we escorted the expat refugees on foot across the 500 metres from the Aero Club to the main runway to embark on the Transall C160, its propellers already turning so as to spend as little time on the ground as possible, some of the women could be heard inconsolably sobbing. It was pretty obvious why. We later learned that at least one of these women, unable to come to terms with her ordeal, had committed suicide.

On a positive note, we managed to evacuate five thousand people in just one week, the military flights stacking up high in the skies above Brazzaville, waiting their turn to land. Once down, they'd put the brakes on, open their tailgates, embark the expats, close their tailgates and take off. This went on throughout the day, unless the fighting encroached on our positions at the airstrip, which it did on several occasions. We would fight the rebels off if they attacked us, or go firm when the different factions were having a go at each other close by. As soon as the fighting ceased, the evacuations would speedily recommence.

With all the drama, there was, of course, a heavy press presence, who for the most part attached themselves to our position at the Aero Club. At the drop of a hat, though, they would tear off, armed only with their cameras, to film and photograph any scraps between the warring elements in downtown Brazzaville. They seemed to have scant regard for their own safety, clicking away alone amidst drugged and drunken savages. One of these was the BBC correspondent Dave Chasm. I noticed he had a mobile phone that actually worked, since he was always talking to one person or another on it. This was still early days for mobiles – well, in the Legion, anyway – and I thought it would be nice to ring up my family back in the UK, just to let them know everything was OK with me. Dave Chasm had earlier asked me to get him a camp bed, which I had done. I therefore asked him if he could now scratch my back. ''Ere, Dave,' I said. 'Gis a lend of your phone for a couple of minutes, just to ring home.'

'I'd love to, but the BBC are pretty strict on its use,' he replied.

With that an American voice piped up, 'Here, man, use mine. Catch. Let me have it back when you're done. Take your time.'

I deftly caught the flying mobile phone. The person who'd casually chucked it was an unassuming reporter called Will from World Television News (now APTN) – he was a real-life maverick. Needless to say, from then on he was well looked after. On one occasion, my section (equivalent to a platoon), of which I was second in command, was only a few hundred metres from the warring factions' front lines. We had dug in to hinder any rebels trying to advance on the Aero Club. The factions were involved in a heavy exchange of fire, so I sent a discreet word back for Will and his cameraman Mohammed to get themselves up to my position. They soon joined us, along with a South African journalist friend of Will's who had literally just stepped off a flight in. Within half an hour, he had exclusive footage of intense fighting, with one unlucky rebel getting filmed as he took a direct hit from an RPG. Later, during a quiet spell back at the Aero Club, my section having been rotated from forward positions, Will casually came up to me and in true Hollywood style whispered, 'I know where the beer is, man.' He wasn't joking. Supplies were off-loaded from every flight coming in to rescue the expats. Will had noticed several green-and-white cardboard cases of Heineken. His investigative instincts had taken over, and he had followed them closely to their hiding place, a large walk-in cupboard beneath some stairs that led up to the generals' commandeered accommodation. With the help of a few shoulders and the point of my bayonet, the cupboard door opened to reveal two seven-feet stacks of mouth-watering beer cans. With discreetly muffled ecstasy, we punched the air and did several war-dancing tours around the beer, then set about removing several of the cases. The only thing to do now was dispose of the evidence, which was a tough job for a bunch of thirsty legionnaires and newshounds, but someone had to do it. I don't think the beer was missed, as there was no accounting of goods coming in. The objective of Operation Pelican II was not to scrutinise beer supplies but to get all expats out alive, which was where the exercise of counting really counted, as it were.

On 12 June 1997, our mission was to defend the runway used for evacuating expats by our presence and by firepower, if we came under attack. As second in command of my section, I positioned myself between the second and third groups (equivalent sections in the British Army), the first group being about 200 metres off to my left flank. The *chef de section* (platoon commander) had remained at the HQ for a briefing by the general, leaving me in charge. My section was dug in on line and faced a Congolese Military Air Force base, some 400 metres to our front. The runway was 500 metres to our rear. The Congolese air base was occupied, but, as yet, no shots had been fired on our positions. The problem was that there was no clearly good-guy or bad-guy Congolese. They all just seemed to be happily taking each other on, while sometimes having a pop at us in the middle.

It was now mid-morning, and the evacuation was in full swing, with military transport planes stacking high in the clear African sky, awaiting their turn to land and gobble up more fleeing expats. Nothing out of the ordinary was going on: Hercules and Transalls were coming and going as if on a conveyor belt, and the ever-present sound of gun battles could be heard not far off. But even above all the noise, it didn't take us long to hear what sounded like a T72 tank manoeuvring behind the walls of the Congolese base directly to our front. I shouted out for a sit-rep on the tank, but from our position we were unable to locate it by sight, and it was proving nigh on impossible to get a fix on its position from the engine noise alone. I radioed back to our HQ at the Aero Club, where legionnaires were posted on a number of the buildings. I hoped that they would be able to give us a fix.

At first, I wasn't too concerned, as the tank wasn't in a rebel position. The air base was occupied by elements of the Congolese Air Force, who, like ourselves, were just defending their positions from attack. How wrong could I be? Obviously feeling left out of the general anarchy, these air-force boys had decided to take us on, and the next minute let rip with the 14.5-mm Russian machine gun mounted on the tank. From several points along the wall of the base, they then opened up with AK-47 small-arms fire. Incoming small-arms fire never feels small; in fact, it makes a sickening, bowel-loosening, sharp, dry cracking noise as the rounds hurtle in at bone-smashing speed. Our workaday world had changed from peaceful observation to instant, adrenalin-pumping combat in the blink of an eye. A crescendo of incoming rounds crept up to and through our position, their advance marked by the clouds of dust kicked up by their impact with the ground. Our reflexes took over and we returned fire, putting down an effective blanket of rounds; this gave me time to observe the air-force base. I still couldn't get a fix on the location of the tank, though.

The first group had taken the brunt of the incoming, resulting in the *chef de group* (section commander) being hit. This group was on the extremity of the line, some 200 metres to my left. I decided I would have to break cover to take command of the group. I gave preparatory orders to intensify firing on my command. I also gave orders for the 112-mm anti-tank rocket to be armed ready to fire, instructing the legionnaire to aim to hit an area of the air-force base perimeter wall where previous movement had been seen. This action, along with the rest of the sections' firepower raining down on the Congolese, should afford me freedom from incoming rounds whilst making the 200-metre dash to the first group's position and keep my precious skin intact.

We were still taking incoming, although it was fairly sporadic and wild. I prepared myself for the 200-metre dash.

Caporal Ojescu, the platoon medic, was coming with me, and to gain a bit of speed we both ditched our day sacks. I was feeling good – so good, in fact, that I was actually relishing the prospect of running through incoming fire. How different it all is when you're among well-trained, highly motivated soldiers, confident that everyone around you will do their bit! I looked at Caporal Ojescu, who like me was smiling and enjoying the moment. I had total confidence in him, as we'd both been involved in fighting in the Central African Republic the previous year.

Reports had reached the French government that a military coup had been instigated in the Central African Republic, their former colony and now ally. When it looked as though this coup might very well succeed and topple the Central African Republic government, the head-sheds in Paris decided it was time to send in the troops. My company was then serving in Gabon so was ideally situated to go in and sort out the mess. Obviously, it was going to take more than a company, but with reports that the rebels were now in spitting distance of the presidential palace – a gaff which though resembling an oversized holiday villa was kind of crucial to keep hold of – things were looking urgent. A ground presence was requested immediately, and so one dark night we found ourselves piling into two Transalls and taking off from Libreville Airport. A few hours later, the pilot came on the intercom and said, 'Bangui' – the Central African Republic capital – before plunging the droning shell of the plane into complete darkness. Then, just like a fairground big dipper, we took a hurtling nosedive towards terra firma. Cocooned in the pitch dark, I screwed my eyes tight shut and thought of the water chute at Battersea Fun Fair, where my mum used to treat me and my two sisters when we were kids to a day out on bank holidays. The open-top train on the water chute would slowly ascend the ramp, a large turning cog pulling it higher up the rails, tension building as it neared the dizzy summit. Most of us on board were silent, nervously waiting for the gut-lifting drop over the other side, though a few people would let rip as soon as the climb began, really getting their money's worth and screaming hysterically like extras in an American B-movie. Edging over the precipice, the train would seem to bottle it for a moment, before finally deciding to go for it, sending us all into a massive, thrill-seeking fit of terrified, screaming exhilaration as we dropped at breakneck speed down towards the awaiting tank of water. Those that hadn't already wet themselves were soon drenched, everyone laughing and jubilant with relief as they staggered out of the trucks and off to grab a burger and a Pepsi. Good old British fun.

Going down the water chute was just how I felt that night coming in over Bangui, until the plane lifted its nose at the last minute, and I heard the reassuring screech of tyres connecting with the runway. As an infantry soldier, I prefer to get around the way nature intended, with my size nines firmly on the ground.

Sadly, Battersea Fun Fair is no more, closed down after a fatality on the big dipper during a bank-holiday weekend. My mum had taken us there only the previous day, as always flatly refusing my whining demands for a go on the dipper . . .

'Right, if you don't let me, I'm gonna join the Foreign Legion when I'm older and nosedive into a war-torn and despotic African republic.'

'Righty-o. Now, what do you want? A toffee apple or candy floss?'

'Candy floss.'

A rumour quickly circulated that the main mission for the company would be to secure the airport to allow more troops to be brought in and for the evacuation of the expat community. This didn't go down well, as we started to think about the fighting we would be missing out on. The concern was short-lived for me and my group; being as I was in the first section and the senior sergeant in charge of the first group, I had the privilege of getting the first mission we were tasked with. Earlier that night, the French ambassador to the Central African Republic had received a telephone call from one of three families living within the compound of the Mocaf beer factory, some four kilometres outside Bangui. Rebel forces had taken over the factory, and the situation was turning nasty, with the lives of the three families – women and children included – in serious jeopardy. The rebels were in a very drunken state, hitting the men and threatening worse for the women. Our mission was to rescue the civilians from a clear and present danger. But not only that, we were also to remain in the factory afterwards and safeguard the beer! A valuable commodity was at stake here. I mean, there's fighting for 'Queen and Country' and there's fighting for beer. Imagine the situation: 'Right, Si. You're off to fight in an African republic to put down a *coup d'état*.'

'All right, let's go, be good.'

'Hold on, that's not all. You'll have to take back a beer factory from the rebels and then occupy it for a week.'

'Bummer.'

Whether it's bayoneting open a cupboard or storming a factory, the liberation of ale is its own reward.

The mission intelligence was sketchy, with the number of rebels and their weapons unknown, but the situation was deemed urgent enough to risk sending in 12 legionnaires to save the families. I gave my group some rapid orders. Not knowing the layout of the factory, all I could rely on was a practised drill – to remain as one fighting block, not splintering and losing control. We were to be dropped in by air, so went hastily through further dry drills, practising our exit from the helicopter then going firm to access the situation. Next, I ran through some actions – no resistance, heavy resistance, wounded, etc. I also asked the helicopter pilot if prior to landing he could give us a good overview of the factory and surrounding area. He agreed, providing we weren't taking incoming fire – a proviso I was happy to agree to!

With the streets of Bangui continually echoing to the sound of gunfire and mortars exploding sporadically all around us, our mood was now deadly serious, the adrenalin already flowing for the assault on the beer factory. We assembled at the helicopter, its rotor blades turning and the engine straining noisily, impatient to be airborne. The sense of urgency and danger was palpable. I caught a whiff of av-gas, the heady aroma taking me straight back, as ever, to Bessbrook Mill, Northern Ireland. Kneeling down at two o'clock from the front of the helicopter, eyes squinting and body pressing back against the rotor downwash that was creating a rush of air like a warm Atlantic gale, I waited for the signal to embark. At the thumbs-up from one of the pilots, I doubled over and sprinted forward. This was made easier by the fact we'd not been issued with body armour and had only our small day sacks strapped tightly onto our backs. I knew my legionnaires would be following me and, more importantly, that one Caporal Waminya would be doubling forward with the other half of the group and embarking in symmetry on the opposite side of the helicopter.

Caporal Waminya was, to be fair, a slightly overweight Polynesian. He had a liking for too much alcohol on occasion but was also capable of ripping heads off at an alarming rate. His physical dimensions made the Minimi machine gun habitually slung round his neck look small and deceptively insignificant! Like all South Seas warriors,

Caporal Waminya was an absolute pleasure to have around in a tight situation.

Reaching the open sliding door of the Puma, I stopped and gave the legionnaires a helping shove into the helicopter, getting in last so as to be first out. Waminya and the lieutenant did likewise on the other side. As soon as I'd firmly slid the door closed, the helicopter lifted slightly, wobbled from side to side then climbed steeply up and forward, the pull of gravity pinning me firmly down in the canvas seating. Up we climbed until we had an unparalleled view of the airport and the now matchbox-size black highway leading into the squared road system of smoking Bangui. We headed away from the city, taking a wide detour to our eventual destination on the banks of the River Ubangi, some four kilometres to the west. The tension remained high as I glanced around at everyone inside the helicopter. Serious expressions and intently staring eyes returned my gaze, mirroring my own face. Even if we were inclined to conversation, the constant roar of the engine and rotor blades made small talk – in fact, any talk below a shout – impossible.

Observing the ground far below us, I was suddenly aware of someone tapping me hard on the shoulder. It was one of the co-pilots trying to hand me a headset. I grabbed it and prised the two olive-green earpieces apart, but the headset wouldn't sit on my ears because of my helmet. Ripping my helmet off and placing it securely at my feet, I positioned the cushioned earpieces over my ears. Instantly, the noise dropped to a hum and the calm voice of the pilot, sounding as though he was talking into a tin can, informed me we were nearing our destination. He said that in order to approach the factory unseen he would descend to grass level and, if safe, perform a lift-up just prior to landing to give me a panoramic. Replacing my helmet, I proceeded to grab the attention of my group, tapping shoulders and gesticulating for the others to do the same, until everyone was paying attention. Shouting and gesticulating, I told them we'd shortly be dropping to grass level and flying tactically over the remaining distance to the factory. As if on cue, the helicopter made a dive towards the ground. Trees and vegetation raced up to meet us with such speed that I thought the pilot must have flipped into kamikaze mode and was taking us with him! Twelve legionnaires hung on for grim life as we performed a series of turns, twisting one way then the other. We could see nothing but the ground only feet away, followed by blue sky as we were pinned down by an incredible force, the helicopter climbing steeply to shave the tops of trees ahead, then immediately dropping down the other side, releasing us to weightlessness. These looping aerobatics grew more extreme, the stakes getting higher and higher with every twist and turn. Racing with the dry African grass close enough to touch, I prepared myself for the worst, which, apart from getting shot down before we landed, included the possibility of going firm on the ground only to realise we were hopelessly outnumbered as the departing helicopter disappeared over the horizon.

We banked hard to the right; the rotors were now much louder and produced an almighty cracking sound as they checked the helicopter's direction and slowed it down, resulting in an incredible g force on all of us inside. Fighting against the force, I strained to find a position from which to see outside, as the helicopter, its rotors still cracking loudly in the displaced air, rose about 100 metres up. Looking down, the scene that met my eyes was surreal. Inside the perimeter walls of the Mocaf beer factory were between 15 and 20 pick-up trucks, haphazardly parked around a compound. Plying to and from the factory were perhaps a dozen or more Action Man-sized-looking black men dressed in an assorted array of uniforms – from tiger-striped to olive green – and some were wearing absurdly shaped red berets. With the swarming efficiency of worker ants, the men were carrying crates of beer and loading them onto the pick-ups. Suddenly, it was apparent that our presence had been spotted. The regular pattern of movement broke out into a panicky chaos, the crates of beer were hastily slung down and the looters began running towards their vehicles. Soon there was a stream of pick-ups retreating through the factory gates. Accelerating wildly and kicking up clouds of dry red dust, they careered recklessly off down a potholed road, away through the ramshackle village of mud and corrugated huts beyond the factory compound.

Our helicopter pilot read the situation well, and seeing the effect of our presence hovered some hundred metres or so from the walls of the factory. We were positioned on the western side and made ready to land just outside the wire perimeter fence. Just inside and to the left of the fence stood three villas, which we understood housed the families. I signalled to one of the pilots to put us down on the open ground below. I was surprised at how carefully he made the descent, manoeuvring the helicopter down to hover about a metre off the ground. We streamed out and dropped into position, lying in line just a few metres from the helicopter, its swooping blades flattening the grass all around us. Facing the factory compound, I aimed my FAMAS assault rifle through the wire perimeter fence, selector on single shot, ready to open up and kill any rebel that showed himself. Meanwhile, the helicopter lifted up and soared off to one side, the surface of the grass wobbling like jelly then stilling, ruffled as though it was having a bad-hair day. The noise of the helicopter quickly faded into the distance, and for a split second there was a loud, humming silence in my ears. Quelling it, I shouted to Waminya to check everything was OK at his end. In his deep, perfect French accent, he replied, *'Oui, Sergent.'*

The lieutenant who was with us hadn't uttered a word since boarding the helicopter, which I didn't find surprising, as he wasn't long out of officer training and looked to be a bit out of his depth – not scared but unsure. Good, I was happy for him to just watch and learn. Looking through the wire-mesh fencing about ten metres in front, I could see the back wall of the factory building. During the aerial view, I'd seen several looting rebels around the other side. Despite the number who had run off at the sight of the helicopter, I had to assume that the place was still overrun with them.

As I was assessing my next move, Sukima, my little Japanese sniper, piped up in his high-pitched pidgin French, 'Sergent, Sergent. Homme, homme, devant!' On the inside of the fence next to a tree, was an old black man wearing a holed T-shirt, greyish slacks and flip-flops. With both arms held high above his head, he was pleading in French for us not to shoot him. Although he clearly posed no threat to us, caution demanded I point my weapon at him. Everyone else thought likewise, and as a dozen guns swivelled towards him, the old man performed a comical nosedive behind the tree. In true Monty Python style, I shouted (in French), 'Who are you?'

He replied, sounding like a Nigerian-speaking Frenchman, 'I am the houseboy. Please don't kill me.'

'OK, mate,' I shouted back, 'you're all right. We're here to help you. Where are the three French families?' Hearing the good news, he came running out from behind the tree and lifted up an unsecured section of the fence. Wondering what they had been using this covert access for, but, more importantly, grateful that it was there, I ordered Waminya and his team under the fence. When they were inside and firm, I followed. The old boy advised us that the three families were all together in the third villa and that the rebels who'd been with them had all run off on hearing the helicopter. The bloke had some guts. He'd been inside with the families, but when the helicopter had arrived had come out to get us, not knowing if we'd shoot him or if the rebels were springing an ambush for us in the compound.

Although he said the rebels had all done a runner, I needed to clear the grounds. I ordered Waminya and his team to double up to positions in front of the villa that faced the entrance to the compound. Once they were in position, I could pass behind them and take up a position further along, establishing a view of the front of the main factory building where the pick-ups had been parked. As Waminya was advancing, a figure came running out of the third villa. He was a white gentleman, extremely fat and sporting a loud blue Hawaiian-style shirt. With both hands held high, he shouted, 'Don't shoot, don't shoot!' If the situation hadn't been so serious, I would have pissed myself laughing at this sight; as it was, I did, for a brief second, see the funny side, letting a wry smile form before I returned to the job in hand. Although he was crying and in great distress, the man proceeded to thank us profusely. I told the lieutenant and the radio operator to take him and the houseboy quickly back into the villa and stay with them while I continued clearing the compound.

We continued to advance stealthily round towards the front of the main building when I heard a car starting up on the other side of the factory. Suddenly, a Toyota Land Cruiser pick-up came hurtling around the corner, full to bursting with tiger-striped rebels and accelerating for the open exit on the perimeter. On sighting us, those crammed onto the back of the vehicle opened up with their AK-47s. The shooting was wild, rounds kicking up dust way in front of us and yet more ricocheting high off the breeze-block wall of the factory. But it was enough to give them the few vital seconds they needed to make it out of the compound. We returned fire, but it was more of a reflex action than aimed shots. My FAMAS being on single shot, I was able after the first two rounds to aim into the back of the disappearing truck and get off a further six rounds. They'd got away, but, more importantly, we'd sustained no casualties.

Drenched in sweat, we resumed the clearance, moving from cover to cover further into the compound. The sudden firefight, although it was over in a matter of seconds and none of us had been harmed, left a strong smell of cordite in the air, a sobering reminder of our situation. Miles from any back-up, we were cut off in a beer factory, and Bangui was a no-go area swarming with rebels. On top of this, those rebels had just had their loopy-juice supply severed by a mere handful of forces – forces on the side of a government on the brink of collapse. Any rebel, however drunk, would soon realise that a single helicopter doesn't carry that many men. I began to get seriously worried that the enemy would rally and launch a counter-attack on us. True, we had the lieutenant's radio operator, but whether we'd be able to get through and raise the alarm was another matter. I just hoped that the phone lines were still working.

As we continued clearing the compound, I became acutely aware that I simply didn't have enough men to contain the massive expanse of the grounds contained within the walled and fenced perimeter. Even as we moved, the rebels could be infiltrating unseen in another part of the factory. I had already posted three legionnaires facing the metal gates at the entrance, which we had now closed. Their orders were to shoot to kill if any rebel so much as enquired whether the factory was open for business.

With the clearance finally complete, I returned to the gate. I then made the decision to only defend the main entrance and villas, which were all within 100 metres of each other and, apart from the first villa, all in line of sight. Posting a further two legionnaires facing the main entrance, along with our full stock of 89-mm anti-tank rockets to repel any rebel charge, I left Caporal Waminya doing a good impression of Michael Caine in Zulu. Then, with the three remaining legionnaires, I doubled over to the villas to have a quiet word with the lieutenant about getting reinforcements in place pronto!

Inside the villa, the families were all grouped in one large open-plan living room. Two sets of French windows led out to a garden, which, in complete contrast to the surrounding vegetation, was lush and green. The air in the villa was thick with the odour of foul-smelling French cigarettes. The men were talking to the lieutenant, as the women quietly comforted the children. I could feel the sense of hushed fear as I entered. One woman showed me her face, which bore a red rash from a hand slap, then she pointed to the ceiling. It was pock-marked with several bullet holes, which she explained had been caused by the drunken rebels firing wildly as they looted and rampaged through the villa. I reassured her that she was now in the safe hands of the Foreign Legion, which, I wanted to add, was commanded by a Brit. Not wishing to cause any misunderstanding and thereby add insult to injury, I refrained.

With the relieved families still in recovery, it was hardly the time to let them know we would be pitifully outnumbered in the event of those savages returning mob-handed. I therefore caught the lieutenant's eye and discreetly jerked my head to the door, raising my eyebrows at the same time. He got the message and excused himself, saying he was going out to 'check things over'. With a polite nod to the families, I followed him out.

'Mon Lieutenant,' I said when we were outside, 'I hope we've got comms with the company, as this is way too big a compound for us to secure, and if the rebels mount a counter-attack, we're doing our own fucking Camerone!' (Camerone is the Legion's Rorke's Drift.)

I always liked to sling in a 'fucking' every now and then, sometimes even speaking French in what I call my Madness accent (the 1980s pop group) just for the hell of seeing a Frenchman screw up his face in pain. This wasn't the moment. The lieutenant, having gained a lot more composure since earlier on – in fact, he had a mad glint in his eyes as if he'd just twigged 'I like this' – said the radio operator had not been able to raise the company. Great. Waminya had better carry on as Caine, and I'll play Hookey in the sick bay . . .

All was not lost, however; not yet, at least. The lieutenant said that the land lines were still working, so he'd call the ambassador's residence and get him to relay a message to the company to send reinforcements or the means to evacuate everyone. I just hoped it wasn't a payphone. 'Anyone got a 50-centime piece?' Perhaps we could reverse the charges! The call discreetly made, we waited.

Within the hour, the morale-boosting whirr of a Puma's rotor blades was heard. The group it disgorged into the compound was commanded by one Caporal Chef B., an Austrian with only one and a half ears, the missing half having been eaten by a hungry Brit many years previously. Also with them was our section second in command Sergent Chef B. (equivalent to a colour sergeant in the British Army), a Spaniard whom I did not exactly see eye to eye with – he was a fine soldier but one vindictive bastard. As a good second in command, though, he had the young lieutenant eating out of his hand. I honestly believe that if he'd told the lieutenant to jump, the man would have asked him how high.

Beefed up and in good shape to hold the beer factory, there was now some optimistic speculation we might sample its wares! Sergent Chef B., who had brought orders from the *capitaine*, advised us that the three families would be evacuated by road in a few days' time, when a military column of armour and infantry was expected to push its way through. Until further orders, we were to remain in position thereafter and deny the rebels access to any Dutch courage. The *sergent chef* also ordered us not to inform the families about the hoped-for rescue column, and for once I thought that he had the best interests of someone else at heart. How wrong I was.

After settling down into all-round defence, I allowed myself a pat on the back, pleased with and proud of the 'thank you for saving our lives' praise heaped on us by the three families. Believing myself to be their rescuing hero, I had no qualms about drinking their beer, once it was offered. The head honcho of the factory lost no time in pointing me out to one of the houseboys, saying, 'See that man? Make sure he has an endless supply of cold beer.' The houseboy was a diamond but took 'endless' to mean what it said. I had to politely chastise him the following morning when he arrived at my position at the front of the compound at around 0800 and proudly plonked down another crateful of the chilled, dark-brown bottles of beer. Now, I'd be lying if I said we'd only had a few beers the previous night, but even with it on tap there had to be some respect for suns and yardarms, not to mention one's liver and the need to carry on guarding it all. 'Oi! Cold beer when the sun's gone and cold Coke when the sun's up,' I said. As the days went on, I began to hope I'd never see another Coke bottle again.

On a few occasions, we took incoming rounds, and sometimes, if we were more or less certain of its origin, we returned fire. But the rebels never did mount a full-on attack. They were too busy in town, first with almost overthrowing the president, then with saving their skins from the assault of the French forces, spearheaded by three companies of my regiment, which had arrived during our occupation of the factory.

The families were evacuated four days after our arrival.

I can still see them running, once again with frightened and bemused looks on their faces, from the villas and out through the gate to the waiting armoured column that had finally made it. It was then that I discovered why Sergent Chef B. had told us not to mention the imminent arrival of the armoured column to the families. It was to deliberately orchestrate an element of surprise. Because they didn't know that they were to be evacuated, they didn't pack any cases, and when the column suddenly turned up they were quickly chivvied out of their homes, taking next to nothing with them. Their belongings would all be sent on or stored. Of course they would. Once the families were gone, I watched the *sergent*'s sham operation of making the houseboys load the pick-ups with mattresses and other non-essential gear from the villas, and then ordering them off to look after it all in their homes in Bangui until order was established. This was a simple but crafty ploy to cover up his thieving. When the loyal and trustworthy houseboys brought back the old mattresses and other stuff, it would be assumed that they'd creamed off all the valuables, which Sergent Chef B. had, in fact, lifted from the villas for himself. It left a foul taste in my mouth. We'd saved these people's lives only to then rob them. All right, I didn't do the stealing, but I had turned a blind eye, as had the lieutenant.

The houseboys were so loyal that even after the families had left they still went about their daily tasks. As much as anything, they were probably trying to keep up some sense of normality amid all the chaos. The old boy who had risked his life coming to find us would stand ironing on the terrace of the villa, neatly and meticulously folding everything. I'm sure he ironed the same clothes over and over again. Just before our departure, the *sergent chef* put the finishing touches of his plan into action, and the houseboys drove off with the 'gash' items. They were cute, though, and suspected they were being set up. From their faces, it was also plain that they knew what the implications might be for them. But what could they do? They were servants, and servants always steal, don't they? Not like the fine officers of the Legion, not like gallant Sergent Chef B. To exploit these innocents and make them fall guys for his greed was to me worse than robbing the families. But rob them he did; when we returned to Gabon, the *sergent chef* had one of their laptops.

Back with the company, I soon learned we had missed out on some good fighting in Bangui, after all. Caporal Ojescu and the others had taken back the radio station, cutting off the rebel broadcasts. Their unofficial propaganda could now be replaced with proper propaganda. Legionnaires involved in the fight for the radio station told us their war stories of who'd done what – so-and-so nearly cutting a rebel in two with an 89-mm rocket, etc., etc. One incident that was recounted to me made my blood boil. After the successful assault on the radio station, the rebels had capitulated and surrendered in droves. Elements from my company in Bangui had been charged with rounding them up and handing them over to the Guard Presidential, the forces that had remained loyal to the government. This force was now strategically positioned throughout Bangui, guarding government buildings, controlling crossroads and generally making their presence felt. Having assembled some stray rebels, who were duly stripped to their underwear and had their hands firmly plasti-cuffed behind their backs, the legionnaires herded them into the back of a VLRA (large open-top Land Rover-type vehicle) and drove around Bangui in search of a group of Guard Presidential to whom they could hand over the prisoners. When an element of Guard Presidential was found securing a sensitive location, the prisoners were taken down off the VLRA to be handed over to them. At that point, the prisoners became very agitated, and one of them tried to make a break for it. This resulted in him being shot and killed by one of the Guard Presidential. Mayhem quickly ensued, with the rest of the plasti-cuffed prisoners bomb-bursting away, running for their lives. They all met the same fate as the first prisoner, each and every one of them being shot and killed by the Guard Presidential as they pathetically tried to run with their hands tied behind their backs. Not one of them made it more than a few metres. In the space of one minute, what had been living human beings were now dead bodies, lying at obscene angles, some twitching and pissing blood. The maddening thing was that these rebels had staged the *coup d'état* because they had received no pay for several months, unlike the well-paid Guard Presidential! No one bites the hand that feeds them, I suppose.

Reinforcements from France soon arrived, freeing us up to return to Gabon and carry on with our jungle training there. However, before we left, we found one resident of the Central African Republic who did bite the hand that fed him – our hands to be precise. We bore no grudges, though. In fact, we took him back home to Gabon with us. He was a foul-mouthed African Grey Parrot who had been saved from the burning Maison Radio. In his new home, he sat proudly in a cage in front of the company lines, telling any admirer who stopped to look at him to 'go fuck yourself'. Well, any fool can say 'pieces of eight'.

With only intermittent fire now coming from the Congolese air base, my section was dominating the firefight. Caporal Ojescu and I ditched our unnecessary kit, and I asked him, '*Prêt, Ojescu?*'

'*Prêt, Sergent.*'

'*Intensification de feu dans quinze secondes,*' I ordered over the radio.

'*Un, reçu.*'

'*Deux, reçu.*'

'*Trois, reçu.*'

Ojescu and I readied ourselves, waiting for the covering fire to intensify. Hopefully, it would keep the heads of the Congolese rammed firmly in the dirt. I knew the groups would first put down an almighty barrage then enough sustained fire to cover our dash to the first group. Boom! The 112-mm anti-tank rocket hurtled towards the wall of the air base, exploding on impact. This was our starting pistol. We sprang off the blocks and were away, neither gravity nor the added kilos of body armour and ammunition any match for the energy now ignited within, a white-hot furnace of fear and excitement driving us on. I was now oblivious to the awesome firepower going down, the only thing audible my own heavy breathing and the clatter of equipment on my back. Totally immersed in my own head space and conscious only of the need to cover the 200 metres of open ground as fast as possible, I locked onto my destination like an Exocet. The realisation that I was now out in the open and that any moment a lump of flying metal could slam into me was utterly exhilarating, the adrenalin pouring through my body quickening the rush, pumping up the thrill. 'Come on then you bastards! Yes . . . yes . . . yes!'

Having reached the first group's emplacement, I set about rapidly organising the men to prepare for withdrawal, at least out of small-arms range. Ojescu took charge of the wounded *chef de group*, cutting off one leg of his combat trousers to gain access to the gunshot wound on his upper thigh then checking there were no further wounds. The incoming rounds having now abated, Adjudant L., a Brazilian, together with Caporal G., a giant of a German, raced out to us with a pick-up and recovered the wounded *chef de group*. Once they left, I gave the order to prepare smoke for our withdrawal to the runway, some 500 metres to the rear. The second and third groups remained in their positions and covered us as we withdrew. The *chef de section*, Adjudant H., an Arab, had got himself and three VABs (armoured troop-carrying vehicles, mounted with 12.7-mm guns) up to the runway by the time we arrived. We were then able to cover the withdrawal of groups two and three.

The wounded *chef de group*, a Dutchman, was flown out on the next flight, making it back to Paris the following day. I only saw him once after that, when I was clearing Aubagne during my last week in the Legion. At first, I didn't recognise him, as he had put on a considerable amount of weight and had quite a pronounced limp. His wound had become badly infected, and the surgeons at the military hospital had been forced to remove a good inch of his thigh bone. This was at least better than a report by a French journalist in *Raids* magazine that said he had received a serious head wound! An error that might be forgiven but for the fact that the journalist had taken photographs of the patient on a stretcher just before he was airlifted out of Brazzaville, bandage plainly visible on his leg. Perhaps the journo thought legionnaires wear their brains in their legs, though obviously his own head was lodged somewhat higher up. Old Dutchy's limp wasn't our only souvenir. Caporal Ojescu received a gallantry medal and citation, as did I.

Blasting down to Nice at 130 mph, all thoughts of Iraq conveniently stowed away, I was determined nothing would hold me back – certainly not speed limits or gendarmes' snares. (The latter are now more common in France than Britain – all good things come to an end. Spain's maybe good for another ten years, till they get civilisation.) I had made the same journey many times while in the Legion.

An hour before Montpellier, I turned left onto a road that must have been designed by a motorbike fanatic, the wide expanse topped with sticky tarmac, running into large sweeping bends with clear visibility on the exits. There was not a soul in sight for well over ten miles. I had looked forward to this stretch of the route, signalling as it did the approach of the coast and the imminent reunion with my good mate Geds – the raucous reminiscences, the catching up on each other's lives, the laughter and, of course, the drinking. I was filled with an immense feeling of euphoria and well-being, the day a joy to be a part of.

When travelling to somewhere or someone special, the anticipation of arrival is a state of mind I always like to savour, pausing from time to time en route to sit with the moment. Simple things like stopping off at a service station are for me not dull necessities but little shots of perfect happiness. Sprawled by the bike on the patchy grass and soaking up the sun, I like to watch the world go by while dragging on a cigarette and sipping good, strong, ground coffee. Ever the sybarite, I always take time out to enjoy small pleasures. Afterwards, I zipped up my leathers and started the bike, its illegal race exhaust growling. I then nailed it onto the approach road and roared back towards the autoroute with a wheelie slung in for good measure. Childish, I know, but, wow, life doesn't get any better!

The ferry for Calvi was due to sail from Nice harbour at 6 a.m. The air was cool with just a light breeze, the dawn beginning to show through the night sky. Sitting astride the bike with my helmet off while I queued on the quay, I could tell that the day was gonna be a scorcher, only growing hotter as we got nearer to Corsica. The early morning sights, sounds and, most redolently, smells around the quay were already transporting me back to earlier days. I saw myself together with five other proud and smartly attired legionnaires in *tenue de sortie* (best-dress uniform) and *képi blancs*, enjoying the nervous glances of civilians waiting, like us, to board the ferry for Corsica. They were off on holiday, while we were hoping to earn our wings and thereby join the Foreign Legion's infamous paratroopers of 2REP. That was sixteen years before. I'd just completed basic training at the Legion base at Castelnaudary. To fulfil my all-consuming ambition, all that remained was to pass the pre-jumps course of three weeks, which started the minute our feet touched down on Corsican soil. Finishing first in basic training had at least assured me a place on the boat to Calvi.

The six of us crossing that day had comprised two Brits, one Spaniard, one ex-French para, one Pole and, last but not least, a German. The ex-French para was my battle partner in training by name of Carrière, a Parisian. He, like every Frenchman who joins the Legion, was immediately given, without exception, a new identity, including a new nationality, from a country such as Canada, Luxembourg or Monaco. In this way, the Legion maintains its tradition of never spilling French blood. New identities are also given to any recruit accepted into the ranks of the Foreign Legion who is on the run from their past – be it criminal or matrimonial. This process is called *Sous Anonymat* (Under Anonymity). These individuals are bound never to break this contract of anonymity, and if they do, they are immediately kicked out of the Legion. It is the sin of all sins, and quite right, too, as the Foreign Legion is prepared to deny your existence to whoever is looking for you. Theoretically, no lie has been told, as the original person no longer exists. What other organisation can offer this as a perk of the job? So, if you're dumb enough to ring your loved ones at home and are caught doing it, fuck off back to 'em, cos your new life has just ended.

Carrière was a tough cookie and a switched-on soldier, but like all Frenchmen got a particularly hard time from the instructors. This was not to change in 2REP, as our section second in command, Sergent Chef J., was the hardest, scariest, nutter I have met – or ever will meet. Ironically, he too was a Parisian. He took an instant dislike to Carrière from day one, and when he discovered that his new charge couldn't swim, he tied his hands behind his back and kicked him into the regimental swimming pool. We stood transfixed as Carrière floundered. I assumed that Sergent Chef J. would jump in at any second, but it soon became clear that he was happy to let the man drown. Carrière and I had watched each other's backs throughout training and had automatically teamed up in 2REP, so I jumped in and pulled him to the side. Coughing and spluttering, he was hauled up and out by the others.

Oddly enough, Sergent Chef J. liked me, although it didn't stop him from smashing me full in the face one day, splitting my bottom lip, because he felt that I hadn't executed an order in the field quickly enough. Needless to say, Carrière remained very wary of him, but always stood his ground and was one of the toughest legionnaires around. Sadly, I lost contact with Carrière when I was posted to French Guiana. I did hear news of him from time to time, but this news eventually dried up, and after some four years in the Legion his trail went cold.

Sitting there on the quay at Nice, a holidaymaker this time – and a relatively well-off and free man – I knew that if I had the chance, I'd do it all again. The ten years I'd spent in the Foreign Legion had more than lived up to the adventurous life I'd sought, leaving the comforts and worries of everyday life far behind. But looking back, the biggest adventure of all was the time spent travelling to join the Foreign Legion. The strong sense of excitement mingled with the fear of the unknown made me feel very much apart from everyone around me safely going about their daily lives. Knowing that I could just turn back and be part of that routine only strengthened the sense of anticipation I was feeling about the ultimate adventure I was voluntarily setting out on. And it all started with a question . . .

'Is that one dead, mate?' I looked up and thought for a second – long enough to make my decision. I nodded and the barman in the Half Moon Tavern in Herne Hill, south London, took my glass, added it to his stack of empties and moved to the next table. I had finally and all of a sudden made up my mind, and nothing could now make me wait. It was unusual for me to leave a pint unfinished, but that night I had unfinished business. Procrastination had held me captive too long.

After seven years in the British Army, I had been working on the roads for the previous few months. Spreading hot tar was hard graft, but the money wasn't bad. However, the Legion thing had been knocking around in my head for quite some time, and that night in the pub I accepted its siren call. I'd be lying if I said that I hadn't thought about the danger, but I also glimpsed a more crushing fate not far off – that of a life unlived. I had finally accepted that I'd rather be a dead legionnaire than a bored and unfulfilled 40-something might-have-been in a few years' time! So I picked up my coat and headed for the exit.

Walking out of the pub, weaving my way through the drinkers, I felt a rush of excitement. Seeing them all sitting there with their real ale and their ready salted, their mortgages and retirement plans, I thought, 'If only they knew where I am going!' I also felt stomach-churning apprehension. I knew that this was it – I was going to do it.

Back at my flat, I grabbed my passport and stuffed a change of clothes into a small grip, then closed the door for the last time. I didn't lock it. The world was welcome to my worldly possessions, such as they were. Clearing customs at Dover,

I was pulled aside and asked my destination, to which I replied France. I was then asked if I was going to join the Foreign Legion. 'Yes,' I replied. I was instructed to wait. A check had to be run on my passport. Five minutes later, I was nodded through. Someone said, sounding genuine, 'Good luck!' I hoped I wouldn't need it.

I did the watching the white cliffs of Dover bit from the back of the ferry, but *sans* the Vera Lynn impression. 'Tomorrow, just you wait and see,' I thought. Adrenalin was bursting through me as I contemplated what was ahead of me. I'd never felt so alive, looking round at the booze cruisers and white-van bootleggers going across the Channel to get their fags and lager, while I was off on one of the last great adventures available to the common man!

I'll join the Legion that's what I'll do,
And in some far distant region, where hearts are staunch and true,
I will start my life anew.
I'll do or die, you'll know the reason why . . .
'Goodbye', as sung by Josef Locke

If there was any doubt about where I was and what I was about to do, it was brought well and truly home as I stepped off the train at Gare du Nord. A large poster showing the head of a legionnaire wearing the famous *képi blanc* and the bold caption 'THE FOREIGN LEGION, THE ADVENTURE OF TODAY' was displayed on the wall. Underneath was the address of Fort de Nogent, the Legion recruitment centre in Paris, in the suburb of Fontenay-sous-Bois.

Standing on the crowded metro platform, which smelled like a sewer, I tried to keep calm. Within half an hour or so, I'd be knocking on the Fort's entrance, signing the next five years of my life over to serve and possibly die for the

Foreign Legion. Never has a tube ride been so nerve-racking; counting the stations still to come, I was aching to get there and get it over with. At the same time, I didn't want the journey to end. When it did, I rapidly climbed the stairs two at a time to ground level. I asked an official-looking chap in a 50-pence-shaped, peaked flat cap directions for the Foreign Legion. *'Où, Légion Etrangère?'* Without batting an eyelid, he pointed along a tree lined road. *'Par là, par là.'*

Two minutes' brisk walk found me staring at a sign above two large wooden arched fort gates – *Légion Etrangère*. Taking a deep breath and holding my grip over my right shoulder, I walked towards the small door set into the larger wooden gates, my heart beating ten to the dozen, and rapped loudly with my knuckles. Immediately, a slit in the door snapped open. A pair of eyes peered from within, scrutinising me. I waited for a few seconds while the eyes continued their hard stare, then, pointing to myself, I said, *'Moi, Légion Etrangère.'* The eyes disappeared, and there was a scraping of bolts before the small wooden door opened inwards. It revealed a legionnaire in combats and *képi*, assault rifle slung across his chest. He motioned me to step inside, where I was first searched and then led into a bare stone-arched room. He uttered two words: *'Assis toi.'* I sat on one of the old wooden chairs positioned against the wall. The legionnaire then left, closing the solid wooden door with a resounding bang. Now alone, I looked up towards the ceiling, stretched my legs out in front of me and breathed out a massive sigh of relief. I had done it. I had crossed the fateful line and into the unknown.

The cars around me had started their engines, and some were already driving at the ferry ramp. Coming out of my daydream, I hit the bike's electric start with my right thumb, pulled in the clutch and selected first gear with a quick downward dab of my left foot. This produced a loud, hollow, metallic, cog-chewing clunk – ouch! Releasing the clutch, I accelerated onto the ferry with my helmet on my left wrist.

The sight of Calvi always takes my breath away, with its citadel built high on the rocky outcrop, sweeping down to the sandy beach below, and the immense bay with its backdrop of sharp-ridged mountains piercing the perfect Mediterranean sky. Standing out on the deck catching a few rays, I ran my eyes eagerly over the town, fondly taking in the familiar places as we drew slowly closer. There was the unmistakable citadel, dominating from on high, and the more discreet Foreign Legion Para base, some three kilometres outside the town, halfway along the bay and a couple of hundred metres back from the beach. The mountain ridges, now some ten kilometres away, were a pleasant reminder of what I wouldn't be doing in Corsica this time round – gruelling Legion-style marching, uphill and in full kit in the heat of the day. This trip was for pure relaxation – downtime with a little bit of alcoholic debauchery thrown in. At the same time, and with a tinge of melancholy, I couldn't help remembering how my eyes had feasted on this same sparkling panorama some 16 years before. Then it had been for the first time. The big adventure was still moving on and the part of my life that was Calvi yet to come . . .

The *caporal chef* in charge of our band of six 'sprog' legionnaires ordered us to get our kit together and, in true Legion style, told us to shut our faces: '*Fermez vos gueules!*' The ferry was now five minutes from docking in Calvi. Our brief reacquaintance with the outside world, travelling by train from Castelnaudary to Nice then sailing across for Calvi, was almost over. It would be another six months before I got any leave, and that would make a year since joining up. Perspiring copiously from the heat and nervous apprehension, we did as the *caporal chef* ordered and, apart from a few grunts, quietly hoisted our packs and *sac marins* (large kitbags) onto our backs, our neck muscles working overtime to keep chins off chests. All hands then took hold of heavy, full-to-bursting grips. We stood silently one behind the other, straining and dripping uncontrollably with sweat, each man now laden with his entire kit issue. We were about to begin our pre-jumps course.

Some old sweats had already given us a foretaste of what might happen next: 'The minute you leave the boat, it starts. Your sergeant instructor will be waiting on the quayside, and, depending on his mood, you could get straight onto the open-backed, four-tonne wagon to the camp. Otherwise, you'll be marching off with all your *paquetage* up the steep hill to Calvi until he decides, or doesn't, to let you get on the wagon.' Thanks, pal. Looking forward to it. 'Be lucky!'

Our instructor came over. A small, swarthy Chilean, Sergent B. did not permit us to put our bags down. He walked slowly along the line, looking at us as if we'd just dropped out of his arse. Stopping at my level, he looked up into my face, then down at my bare forearms, which were at his eye level. My forearms, exposed by *manche courte* (shirt sleeve order, otherwise known as sleeves rolled up), were covered in tattoos.

'*Anglais toi?*' he asked, smirking.

'*Oui, Sergent,*' I shouted, thinking, 'Nah, I'm a fucking wop. What d'you think! Fucking tattoos. There goes the grey man . . .'

'*Ha,*' was his unimpressed reply. He turned to head off. I hoped he was making his way towards the wagon, but he then shouted back over his shoulder, '*Allez dépêchez vous, sac à dos dos, c'est partie!*' (Move it, packs on backs, let's go!)

'Shit,' I mumbled to myself. 'The fucking packs have been

on our backs for the past half-a-fucking hour.' However, having already been singled out, I was fired up and would have marched to Timbuktu and back.

Off we went, sweat-sodden and arms stiff with pain from holding the grips. It was a toss-up which was worse: the aching shoulders from the weight of the packs or trying to keep the grips from banging against my straining legs and constantly throwing me off balance. By that point, my chin was firmly pressed against my chest, and, unable to see ahead, I only had the heels of the legionnaire in front for direction.

Leaving the quay, we climbed steeply up towards Calvi town. The noise of laboured breathing grew louder by the metre. Oh, miracle of miracles – parked up on the right by two public telephones was the best-looking, camouflage-painted, open-backed, four-tonne TRM 4000 I'd ever laid eyes on. 'I hope it isn't a mirage,' I thought. Sergent B., already standing by the wagon's tailgate, ordered, '*Allez embarquez, vite, vite.*' (Get on, move it, move it.) Finally able to sling our packs and grips down, we set about passing them up between us onto the back of the wagon. Enraged by our lack of urgency, Sergent B. screamed out another order: '*Allez sac à dos dos et paquetage à la main, bande de connards!*' (Packs on backs and grab your kitbags, you bunch of tossers!) At the threat of being marched all the way up the hill with full kit, our cooperative loading style was instantly dropped. Galvanised into action, every man now scrambled selfishly and frenetically to get his pack and kitbags back about his person. Within seconds, we stood lined up as before, packs hastily slung on backs, kitbags balanced precariously on high and a grip clenched in each hand. This time the *sergent* looked at us with his head slightly cocked to one side and said, '*Je dis embarque, et putain vite. EMBARQUE!*' The last word was screamed out in maniacal-non-commissioned-officer style. We didn't bother taking our packs off. Slinging the grips in, we scrambled up after them, spilling over the sides and into the wagon. Ripping the packs off our backs, we quickly sat down on the outward-facing bench seats, breathing heavily and looking straight ahead, waiting for the next inevitable bit of ritual unkindness, the not-quick-enough-on-the-wagon scenario. Sergent B. looked at us thoughtfully, as if making up his mind, playing the old string-it-out number, milking it. He then jumped in front next to the driver, who managed to start the engine after two attempts. The exhaust spat out a thick black cloud of smoke, and with a clutch-dumping pull away, we lurched up towards Camp Raffalli. The *caporal chef*, who had boarded the wagon in leisurely fashion, looked at our knackered, sweat-bedraggled faces and said with a laugh, 'Welcome to Calvi!'

With a flick of the wrist, the bike roared at head-turning decibels off the quay and tore up the hill. 'Anyone can do it this way, though,' I thought. 'Only a few get the chance to go up in style – Legion style!' Passing Calvi, I followed the coast road towards Camp Raffalli, turning right just before the large DZ (drop zone). With the DZ now on my left, the road stretched ahead towards the wall of mountains about ten kilometres away. Nestled some 15 miles further on, high up on the mountain road, is where Geds and his wife Sarah had made their home. They had both lived on the island for some time and had been married two years before.

Meeting up with Geds always involves a good drink, and this visit looked like being no exception. We started with a couple of beers in the local village bar, then went back to his old three-storey stone house and cracked open some more. Out came the photo albums and the animated talk of good-times past. The beer continued to flow, Sarah knocking them back as well. We decided to continue the trip down memory lane with a trip into Calvi to revisit a few of the old haunts, even though Geds was saying that, sadly, they were no longer the same . . .

For a new legionnaire in the parachute regiment, time off was rare. What R & R time there was, was inevitably spent in a bar. But before the thought of relaxation and cold beers, there was the three week pre-jumps course (promo) to complete. After that, we all had to complete six jumps to obtain our coveted wings. Only then could there be beer.

Having finally arrived at Camp Raffalli, the TRM 4000 stopped beside what was to be our accommodation for the promo jumps course, a single-storey building next to the DZ, comprising one large dormitory with old metal bunk beds separated by door-less lockers and not a lot else. Some of the lockers were already full with immaculately folded kit, each set of which was identical in terms of the size of the folded items and the order in which they were stacked. We knew all too well that this was the result of hours of painstaking work, for these lockers belonged to the ten legionnaires who had finished instruction only two weeks previously. They had had the heel-kicking misfortune of having to await our arrival to make up the numbers for the promo. Not that they'd been left to kick their heels!

No sooner had we assembled in front of the accommodation than Sergent B. gave the order 'Sac à dos dos. C'est partie pour un tour d'horizon.' (Packs on backs for a tour of the camp.) This choice of phrasing for the guided tour – tour d'horizon – would later make more sense to us in another more important context. A tour d'horizon is the check carried out just after your parachute opens following your exit from a plane.

Off we marched, still in tenue de sortie but minus our

képis. The packs, at some 20-odd kilograms, soon began taking their toll as we tried to take in the different locations being pointed out – combat company lines, the med centre, foyer (NAAFI), gym, etc. The *sergent*, though only small, was a real live wire, his every movement dynamic. Even when he was just pointing something out, he would give the impression that he was about to forward roll into a kneeling position, 9-mm pistol already double tapping! If I wasn't mistaken, I thought he was gonna be a good instructor. I wasn't.

The days on the promo were well-structured, and a routine was quickly established. It began with us rising at 0500 and donning full combats for roll call (*appel*), which was taken on the small area set aside for the promo courses. Just before the roll was called, we would line up in two columns, warming up our arms and performing ten or so straight-arm pull-ups to the bar and two four-metre hands-only rope climbs. Throughout every day of the promo, each of us did something in the region of a couple of hundred pull-ups, ten or so arm-only rope climbs, plus any number of press-ups and sit-ups. The press-ups (or pumps) would either be part of the scheduled training regime or punishments, which were frequent. The pull-ups were always undertaken at least ten at a time before or after runs (known as tabs) and meals. Though my upper-body strength had always been good, I tried to avoid doing too many arm-only rope climbs, as they would adversely affect the muscles and tendons around my elbow, causing swelling and a constant dull pain. This would occur no matter how much I warmed up beforehand.

The roll call would be overseen by the duty *caporal*, after which there would be a mad rush to grab some breakfast and complete all the block jobs and area cleaning (*corvée bâtiment* and *corvée quartier*). If any dirt was found on a later inspection by Sergent B., our precious downtime would be replaced by tabbing with full packs in the scorching sun across the DZ, a knackering and pointless punishment.

At 0600 we would all assemble in full combats, helmets on our heads and 14-kilogram sacks on our backs, standing at ease (*repos*) in total silence waiting for Sergent B. to arrive and take command for another day's training. Sergent B. seemed to radiate energy, morning, noon and night. At 0600, we'd be like the living dead, but from the minute he took over command of the promo from the *caporal*, he'd instantly burst into life and order press-ups out of us to the point that we'd collapse to the ground under the weight of our packs. He'd then order us to ditch them and do a whole series of pull-ups, rope climbs and sit-ups, before getting us to sling our packs on again and try to keep up with him as he 'doubled off' onto the dusty DZ. Thankfully, it would still be the half-light of early morning at that time, and the air would be warm, as opposed to stiflingly hot, as it was guaranteed to be a few hours later. When we did catch Sergent B. up, it was straight on to the next treat – an eight-kilometre tab, known in the Legion as a *huit mille T.A.P.* The pace, at first, would be a gentle jog, warming up joints and muscles as the straps on the 14-kilogram packs were given little tugs of adjustment to settle them comfortably on our backs. However, within a few hundred metres, the pace would pick up, and after five minutes it was every man for himself, each aiming to improve on his finishing time in the previous day's two four-kilometre circuits of the DZ. A gazelle would complete this circuit in anything under 38 minutes – a respectable time was under 42. Anything over this, and your arms would be pumping out press-ups later on. I normally turned in at around the 40-minute mark, on a good day just shy of 39.

During the first circuit of the DZ, everyone would be getting into their stride, and this is when I would let my mind wander a bit, as it was one of the few times when I would be on my own with no *caporal* or *sergent* in my face. I would enjoy the sweet smell of the gorse and would pull in the air deeply through my nose, controlling the out-breath through my mouth, each breathing cycle taking several striding paces. Daydreamer that I am, my mind would drift back home and to thoughts of the family and my mum – I hoped that she'd still be around when I eventually went back. The rhythm of the tab would then take over, the river of memory tripping off into abandoned inlets, tributaries of the past. My early school days, those long-forgotten classmates: where are they all now, those children of Camberwell, whose names and faces drift through my mind as I run around the rocky sand track, lost to the present on an island far from home? The second lap would be my cue to snap out of the dreaming, increase the pace and pick off the legionnaires in front of me. One, Sigue the Spaniard, I would always try to pass but without success. A gazelle on two legs, he would come in at just under 39 minutes on a bad day.

After the tab, there would be a series of sprints with fireman's carries, sit-ups, etc., then it would be off for a shower, only to assemble 30 minutes later in sports kit for circuit training in the gym, finishing off with either boxing or kick-boxing, depending on the instructor. We used to call this part 'getting punched and kicked in the head' time.

From the second week on, the afternoons were given over to jump drills, in which we'd exit a metal-framed mock-up of a Transall C160 military plane, practising procedures exactly as in the real jumps, now only two weeks away. Jump drills also included a 50-metre tower with a 'death slide'. After scaling the tower, you'd hook onto a metal cable and jump off, sometimes facing forward, sometimes backwards. This was to perfect the correct landing position of legs and feet together with knees slightly bent to absorb the shock. The ideal landing should be feet first, followed by side of one thigh, then rolling onto your side and the back of your shoulder. Then there was the endless practice of kitting up with the main and reserve parachutes, with even the slightest error punished by press-ups – habitual offenders were ordered to stay in the press-up position till Sergent B. was satisfied that the culprit was genuinely suffering and barely able to stop his shaking body from collapsing in a sweat-soaked heap. Believe me, being left in the stress position soon hammers home the correct and only way to do things.

The days ended at 2200, signalled by the regimental bugler sounding lights out. All lights had to be extinguished, and if you were lucky, your head would hit your pillow and you would fall asleep. If, however, some piece of kit or material needed repairing, you had to crack on with it, by the light of a head torch, into the small hours of the morning if necessary. The promo was no exception: uniforms needed new braids to be sewn onto them for the hoped-for wings and regimental insignias; and lockers needed redoing after the day's scramble for kit. That being the case, 2200 didn't signal the end of work, it just meant working in bad light.

The bugler would also sound the wake-up, or reveille, at 0500, backed up by the duty *caporals* blowing loud whistles in front of the company lines. Being woken so shrilly, feeling that I'd only just closed my eyes, always made me question what the fuck was I doing there, with not even a minute to lie in bed and come to. Instead, a minute was about the amount of time I had to get dressed in full combats and go outside, before it was even light, for the *appel*. 'I volunteered for this? I must be mad!' But once I was outdoors and had fallen in, breathing in the sweet smell of the gorse in the warm Corsican morning, I knew I was bang in the right place. Another day was about to begin.

The third week of the promo was fast coming to an end

and all talk was of the forthcoming six jumps that would earn us our wings. There was also a rumour going round that we were to be posted to the third combat company, specialising in amphibious warfare. In two months' time, this company was due to go on a four-month operational tour of duty in Chad. Carrière being a non-swimmer was trying to get posted to the second combat company, which specialised in mountain warfare. But in true Legion spirit, being a non-swimmer was not deemed sufficient reason to avoid being posted to the third company! Carrière resigned himself to his fate, thinking that he was maybe being sent to Chad to make up the numbers, after which he would hopefully be posted to the second company.

The day of the jumps finally arrived and with it a set-back. Thousands of press-ups and back-breaking physical exertion and we found ourselves stymied by what? The answer, my friend, was blowing in the fucking wind. The tricolour on the tall white regimental flagpole was flapping around like the torn sail of a ship, and we would have to jump out somewhere over Italy to land on the DZ in such conditions! It seemed doubtful that we'd even get kitted out, let alone take off. The morning was spent waiting around, hoping that the wind would maybe just blow itself out. Everyone listened out for stillness and the following cry of *'Equipez vous'* (harness parachutes). It didn't happen – the wind blew hard all day and on into the night.

At reveille the following morning, Carrière was out of his pit with the speed of foul-smelling body waste off a shiny garden implement. Flinging open the large wooden door, he announced *'Pas de vent, en va sautez'* (No wind, we're jumping). And I never even heard Santa come down the chimney! From *appel* to *rassemblement* I was half expecting the gusts to return crashing back through the camp and crush our hopes for a second day running. But the calm

Spinney.

Akihiko Saito: KIA on convoy near Ramadi.
(© AP/EMPICS)

Allah on my right, Abid One on my left.

En route to Ramadi from the Jordanian border,
some three hours before the ambush.

Abid One's headrest after the ambush. Two asprins twice a day!

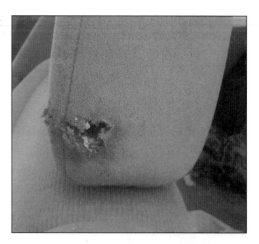

A convoy nearing Mosul.

En route to Najaf.

No, sonny, we don't take
you to cash points here!

I'd like to
teach the
world to sing
in Bangui.

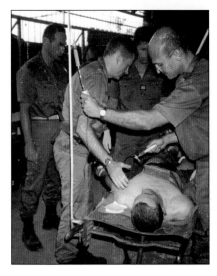

Dutch legionnaire receiving
treatment in the Congo.

Képi blanc ceremony.

My group on Mount Igman, Sarajevo,
one year before we were posted to Bangui.

My citation.

Legionnaires getting ready for
parade in French Guiana.

Me and my reporter mates
in Brazzaville.

Out in the oulou, south Basra way.

A downtown mosque in Baghdad.

Captured insurgents – Chas on radio, Jake stamping his authority!

Take 'em away
(all of the insurgents are alive –
no shots were fired in their capture).

held, and before long I found myself, still in the pitch black, in a rapidly diminishing queue by two portable containers housing the parachutes – dorsal (main) and ventral (reserve). Arriving at the front of the first container, I only just caught the flying main parachute that was slung at me at chest height. A disembodied voice from within the container bawled out a number, which I repeated as I recoiled from the force of the throw, regaining my balance just as the reserve parachute flew out at me from the second container. With dorsal and ventral (weren't they a 1970s comedy duo?) both clutched firmly against my chest, I doubled over to the TRM 4000 and scrambled up. Sitting with the two parachutes on my knees, I felt the first butterflies in my stomach. In about 30 minutes, I was going to hurl myself out of a hole in a plane some 500 metres off the ground, with only a flimsy piece of silk to stop me plummeting to earth and smashing into the Corsican soil. Looking down at my two life-preservers, I only hoped that if dorsal did try any funny business, ventral would play it straight.

We were not the only ones jumping that day. The fourth combat company, which specialises in snipers and explosives, was filling some empty spaces, with two of their sections joining us. A Brit from one of these sections who was already on the back of the TRM 4000 must have read my thoughts, as he leaned over and imparted some valuable knowledge: ''Ere, mate. If they both don't open, make sure you grab hold of the ground on impact and you'll be all right, as it's the bounce that kills you.' He then emitted a loud rasping laugh and proceeded thereafter to ignore us lower forms of life.

I felt happy, in a way, to just sit there, letting destiny carry me along. Deep in thought, I watched the dramatic scene being played out in the early morning darkness, the seriousness of the mood cranking up my apprehension over the impending jumps.

Sergent B., plugged into the mains as usual and more electrically alive than ever, 'controlled' that we'd all been issued our parachutes and were on the truck. 'Ah, Johnny today jump,' he said in pidgin English, looking at me with a beaming smile on his face. He then bounded over to the fourth company's senior NCOs, talking and laughing loudly amongst themselves as only those in command can. The order to depart for the airstrip rang out: '*Allez moteur en route, c'est partir.*' (Engines on, we're off.)

The NCOs abruptly stopped chatting and jumped into the fronts of their respective trucks, which fired immediately into life, shattering the dawn peace and revving hard to increase air pressure before moving off. The fragrant Corsican air was filled with thick black exhaust fumes, stinging the eyes and nauseating the senses. We exited the camp under the raised red-and-white barrier at the main gate, the legionnaire on duty standing stiffly to attention in full *tenue de parade* (parade uniform), his white *képi* and red shoulder epaulettes splendid to behold. Here was tradition embodied, reminding me of where I was, miles from my homeland wearing a foreign uniform, ready and committed to fight for another country. Now, surrounded by disparate nationalities talking in strange tongues, I was being driven along a coast road at dawn, on one side the dark glimmer of the sea, on the other the high and ominous shadow of distant mountains. This was the adventure I craved – my dream come true, my match-winning goal at Wembley, my lead-guitar solo at Hammersmith Odeon – and, thankfully, I had the good fortune to know it. During that five-minute journey to the airstrip, I was granted a transcendent experience, a unique personal moment in my life that was unsurpassed then and remains so to this day.

By the time we reached the airstrip, the dark grey of dawn had lifted considerably, the barren DZ and our camp to the other side now emerging into the daylight. The CCS (HQ) building was slowly revealing its orange roof tiles, and the distinctive tower used for hanging up the parachutes before repacking was starting to take shape. The trucks pulled onto a large tarmac area, at one end of which stood the Transall. There was no sign of life from the aircraft. Red tape fluttered lazily from the two propellers, one on each wing. A large wooden chock was wedged up under the twin tyres directly beneath the cockpit, and all the doors and the rear tail ramp were closed for business. Our sudden noisy arrival, with shouted commands to get off the trucks and form up, did nothing to change the abandoned look of the plane. Jumping down from the back of the truck, I felt as though I was the only one who didn't know what the hell was happening. Seeing parachute-hugging bodies dashing to file up across the tarmac square, I broke into a run and began to follow them, but on hearing Sergent B. shout out, *'Promo par ici,'* I got a fix on him and some of the promo already lining up. I doubled over, relieved not to have to think for myself, and joined the line of lowlifes yet to get their wings.

The fourth company had already fallen in, with their jump monitors out in front, wearing orange helmets – like old-style leather crash hats – and shouting loud commands to get kitted up. The legionnaires in the line began their speedy but confident kitting-up procedure, wrapping their large backpacks and weapons in a 'gain', which would be hooked onto the parachute harness and secured in front of their legs. The gain would remain in this position when the jumper exited the plane, before being released to dangle on a cord some six metres below them during descent. Some were a lot quicker than others, finishing their gains and promptly jumping up to sling their main parachutes and harnesses onto their backs with smooth, practised movements, arms outstretched up and behind their heads to allow the straps of their harnesses to slide down and come to rest on their shoulders.

Sergent B. snapped me out of my mesmerised absorption in the scene. *'Equipez vous,'* he barked. Now it was our turn to perform the drill of kitting up with our parachutes, the difference being that as it was our first jump, we had no gain to prepare. This type of jump had the mildly derisive nickname of *saut touristique* (tourist jump). Another difference between us and the legionnaires we'd just watched was that as jump virgins all our drills to date had been dry. Now it was for real. Knowing that within the next hour I'd be slinging myself out of the large Transall some 500 dizzy metres above the DZ, I rechecked and secured every strap and buckle several times. Standing there with the tightly secured chin strap of my helmet forcing my lower jaw hard against my upper, and hugged firmly by dorsal on my back and ventral on my front, I waited in line for a jump instructor to control that everyone was correctly rigged up. This control was exactly the same for everyone, whether it was your thousandth jump or your first. Anyone found with badly rigged-up kit was unceremoniously pulled out of line and left to readjust the offending item three paces out front. He then had to remain there until the jump instructor returned to control the offenders. If satisfactory, they'd be pushed back into line, leper status lifted. None of us on the promo were pulled out that day, but a couple from the company were.

Satisfied that everyone was correctly kitted up, one of the orange-helmeted jump instructors then shouted the command to form up. We had practised executing this command umpteen times throughout the promo and moved forward in line to be corralled into four 'sticks', which would be our formation inside the aircraft. The instructor, clearly pointing with his arm outstretched and forefinger rigid, then gave the order in which each stick would exit the plane: *'Premier passage . . . deuxième passage . . . troisième passage.'* There had to be three flypasts over the DZ, as it wasn't long enough to exit everyone in one passing. As the promo, we would be the *premier passage* (first tour), and I was third in line, so I'd be the third out of the plane. The privilege of being first out was given to the Spaniard for finishing first on the pre-jumps course.

We were now kitted up, fully briefed and ready to embark the plane. There was only one problem: the plane was still lying abandoned and not showing any interest in the proceedings. The flight crew had not yet made an appearance and were presumed to be still having breakfast in the *sergents'* mess, where they were housed when attached to the REP for a series of jumps, which was nigh on every other week. Meanwhile, we were all dressed up with nowhere to go, and the brutally early start to the day, in order to get in as many jumps as possible, now seemed a waste of precious sleep. The legionnaires from the fourth company stood with two parachutes, their weapon and pack – a considerable, back-breaking weight to bear needlessly for what could be some time. The command was issued to sit on the ground, back to back with legs outstretched. With instant relief from the weight and a 'why are we waiting' mood, it wasn't long before some banter started up. One Brit with a macabre sense of humour who was not bothered about only speaking French as we were supposed to (perhaps like me, he couldn't) called out, 'Is it me, or can anyone else smell death?'

This brought a reply from an anonymous voice somewhere behind: 'Thank fuck for that. I thought I was the only one!' Oh, the timeless wit of the British Tommy. Utterly hilarious. I hope they forgave me for not laughing. This was unwished-for time to reflect, the only comfort the warmth of the rising sun.

A jeep eventually turned up, and out sauntered the flight crew, each sporting a very American-looking leather jacket. It would still be a good 15 minutes before the plane would be ready, so we remained seated. In unhurried fashion, the crew went about their start-up checks, removing the tape from the propellers and walking the length of the plane examining it for any visible faults. A whirring noise came from the front, then one of the propellers started to turn, slowly at first, before building up to a speed at which my eyes could no longer see the blades or follow their direction. The propeller on the other wing also slowly turned into life.

'*Debout*' (Get up). The ensuing execution of this order was not carried out with what you'd call soldierly agility by most of the legionnaires in full jump order, but that was hardly surprising – the weight and awkwardness of their kit was a serious hindrance. For us virgins on the promo doing our *saut touristique*, there was no restricting gain on our legs, and we were straight up and ready, able to watch the other legionnaires struggle. However, some of them did manage to make it look effortless, pushing up on their arms and shouldering the weight of their equipment in a few smooth moves. Would I be as slick?

Formed up, the same jump instructor went through the motions of indicating our positions and order of jumping, this time accompanied by the heady smell of aviation fuel, once again an instant reminder of Bessbrook Mill in Northern Ireland. The image was gone as quickly as it came, and I was now looking at the Transall's rear end as it swung round in front of us. The engines' deep droning rose to a crescendo as the plane came to a halt, and we were hit with a warm, body-bracing current of av-gas-filled rotor wash. The tail ramp was down, the guts of the aircraft open towards us. The noise and smell heightening the sense of danger and urgency, a jump instructor standing on the tail ramp motioned us forward. We shuffled onto the ramp and out of the blasting rotor wash.

Once in the belly of the plane, the noise dropped to a steady, vibrating hum. Being the first to jump on our side, we were last to embark. I found myself sitting some two metres from the side door, which I'd be leaping out of in a matter of minutes. Facing me on the cramped red canvas bench seats opposite, was another row of helmeted legionnaires, most of them looking very serious. Through on the other side of the plane, I knew there would be an identical line-up of bodies, ready to exit the other side door. Adding to the discomfort in the crowded fuselage, one of the jump instructors was casually making his way through the plane, climbing across the tops of the bench seats while using the helmeted legionnaires' heads as a hand rail.

The tail gate moved up and closed with an ominous finality. Cocooned in the vibrating shell, we sat silently with our thoughts. My own thoughts were again of how often I'd imagined becoming a Foreign Legion paratrooper, and how the overwhelming romantic urge to be a part of that shadowy entity had beguiled my soul. I'd always known that this was 'the only thing', the ultimate journey, my *Boys' Own* dream, 'Promised Land' and 'Wheels of Terror' rolled all into one. If my eyes alighted on the words 'foreign' or 'legion' in a book or paper when I was a kid, I'd be really disappointed if it had nothing to do with the Foreign Legion; however, if it was, I'd pore over it again and again, absorbing every word, filling myself with the 'lure of the Legion'.

Now, crammed into the Transall, minutes away from fulfilling my destiny, I wanted, as on the truck, to savour the moment. But, like the perfect wave on the sand, the feeling wouldn't reappear, and with so many other thoughts battering around my brain and my nerves building up, I was relieved when the plane began to move. No sooner had it done so than it braked sharply and everyone was jolted forward. This apparently was a standard procedure to check the brakes. Moving off again, bodies lurched in unison as the plane turned. Squaring up, it then accelerated, bumping along the taxiway. I tried to figure out where we were now in relation to the runway. I assumed we were still on the taxiway when the engine noise and speed dramatically increased, this time tilting everyone towards the rear as the Transall accelerated hard down the runway for take-off.

The vibrations ceased as we left the ground and were replaced by a more relaxed drone. We climbed steeply for about 20 seconds, then banked hard right. The plane levelled out, and we were ordered to *'Debout, levée le siège, accrocher, série vers l'avant'* (Stand up, lift the seats, clip on, dress forward). With this task accomplished, I found myself next to a gaping hole as the door slid away to reveal clear daylight – a violent rush of air filled the interior. I was feet away from nothingness, an utter void that I would fling myself into a few seconds later. Wild excitement was coursing through me. This was it! Eyes wide open, I looked out and saw it was not quite empty space, catching glimpses of the greenish-blue sea below. Any second, the red light above the door would flick from red to green and a buzzer would sound, signalling us to 'go, go, go'.

The Spaniard was now in position with his arms braced either side of the hole, ready to launch himself out. As soon as the light changed, he was gone. Without thinking, I pushed forward close behind Carrière, who also slipped silently away a second later. It was now my turn. I moved into the space left by Carrière and threw myself out. With my eyes screwed shut and arms automatically crossed, my hands grabbing hold above the elbows. My head was rammed hard down into my chest, and my legs were held tightly together. A violent wind seemed to be sweeping me off down a tunnel, shaking me roughly about and lifting my legs up as my torso was thrown around. The sensation came to an end with an almighty jerk, and instead of flailing uncontrollably around I was sedately swinging to and fro. My parachute had deployed, the static line hooked on in the plane doing its job!

On opening my eyes, I was surprised to see the lumbering Transall was now quite far off, its underbelly still spewing out bodies. The fading drone of the distant Transall and the bird's-eye view of the slowly approaching ground, signalled to my well-programmed reflexes. I immediately put into practice the drummed-in drills from the promo, first looking up into the dark olive dome of the parachute, its cathedral-like interior surprising me by its dimensions, to check that it was fully open. I also checked that none of the parachute cord had become tangled over the top, as this would severely cut down the wind resistance and send me falling to the ground at a speed liable to break legs or back. All was OK. I then did a *tour d'horizon*, checking that none of the other jumpers around me were too close – good.

The ground was getting rapidly closer. I prepared myself for landing: legs together and slightly bent to absorb the impact. Tucking my chin firmly into my chest, I grabbed a handful of the paracord immediately above, tilting the open end of the parachute away from the wind, which, in theory, was meant to slow down both my downward and sideways contact with the ground. Bracing myself for impact, I tried not to look as the ground raced up, concentrating instead on letting my legs tell me when I'd made contact. Crunch! I hit the ground hard, knocking the wind out of me and jarring my head back painfully. I was then dragged along the hard stony ground. I knew that I had to do one of two things: pull the quick-release strap on my shoulder, freeing the harness and collapsing the parachute; or scramble to my feet and chase the wind-filled parachute, getting around it and collapsing it from the other side. I chose the first option and yanked on the quick-release strap. The tension on one set of paracords immediately slackened, and the parachute deflated.

Still winded, I lay on the ground for a couple of seconds then jumped to my feet. I was aware of a dull pain in my left arse cheek, which had borne the brunt of the landing, my legs having been bent too far to absorb my impact with the ground. Having endlessly practised the drill, I was soon straightening out and bunching together the cords and parachute, gathering it in then winding it around my forearms. It wasn't till another legionnaire landed close by that I remembered the other vital drill: to check that nothing was beelining my way – for example, descending hardware or a fellow jumper.

With my parachute gathered up, I set off at the double across the open DZ towards the camp, where another two parachutes were waiting to be slung at me so that I could do it all again. Looking up, I saw the Transall directly overhead, disgorging more tiny figures, whose flapping parachutes streamed in its wake. As the air punched open the parachutes, I was amazed at the loudness of the crump, which sounded like someone stamping on an inflated crisp packet. Arriving back at camp, I dropped the parachute off and joined the file to catch the new parachutes slung again from the two containers. Then it was back on the now returned and waiting trucks, out through the raised barrier and onto the coast road, the sea an enticing cool blue and the mountains shimmering in a heat haze. Back at the airstrip, I jumped smartly down; I was no longer the headless chicken this time, knowing exactly where to go and what to do.

That day, we got in four of our six required jumps: three in the morning and one in the afternoon. Come lunchtime,

I had to sit with only one arse cheek perched on the hard wooden cookhouse chair, the result of my incorrectly bent legs failing to absorb the impact of my first landings. This pain was to be a good lesson, helping me to gradually master the right angle for my legs. The topic of conversation that lunchtime was inevitably of the 'how was it for you' kind. Some of the lads said they'd kept their eyes open on exiting the plane and had been bombarded by images of the sky, sea, mountains, ground and even the belly of the Transall. Try as I might, from that first jump I've never been able to do this. At the moment of jumping, I always think, 'Eyes – keep 'em open,' only for them to involuntarily snap shut till the tug of the open parachute tells them otherwise.

We got the two remaining jumps, and a further two, in the next day. The day after that, in a small ceremony on the regimental *Place D'Arme* (Parade Square), we were presented with our wings. I remember looking down proudly at the new addition on my chest and thinking I could now get out on the town for a bit of R & R. 'May I ask what it means to you having your Foreign Legion wings?'

'Beer.'

'What about that time we . . .' Already buzzing from the beers at Geds' place, our taxi ride into Calvi was speeding by in a warm haze of nostalgic banter, the fondly recalled Corsican scenery the perfect backdrop for reliving the great rollicking hilarities of 'those were the fucking days'. Fucking A!

Passing the DZ, I could see myself falling, falling, slamming into the ground, picking myself up, gathering the parachute, then doubling across the DZ with the others to start all over again. The others, my fellow legionnaires, we band of rookies who'd proudly got our wings only to get promptly but no less proudly legless in Calvi: where were they all now? As the taxi ground on, the DZ soon out of sight, I was visited by an overwhelming melancholy. With the effects of alcohol and memory and friendship, and a startled realisation that the years had gone by in the blink of an eye, I felt a rush of sentiment for those men and the short, irreplaceably special time we'd shared. And with these wistful thoughts of the past, there came, like poison dropping into milk or an over-powerful chaser between pints, which rather than enlivening, sickens the stomach, a reminder of what lay ahead for me: the return tour that dared not speak its name right now, not even in my head.

Snapping out of it, I turned my attention to Geds' commentary on the current social scene in Calvi: 'The PMs [military police] still patrol in town, but since most of the Brits have now left the Legion, there's not the same amount of drinking and trouble.' I got the distinct feeling that he said this with a regretful longing – not for the trouble itself but in mourning for the good old days. The good old days – I had a flashback to one particularly memorable Saturday afternoon drinking session in Calvi, 1988 . . .

Calvi is a small Corsican coastal town (or it was back in 1988) that survives by virtue of the hordes of tourists that swarm through it during the short summer months. When the tourists depart, the town goes into hibernation, with only a handful of bars and shops remaining open for the locals and, of course, the legionnaires. The Saturday in question was in August, and Calvi was awash with holidaymakers. The shops in the narrow walkways of the pedestrianised town centre – OK, loud mopeds driven by local underaged kids were also in abundance – were proudly displaying their tat, and the mass of meandering, shop-till-your-flip-flops-wear-out tourists were unashamedly buying it. Working our way through the milling crowds, this was a side of Calvi that barely registered with us, the throngs of docile gawping Alfs and Ritas merely an obstacle to be negotiated en route to the bars and our side of Calvi.

That Saturday, Carrière, Winstone and I were out to get drunk. Not only was this our first sortie into Calvi, it was our first time out on the town – any town – since joining the Legion. We were attired in our *tenue de sortie*, because we were not entitled to wear civilian clothes for five years, according to Legion tradition. Brilliant! I knew I looked the bee's knees, and I felt then as though I'd be happy to wear the uniform for life.

Bars in Calvi were either for legionnaires, local Corsicans or tourists. In the interests of health and safety, these demarcations were to be strictly adhered to – everyone knew that. Although rookies until only recently, we knew because we'd been told, but that Saturday, Legion wings on show and on a high, we were hardly in the frame of mind to remember rules laid down by our regiment vis-à-vis bars, or any kind of rules for that matter. In the interests of research, we had decided to sample as many bars as our beer consumption would allow. In the first one we set foot in, the barman's manner seemed distinctly off-hand. Putting this down to spic etiquette, we thought no more of it and continued supping, enjoying our new-found freedom and sense of discovery.

What we had failed to appreciate was the hatred held towards France by many Corsicans. Added to this issue of nationalism was the mutual antipathy between soldiers and local residents, typical of a garrison town. This can remain a cold war of frosty looks and turned backs in a sober situation, but throw alcohol into the ring and things hot up, turned backs turning into squared-up opponents. Fighting between Legionnaires and the Corsicans happened fairly regularly and was usually pretty violent. The Corsicans were not shy about using guns and knives, and on one occasion a

Scottish legionnaire was shot in the stomach during a scrap. He managed to crawl his way along the beach to a bar frequented by legionnaires and summoned the lads. Revenge was served hot, and the Scotsman lived. Mind you, there must have been some very disturbed tourists trying to come to terms with certain events that interrupted their sunbathing that day. 'I don't remember anything in the brochure about pitched battles on the beach, love . . .'

Sitting at a table overlooking the road, it wasn't long before a Willis jeep rolled by carrying a Legion military-police patrol. The jeep pulled up sharp. We were three smartly dressed legionnaires downing cold glasses of beer in an out-of-bounds bar. Had we been spotted? The jeep reversed a few metres and all three occupants, wearing combat uniform with arm brassards emblazoned in large red lettering PM, looked directly at us. The PM in the front passenger seat was the largest human being I've ever laid eyes on. The most striking thing about him was his neck. Being bigger than his head, it gave the overall impression that even a well-aimed slug with a sledgehammer would have little effect on the man. Mind you, by the look of his face, many fists had tried their luck. His nose was hideously twisted, complementing numerous scars and pock marks framed between a pair of matching cauliflower ears. The shape of him below the neck was equally forbidding: a massive barrel chest, and arms and legs immensely disproportionate to his five-feet-ten-inch height. The man's reputation (as if it needed to) preceded him, and we were already familiar with the legend of the Polynesian kick-boxing champion who had been shot by a Corsican but had picked himself up and, oozing blood, annihilated his poor, naive assailant. Rumour had it that he spent his entire leave kicking and punching Thai boxers into the middle of next week.

Now, here he was, alarmingly involved in my life and looking directly at us. A furrowed expression on his face suggested that he was struggling to decide, in his absurd-looking head, what to do about us. With deliberate slowness, he beckoned us over with his right index finger. Wooden chairs scraping back, we stood to obey his command. Carefully putting on our *képi blancs*, we left the bar and, approaching Godzilla, executed textbook salutes and stood rigidly to attention. Godzilla's constipated look remained, although whether this was mental or literal was becoming increasingly hard to tell. Perhaps, in a best-case scenario, he just wanted one of us to run to the chemist for him.

Carrière came to the rescue and quickly explained that it was our first time out on the town and that we were unaware that this bar was out of bounds. This had the desired effect, relieving the immense brain overload Godzilla had clearly been suffering. His faced regained what I took to be his default mode of 'when's that fucking bell gonna ring'. We were not yet out of the *merde*, though. He now set about slowly checking our dress for the slightest of imperfections. Any trace of dirt or irregularity with our uniforms would mean getting hauled straight back to camp, slung in the nick till Monday morning, released to pass '*report capitaine*' and at least seven days in the slammer for our troubles.

Throughout Godzilla's meticulous inspection, I nevertheless felt we were still on course for a good drinking session. I played along with the game, looking worried and obedient, though inwardly vowing never to be in a position to exercise his thoughts again. We eventually made it to a bar that was most definitely not out of bounds, Le Son des Guitars. On entering a haze of cigarette smoke, we found numerous legionnaires in uniform, some standing at the bar others sitting around tables in groups of five or six. The music was pitched just right – not too loud for some lively chatter. A conversation in deep guttural German was taking place between several legionnaires sitting in the left-hand corner, and a group of loud Spanish legionnaires were trying to come to terms with a game of American pool, but the largest presence was that of the British legionnaires, who outnumbered all others in the bar and were notably more boisterous, here and there to the point of aggression. The heavy Brit presence was not surprising. During the latter part of the 1980s, it wasn't uncommon for sections to have several British legionnaires. Whether they were refugees from Maggie Thatcher's proud achievement of consigning working men to the scrapheap, I don't know.

Behind the bar, several flags adorned the wall: the Irish tricolour, the Red Hand of Ulster, the Scottish Saltire, the Cross of St George, the Welsh Dragon, even the Isle of Man 'Legs'. Displayed up high, the Union Jack made the German flag next to it look really plain and uninteresting – no reflection on the Kraut character, of course. *Képi blancs* were stuck all over the place, with Foreign Legion memorabilia, including plaques and old photos of legionnaires in remote parts of the globe, dotted around the old stone walls. In short, it was a Foreign Legion oasis smack-bang in the middle of Calvi.

Feeling immediately at home, we ordered three beers. Sensing our sprog status, we wisely took a table just to the right of the entrance and quietly absorbed the atmosphere. The excited Spaniards over at the far end were having no difficulty in ruining what should be the precise game that is pool. Just opposite our table on the other side of the entrance, the seven or eight Germans sat calmly around two small round tables drawn up together and precariously loaded with glasses of beer. They were deeply engrossed in what sounded to me like the planning of World War Three. But the Brits stole the biscuit – some were standing at the bar, others in groups of three and four, and yet more were seated.

The English tongue seemed to be audible in every corner of the bar, and every now and then a loud voice hurled out a comment to some mate or other.

'Oi, John, you made it, then!'

'Yeh, she's fucked off and left me.'

'Not as dumb as she fucking looks, then.'

In the midst of all this banter and rough soldierly bonhomie, a relaxed and smiling British family – husband, wife and two teenage kids, dressed as only Brits on a Mediterranean holiday can – walked into the bar. As the door closed behind them, the same look of unbelieving horror registered on their faces. Uncomfortable would not do it justice. After a few confused, awkward glances, they sort of huddled together and slowly shuffled themselves around, back out to their dream holiday. 'I don't recall any mention of 1,200 legionnaires stationed in Calvi in the holiday brochure. Do you, dear?'

The taxi stopped in exactly the same spot Godzilla had all those years before. The bar didn't seem to have altered dramatically, but Geds did say it was no longer out of bounds. So we went in and had a beer. It wasn't the same barman, and the service was very courteous. When we left, I purposely made my chair scrape across the parquet flooring. Carrière and Winstone were immediately by my side. Where's fucking Godzilla now then, eh?

Geds and I had calmed down a bit after the taxi ride into Calvi, but it didn't take long before we were back in the nostalgic swing of things, grabbing a quick beer here, another there, promenading our way along the small bars dotted around the town centre. Something wasn't right, and it wasn't long before the penny dropped. Although there were only two companies on overseas operational duty, there was a marked absence of legionnaires. The answer to the conundrum was, in fact, obvious. I had started to see a change in the Legion towards the end of my service, when the ranks slowly, but perhaps inevitably after the fall of the Berlin Wall, began to swell with Eastern-bloc recruits. This new intake was curiously ascetic and tended to do things like pump iron, rather than the Brit preference of binge drinking. I know that the Brits did untold damage and were the bane of the officers and PMs, but you can't expect clean-living bodies to win dirty fights. Mind you, a lot of those Brits joining up back then were just plain, dog-rough dangerous, many of them too far gone for even the tough Legion discipline to knock into shape.

I think there's something to be said for not visiting old haunts, which sounds strange, but I say it with the benefit of hindsight. I wished I'd given the night out in Calvi with Geds a miss. Not only was it a bit sad to see how the place had changed, but we also managed to cause some good old Brit trouble – yep, in a bar and, yep, pissed. You can't teach an old dog new tricks – or make him forget the ones he's best at.

The bar, lo and behold, was Le Son des Guitars. There were no flags or legion memorabilia, which had apparently been long since shed, nor were there hordes of uniformed legionnaires, also a thing of the past. (That night, only one uniformed legionnaire was to come through the door, but more of that later.) By the time Geds and I made it to the Le Son des Guitars, we were past the point of celebratory drinking and firmly on the road to alcoholic oblivion. On entering the bar, I was immediately struck by the bareness of the walls and the lack of life; in fact, the whole place, except for one lone drinker at the end of the bar and a flat-chested barmaid, was devoid of people full stop, let alone legionnaires. New-looking plastic stools topped with circular cushions were the only things sitting round the barren tables. Gone were the

Germans finalising the order of invasion for the next world war, gone were the Spaniards refining the rules of pool and, most poignant of all, gone were the Brits who had given the place its raw aggressive edge. As Wellington once said of the fighting men of Britain, 'I don't know if they frighten the enemy, but by God they terrify me.'

Still, there was beer to be drunk, and we'd now been joined by Bob P., a man I'd always looked up to. We had served together for a year instructing basic training at Castelnaudary, and I did my best to emulate his style of commanding troops. Plus, he was a big Ian Dury fan, and his tales of what he got up to before joining the Legion, be it making babies up in Blackpool or sleeping on the job down in Billericay, were always told by a master of the art. Bob and I ended up down one end of the bar, while Sarah, being tired, decided it was time for bed. She sat herself on one of the swanky new plastic stools, leaned back against the wall and plonked her two beer-filled legs on the bare table in front of her. I watched her lining up to achieve this posture, her uncoordinated movements like those of an abandoned marionette. I could imagine her springing up from the table when the puppet master tugged on the strings. Though perhaps not strictly decorous slumped there half-conscious, she was doing no harm, and we were all paying customers. The barmaid, however, having little better to do, took a different view and objected to Sarah's relaxed attitude. Inevitably, it wasn't long before Geds, in rightful defence of his missus's rights, was arguing boisterously with the remonstrating barmaid.

With such a scene playing, anyone entering the bar would have straight away realised an alcohol-fuelled argument was in full swing, but a Legion *caporal* in uniform should also have realised that one of the actors was an off-duty senior NCO in the Legion and to therefore not get involved.

Unfortunately, the *caporal* who did walk in was not of the quick-to-realise-what's-savvy breed and voiced his displeasure. Geds, preoccupied with his argument, paid no attention to the *caporal*. Now firmly on his white horse, the gallant *caporal* rounded on Geds, looking as if he was going to physically do something about it. Geds, who was no slouch, had been aware of the *caporal's* presence from the off, and he turned on him, his expression rather like that of a kid seeing a bigger, brighter sweet than the one he's enjoying, and let off two swift but hard punches, bang-bang, which sat the dazed legionnaire down on his arse. Geds followed this with a quick brutal kick to the face, putting any thoughts of reprisal far from the *caporal's* blood-soaked head. The barmaid had by now called the *Police Militaire*, who arrived and carted the worse-for-wear *caporal* back to camp. Waking Sarah gently up, we left the bar, and with the barmaid hurling insults after us, headed off to a nightclub to round off the evening. Remorse could wait until tomorrow.

The following morning, we all sat round the kitchen table feeling hung-over. The conversation came in quiet spurts, and the unravelling of the previous night's events had Sarah close to tears. Geds was dryly philosophical about what had happened and, along with me, was satisfied that the *caporal* got his just rewards. Drunk or not, rank comes before refinement and is to be respected whatever the circumstances. Going on our past record, the *caporal* got off lightly. Despite all the self-justification, we did feel pretty stupid about our actions, but it was on the cards from the first nostalgic beer that passed our lips, having unconsciously, though probably not unwillingly, slipped back into our former selves.

Feeling rather like a rat leaving a sinking ship, it was back to the UK for me that day, leaving Geds to face the music from his commanding officer. It was not the done thing for a sergeant major to brawl in town, drunkenly or otherwise.

Sailing away on the afternoon ferry, my mood was raw, my mind ruminant and troubled. The sensation was not unfamiliar after a heavy drinking session. This time, though, it was coming on in spades, and I knew why. My three weeks' leave from Iraq was drawing to a close, and with all fond remembrances of the past now over, the future was racing up to meet me, cloaking me in a dark and threatening anxiety. Along the fast-approaching coastline, behind the bright canopy of sunshine, I saw only a gathering storm. The film was on rewind, the scenic backdrop filled with foreboding.

5

BACK TO BAGHDAD

Emerging from the guts of the Royal Air Force Hercules C130 at BIAP, the hot afternoon air slapped me gently across the face. Welcome back. In two columns, we snaked towards the all-too-familiar gathering of private-military contractors and their pick-up vehicles parked within the two-feet high cordon of concrete blast barriers. At one end of this parking area, a PX (NAAFI) trailer was selling everything from underwear to top-of-the-range global-positioning systems and sheath knives for any Rambo or PMC with money to burn. Trudging across the deep gravel, just one thought ran through my brain: 'What the fuck am I doing back here?' This was swiftly followed by, 'Well, you fucking are, so switch on.' There was simply no more time to shroud myself in morbid thoughts of dying. If I was to stay alive, I had to instantly tune in to all the hidden dangers I knew were out there waiting for me.

Resigned now to my fate, and with my soldiering head firmly back on, I approached the mustered *Who's Who* of the security world. Now, where was Dave? Some of the contractors had ditched their paraphernalia of weaponry and webbing into the backs of their pick-ups and 4x4 station wagons, happy to be in a safe area where they were able to wind down a little before the stressful return to the streets of Baghdad. Others strutted about, tooled up with weapons slung across their shoulders, oversized pistols strapped to their thighs and chest webbing cumbersomely laden with every conceivable gadget they could buy in the PX surrounding their torsos. The effect was to make just walking look extremely arduous. These super-hero, ultimate-fighting, action men clearly weren't going to be caught napping during an insurgent invasion that might at any moment come streaming across this vast airfield deep in the heart of the heavily protected base that was Camp Victory.

Dave was amongst the take-a-break, poser-free fraternity and greeted me with a big warm genuine smile: 'Simon, good to have you back. I've missed you.'

'Great to be back, Dave. Did my nose just grow then?'

Having already picked up my body armour and helmet in Kuwait, I only had to wait for the RAF fork-lift driver to arrive with the pallet from the back of the Hercules to retrieve my black backpack. There were already several bods standing in the baggage area for the same reason, so that as soon as the pallet was lowered to the ground several eager hands fell on it, undoing the large yellow tension straps. Packs and grips were pulled indiscriminately to the ground, and it was every man for himself. Dave reunited me with my AK-47 and chest webbing, and I sarcastically enquired as to where our reinstated Iraqis were as I threw my pack into the small white pick-up. He informed me that Iraqis were no longer allowed into this part of the camp, so they were waiting patiently in the other pick-up about 200 metres away. Dave said that the Americans were now denying access to

Iraqis working with private-military contractors into several camps and other controlled areas. Only those with DOD (Department of Defence) ID cards were allowed access, and our Iraqis weren't at a level to get these.

Pulling out of the car park, along with a stream of gigantic four-wheel drives, we passed the US Air Force inner checkpoint, where six of our reinstated Iraqis stood next to our other small white pick-up. Against the grandiose cavalcade of security vehicles sweeping by, they looked very much like second-class citizens, not to say outcasts. Dave pulled up, and I got out to greet them, albeit with strong reservations. They came over with an embarrassing display of excitable affection. It was like my mum kissing me in front of my schoolmates all over again. Allah was amongst them, and I'd be lying if I said I wasn't pleased to see him. Although I returned their embraces, I kept my face in a cold stare, hiding my involuntary pleasure at finding them so genuinely pleased to see me back. I felt let down by them but also understood their plight, and even though I knew that one or more of them could have set us up, I was also keenly aware of feeling part of something again, of belonging. The homesickness which had been plaguing me from the moment I'd left Britain started to lift.

After a day back at the villa, it was as if I'd never been away. In my head, I started to calculate how much money would be waiting for me on my next leave in nine weeks' time. I made it the best part of 20 grand. Once again, I pulled the handle of my imaginary fruit machine, seeing the cash jackpot gush out. What would £20,000 look like in pound coins?

Catching up on the fallout from our ambush up at Samara, I was, on the whole, happy with the news. Dave had put his foot down with the firm and made it clear that until we received the appropriate vehicles and armaments, we would do no further convoys north or west of Baghdad. He gave me strict orders that I was to stick to these conditions when I took over as team leader during his leave, commencing in three days' time. As for our Iraqis that had walked out over the helmets, I thought we'd seen the last of them, but the big boss had other ideas and reinstated them. To be honest, he had put the ball in Dave's court, saying that the decision was his. Dave, after weighing it up and dismissing the theory that one or more of them had betrayed us, took them back on the basis of 'better the devil you know'. To find 20 other Iraqis, complete strangers to us, and be able to deploy with them straight away on missions deep into country controlled by insurgents was at best a folly, at worst a suicide pact. So, if we wanted to keep on earning, we had little choice but to run with the boys we knew.

From time to time when I was on leave, I had called Dave on his mobile to find out how things were going. I'd therefore known prior to returning to Iraq that it would soon be me heading the team. If I was lucky, I'd have a good stand-in, an expat security contractor I could rely on. Dave had had a series of stand-ins while I'd been off. One had gone as far as to fall out of a stationary pick-up on the morning of deployment then claim that he'd strained his neck and couldn't take part.

The team had been involved in one contact during my absence, an IED aimed at the last escort vehicle in the vicinity of Najaf. The device detonated but, fortunately, was badly timed. No small-arms fire accompanied the attack, and the IED had exploded well after the last vehicle had passed, inflicting only nerve-jangling relief at the narrow escape. This miscalculation on the part of the insurgents was most likely to have been caused by the bomber pressing the call button on a mobile phone too late. With a pre-dialled number in the mobile linked to set off the detonator, it would be crucial to take the time-lag factor into account. This would only be a matter of seconds – the few seconds it takes for the phone to bleep its way through the digits of the number before going live and transmitting – but possibly, in this case, a matter of life or death. Either that or the bomber was severely cross-eyed or fat fingered. It wasn't uncommon for IEDs detonated in this fashion to be off the mark; nevertheless, it was the insurgents who paced the coalition, constantly upgrading their operational methods.

The problem of a stand-in for Dave was solved by the addition of two permanent private-security contractors, both with time in Iraq under their belts. Their arrival was surprising, as we'd been seeking reinforcements for some time and had received no volunteers, even from other projects kicking their heels and waiting for assignments. Bob and Vinny were both volunteers and glad to be on our team. Bob was in his mid-twenties, five-feet-nine-inches tall and stocky, and he had a stomach that was finally being allowed to grow, as well as long ginger sideburns, oddly out of place on one so young. He was ex-KOSB (King's Own Scottish Borderers), and from the outset I saw in him a rough and ready squaddie with 'I'm fucking trouble but boy can I soldier' written all over his ugly face. A north-of-the-border savage, he'd not fitted in with the more refined, kit-accumulating specialists on his previous contract. And with the threat of early retirement looming he'd jumped at the chance to get out and about and meet interesting people!

Vinny, in his early 40s, was of insignificant build and presence, but along with a saxophone case he also carried a 'I don't give a fuck, I'll do it' attitude. Not having blended as a 'team player' on his previous contract, and quick to speak his mind between blowing his saxophone, he was also to find a permanent niche in convoy. When he arrived at the villa clad in body armour and chest webbing with an AK-47 in one hand and a saxophone case in the other, I greeted him with, 'Fuck me, it's the Ant Hill Mob. I hope you've brought Professor fucking Pat Pending with yer.' From then on, not only did we have to endure the daily noise of bombs exploding close by, but also the harrowing racket of someone *learning* to play an instrument.

Both boys were well and truly welcome. Bob being Scottish, I was already on his side, having grown up on stories of my mum's childhood in the 'Highlands', so much so that her village of Monymusk in Aberdeenshire feels like home to me when I'm fortunate enough to be north of the border, and my ashes will be scattered on my granddad and grandma's grave. As a wide-eyed kid, I'd feast on stories about the prisoner-of-war camp in Monymusk and my granddad and uncles' time serving in the Gordon Highlanders. I've always had a soft spot for 'Bonny Scotland', oh, except on the days that England played Scotland in the Home Internationals – I nearly ran away from home when England were soundly thumped 5–0 at Wembley. Bob couldn't be described as bonny, but he was a hairy-arsed jock who soon proved me right in my assessment of his soldiering abilities, and Vinny, though different in his ways, also proved capable when the chips were down.

There was only one mission in the pipeline: twenty Russian military vehicles needed to be escorted on five transporters from the port of Umm Qasr to the Polish contingent at Camp Charlie in Al Hillah, a couple of hours south of Baghdad. Given a choice of missions to command, this was about as good as it got. First, I knew the roads well from Umm Qasr to Camp Charlie, having done umpteen convoy missions to both locations. And second, it was south of Baghdad, a psychological morale booster, as Umm Qasr, along with Basra, was then fairly tame compared with Baghdad and northern Iraq. And although trouble flared at Al Hillah on a regular basis, it didn't hold the same dread for me as numerous destinations up north and west, such as Mosul and Ramadi. All in all, it was a good mission to get back into the swing of things, and because it was not taking place for a few days there was ample time to plan and coordinate the job.

Just before departing, Dave issued me with a reminder not to accept any missions, whether out of loyalty, money, bravado or whatever, unless the proper back-up was in place. His final words to me in private before leaving were more pointed: 'Stay alive, Simon. You've nothing to prove.'

With all the extra organisational work of setting up the mission to Al Hillah – admin stuff I never usually got involved with, including phone calls to the officers in the J4 Logistics unit and endless emails to endless officials in Umm Qasr, Al Hillah and the distribution warehouse at Abu Ghraib – I was fortunate to be able to leave the vehicle and material side of the preparation in Bob and Vinny's capable hands. During this time, life in the villa went along much as always, that is until the afternoon before the mission. On returning from a trip to the Green Zone, Bob, Vinny and I found Emina the cleaner sitting sobbing on the large sofa in front of the 24-inch television screen, which was blaring out music from some Arab pop video. Since part of Emina's cleaning duties had always seemed to involve watching a lot of television, the only unusual thing now was her sobbing. Sending for Ahmed, our translator, I stood beside Emina and, with some embarrassment, put into practice my first-aid for sobbing, which consisted of me regularly repeating 'There, there, don't cry'.

When she was a little calmer, we tentatively elicited her story. On walking to her home only a few streets away, a car with two men in it had pulled alongside her. The passenger had then got out and grabbed hold of Emina, attempting to drag her into the car. Emina, with the kind of strength only available when your life is in danger, had kicked, bitten, slapped and screamed herself free and had run back to our villa, panicking for her life. One of our armed guards immediately ran to the scene of the incident but found only some neighbours, who confirmed Emina's story. Now, deeply shocked and sitting on the sofa surrounded by men and guns, she looked pitiably timid and vulnerable.

I was enraged but also felt guilty. I knew that this wasn't a politically motivated attempt to kidnap an Iraqi working for the invaders, although, if need be, it was a handy excuse – an excuse for all the freaks to come out of the woodwork and rape, rob, torture and kill. In the early stages of a civil war, when a country is in free-fall with bombs killing sometimes hundreds of civilians in a single day and soldiers' deaths now only making the news after the commercial break, your common-or-garden-variety violent criminal fails to register on the consciousness of the international media. The kind of vicious robbery and carving up that Emina so narrowly escaped goes unreported to the families sitting comfortably watching the six o'clock news. The latent anarchy which a stable country, despotic or democratic, keeps in check is freed to run amok the minute the governing body gets blasted out of existence. In the case of Iraq's former regime, yes, the Butcher of Baghdad and his cronies were responsible for untold heinous crimes, but the explicit pretext for the invasion was the threat from weapons of mass destruction, and, as Ahmed once said to me, 'Under Saddam, my wife and I could go out to a restaurant and eat. Now we don't even go out!' Many of the acts committed by deviants – robbery, murder, rape, child abduction and, as Ian Dury would say, 'other misdemeanours' – go largely unrecorded or even acknowledged by the 'authorities'. These authorities – and I use the term loosely – are caught up in the bedlam of lawlessness that has befallen an Iraq suddenly freed from a dictator by an invasion force unsure of its direction and inadequate in its prosecution of the war.

I felt guilty about Emina because I now had first-hand experience of an Iraqi who was not involved in guns and fighting, someone just trying to make a living in this madness, but who was, nevertheless, at the mercy of indiscriminate bombings and prey to the degenerates left free to pursue their pitiless acts of barbarism. There she was sitting in front of me sobbing, her shoulders heaving in fear and utter despair at the hopeless situation she and other defenceless Iraqis were now in, all because the invaders had not fulfilled their promise to protect and secure the country they had attacked. So, I was guilty because these people were now plunged into living with guns, bombs, brutality and death. Guilty because, like all the Western companies making a killing, I was only really concerned with pursuing my adventure and with the wads of cash I was making. Guilty because I knew things were only getting worse and that the Eminas of Iraq would be left high and dry in the midst of civil war long after me, and the likes of me, were over the hill and counting our cash, not to mention our blessings.

After this incident, we made sure that Emina was picked up each morning, either by one of us or our Iraqis. Then when she'd finished for the day, we'd drop her home. We also submitted a full incident report, which although taken very seriously by Armor Group, was just another of the ever-increasing criminal attacks that wasn't investigated by the Iraqi Police, who were stretched way beyond what even an honest police force could hope to cope with.

From that day on, I noticed a change in Emina. No more did she smile, seeming now always to be deep in thought. A cloud hung about her, and she no longer brightened our all-male household with her fragrant female presence. I did take some comfort from the fact that she still managed to watch a considerable amount of TV with the volume high, playing the annoying Arab pop videos that made Indian ones look half decent. But I could no longer ignore the fact that the brunt of the suffering fell upon people like her, the ordinary citizens of Iraq, the families just wanting to live and work together in peace. Now they were shark meat. Foreign armies, big business, hired guns, insurgents, criminals – all of them were taking their bite out of the new Iraq. Then there were the good old adrenalin junkies like me. Emina hit my conscience pretty hard, but the fat pay packet at the end of each and every month softened the blow. But then how would my jacking it in help her and those like her? I gave Emina a paid break, assuring her that once we were back from our next mission I'd send someone round to pick her up for work again. I'd always been Emina's favourite – well, it was only ever gonna be me or Dave!

The long run down to Umm Qasr was mainly on dirt roads that kicked up clouds of light-grey dust. Due to these dust clouds, there was as much risk of being killed or injured in a head-on collision as from insurgents. The prime hazard was the large American military convoys coming up from Kuwait en route to Baghdad. Their lane discipline was non-existent, and large tank transporters would stretch across the wrong side of the road in a suicidal attempt to see past the fog of dust. Wacky races for real. The other danger was of our drivers falling asleep at the wheel, resulting in the unnerving experience of your pick-up veering off either into the path of an oncoming vehicle or bumping suddenly over rocky terrain. Preoccupied with observing the flanks rather than the forward path of the vehicle, you might only realise what had happened when the situation was well on its way, prompting a lively 'Fucking wake up you twat! What're you doing?' The poor driver, overcome with fatigue from watching the road stretching forever into the distance, would try frantically to revive himself. More water was poured on heads than down throats on the long, slow, grinding crawl down to the port of Umm Qasr. But on the journey down to get the Russian military vehicles, conditions were good, and we did it in about seven hours, meeting the Iraqi transporters at the docks.

The port of Umm Qasr was under the authority of the British military, meaning that we were able to bring the Iraqis and their transporters in for the overnight stay. This was a big help, as it meant that the Russian military trucks could be loaded and secured onto the transporters that night, ready for an early start up to Al Hillah the following morning. After the loading, there was still ample time to clean and check our weapons and material, always a reassuring activity keeping the house in order and the men switched on to the job in hand.

That evening, sitting alone on the quayside enjoying the lack of any company except the calm, quiet waters of the estuary, I reflected on the day's events. I couldn't have asked for a smoother start to the mission. Thinking through what was to come next, I visualised the convoy trundling out of the docks at sparrow's fart and in good order, starting the move up to Al Hillah. Pushing the bounds of probability, I even dared imagine a late afternoon arrival at Camp Charlie, where a well-oiled Polish green machine, eager to get their mitts on the merchandise, would allow us to make our way home – well, to Baghdad, at least – in time for supper.

The Russian trucks were, in fact, troop transporters, similar in function to the old round-fronted Bedford four-tonner, except that these were half the size and looked as if they'd played a major role in the push for Berlin. Not that it mattered. They could have been top of the range Hummers as far as I was concerned. Being around to read my bank statement and having my body intact to spend the money once my contract was over was all that mattered.

At bedtime, the small British naval contingent kindly offered us and our Iraqis accommodation in a single-block building, containing several rooms normally used for teaching. The heat this far south was stifling, up in the high 40s centigrade, and showed no sign of cooling down during the night. It made the prospect of sleeping with a lot of sweating bodies, socks and all, in a four-walled classroom decidedly nauseous. Bob, Vinny and I crashed head to toe down the corridor for the night, with only the sporadic double bleep of Vinny's mobile phone (volume set to five) announcing yet another text from his beloved to disturb us. Till recently, Vinny had been having withdrawal symptoms from the loss of comms with his HQ, but we were now a stone's throw from Kuwait, and one of their phone networks had unexpectedly lit up on his mobile. This was manna from heaven for Vinny and had given him back the will to live. By the same token, had he brought his sax with him, *we* would have lost the will.

Up early next morning, with the multitude of stars still flickering brightly away in the big, dark, cloudless sky, we began the familiar routine of packing our kit and loading it onto the vehicles. With our teeth cleaned and prayers dutifully offered, we formed up in convoy. I was up front with Allah by my side – well, in the back. Vinny's vehicle was immediately behind mine, Ahmed's was sandwiched in between the five transporters and their cargo of trucks, and Bob's CAT vehicle closed the march.

Standing by my vehicle, Motorola handset in hand, with its twisted black lead stretching through the open door, I surveyed the convoy. It lined up over about 100 metres, with the road-weary transporters now being revved mercilessly by their Iraqi taskmasters. The transporters' dilapidated appearance, and that of the Iraqis, was already filling me with trepidation. I couldn't help but see images of them broken down and lost all over southern Iraq, the Russian trucks spirited off to some second-hand-car lot owned by a fat, enterprising, moustachioed rogue of an Iraqi, with me slipping quietly out of the country and into retirement. But slipping quietly out of Umm Qasr just as the first sparrow was contemplating lifting his delicate little leg to officially pipe in the morning, I felt confident enough that the convoy and I would be in Camp Charlie, in one piece, long before sundown. Knowing Bob was bringing up the rear, and that Vinny was tucked some 50 metres directly behind me, was of considerable reassurance.

We might have left Umm Qasr quietly, cruising along at a nifty 60 kilometres per hour, but it would not have gone unnoticed. There were two Iraqi Police checkpoints on the access road to and from the port, so I knew our presence on the main Kuwait–Baghdad highway would be known to those that didn't need to know! The thought wasn't perturbing, as I hadn't heard or read any int-reps about convoys getting hit this far south. I was more worried that one or more of the lorries would break down. If they did, the nightmare scenario would start to unfold. With no spare unit to hitch up to the trailer and continue, the only recourse, which we'd followed on several previous occasions, would be for one of the other lorries to tow the broken one. This would dramatically slow us down, to something like 30 kilometres per hour, and we'd then be running late. There'd be added strain on the towing lorry, and the risk of the other lorries overheating in the blazing sun would be increased. Before long, it would get dark, and we'd still be a long way from Camp Charlie, a straggling, slow-moving, easy target for any self-respecting insurgent or fat, moustachioed second-hand-car dealer. Once again, images of doom and disaster were flashing up in my mind.

The old currant bun was now out, and we were slowly but surely eating up the miles of the two-lane highway that curved its way across the desert. The condition of the road was excellent, with nice new sticky black tarmac and a central reservation separating us from the southbound lanes. The luxury wouldn't last long, though, and at our current speed we had about two hours before the surface disintegrated into a wide, dry dusty track cut into the wilderness. Hopefully, any latent mechanical faults would manifest themselves in the good conditions before we reached the dust bowl ahead.

We'd been on the road about half an hour when Bob came on the radio with the message I'd been dreading: 'One of the lorries has pulled up.' When this type of incident occurred, our SOP would very much depend on where we found ourselves. If we were up north, we would run the rest of the convoy to the nearest military or police presence, leaving a two-vehicle armed guard deployed in defensive positions next to the lorries and off on dominating ground. Our current location, about 20 kilometres north of the turning for Basra Airport, was one I deemed to be fairly safe. I got the convoy over to the edge of the highway and deployed into defensive positions to await the sit-rep from Bob.

Now it was me making the decisions, the responsibility entirely mine, the onus on me. 'Fucking hell, Dave, what did you have to go on leave for?' I'd always been the one relaying the news up to Dave and then waiting for further orders, my main concern the immediate dangers surrounding me. Not only was I still concerned with the dangers, albeit that they were rather low risk here (I wasn't complacent, but a spade is a spade, and this neck of the woods was nowhere near as dangerous as a few hours' drive up north, no matter how much certain individuals tried to talk it up) but I was also now calling the shots as well. Contingency plans were already set and formulated in my head. I was determined to arrive at Camp Charlie with all the Russian trucks, even if it meant just one lorry towing all the other heaps of shit behind it, like some sad impression of an Australian road train. Bob's warm Scottish brogue came over the radio again: 'That's the truck running again. Seemed to me to be some sort of fuel starvation problem.'

This cheered me up no end, my mood instantly lightening as the positive thoughts rallied. I gave the order to mount up and continue. Having picked up where we left off, the five-minute stop would not eat into any of my time-and-distance calculations. I'd broken the mission down into estimated times of arrival at a series of staging areas along the route. Any of these could accommodate an overnight stay if required. I'd also established cut-off times within which each of these locations could still be reached in daylight. Moving at night is a big no-no, and not just from the insurgency point of view. There was also the spotty-faced, 18-year-old, shit-scared Yank on a checkpoint all alone with his feverish imagination and a big fucking gun to consider.

The traffic was light. Only the occasional beat-up old orange-and-white taxi or large 1970s Toyota, amazingly still clinging on to life, passed in the opposite direction. The empty roads and good visibility on either side, plus knowing we were in a predominantly Shiite region, meant that for me the nervous tension just wasn't there. No matter how much I kept reminding myself that anything could happen and we could be the first convoy to be hit hard this far south, I remained far more worried about the lorries, willing them on behind me.

Unfortunately, my worrying wasn't unfounded. A further half-hour up the highway, Bob's now ominous voice returned to the airwaves: 'That fucking lorry has stopped again!' This time it had stopped with all the other lorries piled up behind it, as it had been pushed to the front after the first breakdown to keep the others tight in if the same thing happened again – which it just fucking had, ruining my fucking peace of mind! By the side of the highway, the Iraqis, under Vinny's orders, were taking up defensive positions, leaving me free to walk the hundred or so metres back to the stalled lorry to investigate the problem and give the Iraqi driver a piece of my mind concerning his piece of shit.

The driver was shabbily dressed in Western clothing and was by the look of him new to the trucking profession. A few more years and miles under his belt and he'd evolve into your standard-issue fat-bellied, tooth-sucking, oily, dish-dash-wearing Iraqi trucker. Expecting to see one of the aforementioned, I was surprised by how young this driver was, although he did sport the obligatory black moustache, and also by the look of genuine distress on his face at the failure of his lorry. Winding my neck in, I saw the human side of it and the obvious worry this man was experiencing, with the ever-increasing threat to winning bread for his family writ large all over his face. Even though I'd calmed down, it wouldn't do to express any sympathy, as more often than not this would be interpreted as a sign of weakness and result in a noisy, arm-waving confab among all and sundry. Next they'd be asking to run into the nearest town for spares or to find some Mohammed geezer to come out with his spanners and whip the engine out, only to find he'd forgotten his sky hook. No, neck wound in or not, I still gave him the 'you and lorry no fucking good, fix it or you no good and truck no good' line. This should by rights have been met by an incredulous 'is he for fucking real' look, but it had the desired effect of spurring the driver and his boss, who was now on the scene, into bags of 'sorry, Mr Simon, we fix it, we fix it'.

And fix it they did, only for the same fuel-starvation

problem to reoccur a little further up the road. Again it was rectified, and again, and yet again, the lorry broke down. Its fuel problem became a regular, increasingly frequent occurrence along the road. I was now resigned to the fact we would not reach Camp Charlie, and the large staging area of Scania became my revised target. I also gave orders that if the offending truck broke down within a frequency of less than 20 minutes, it would either have to be towed or left to the mercy of the local tribesmen. This last threat was an idle one, issued out of sheer spiteful frustration. I had no intention of leaving the lorry, or more precisely the Russian truck. I was just venting my annoyance, taking it out on the fretting and unfortunate Iraqi trucker for the headache he was giving me. It made me feel a lot better.

Despite the relatively benign Shiite presence, for the vulnerable this could still be dangerous country. The local tribesmen in this part of Iraq were for the most part unseen. Their minions, however, were paid to sit on their haunches at the side of the road, watching and waiting for vehicles running out of juice or breaking down. The lookouts would then alert their masters, who'd get their arses out there and loot the unfortunate travellers. The carcasses of numerous unrecognisable and burned-out cars littering the highway were a reminder that we were heading north. The frequency with which the faulty lorry was halting grew. The further north we got, the more inclined I was to keep moving. Even a snail's pace was safer than stopping every few miles, so I decided to put the offending lorry on a tow. Once attached, the cab was so close up to the vehicle in front that it looked like it was joined to the back of the towing lorry. It reminded me of the big artics you see on the British motorways, tailgating old retired couples in their blue and silver Micras.

The goalposts having shifted to the staging area of Scania, it now meant that the mission would take a further day to complete and we'd not arrive at Camp Charlie in Al Hillah till the following morning. In truth, this was probably the better course of action, even if we'd not had the breakdowns. It was much better to stay overnight in a safe location and take stock of weapons and material, then do a one-hour or so hop to Al Hillah early in the morning, minus the heap-of-shit transporter and its cargo. I was not going to risk breaking down close to Al Hillah, or worse in Al Hillah itself, as word would quickly spread and an attack follow on not far behind. Scania was a good place to leave the heap-of-shit transporter. The Poles could in their own time run over and collect the trucks, and the offending transporter would bother me no more.

There were two main staging areas on the highway between Kuwait and Baghdad. Scania was the one closest to Al Hillah, approximately thirty miles south-east and some one hour south of Baghdad, with the other staging area a further three hours' journey time south. These areas had been designed for the never-ending stream of convoys bringing in supplies from Kuwait. Some of these convoys had as many as 70 artics in them and were escorted by a handful of US military vehicles. At the staging area, they could refuel, sort out any mechanical problems and eat at the large tented cookhouses, or chow halls as the Americans called them. And, if necessary, they could park up for the night within the huge compound in lanes divided by low concrete blast walls, allowing them to remain in formation ready to roll on the following morning. It wasn't unusual to encounter several hundred artics stationed in these compounds at one time.

Both the staging areas were fenced off and guarded by heavily armed US soldiers, but were also both situated out in the 'oulou'. This made them easy targets for the insurgents, who under the blanket of darkness could mount indiscriminate attacks with gunfire, rockets and the weapons most effective in sapping morale and taking life in a protected area, mortars.

Because we were taking equipment to the Polish contingent, there was no US military presence with us. Therefore, obtaining any assistance other than being given a place to rest and the opportunity to refuel would be nigh on impossible. Anyhow, as long as I left the Russian trucks on the faulty transporter in a safe military location, there should be no problem.

Arriving at Scania with about an hour of daylight left, I breathed one of my many sighs of relief. After refuelling, we regrouped in convoy formation, ready to roll on out the other side for Al Hillah in the morning. I went in search of someone to take responsibility for the heap of shit and its Russian cargo being left there. When I eventually signed over the material to the Poles, I wanted to be able to give them a contact name, unit and location, enabling them to claim the trucks back without too much bother when they came for them. Not that I thought any of the Americans were going to lift the period Russian trucks – or perhaps some re-enactment case might.

Scania was only about one hour's journey from Camp Charlie, and with the heap of shit out of my face, I was already thinking of our return to the villa in Baghdad. What could go wrong?

With the transporters and our vehicles lined up one behind the other in the holding area, I passed an uncomfortable night. Lying next to my pick-up, I woke several times as I drifted in and out of a shallow sleep. Rising at 0400, one hour before everyone else, I made my way in the dark to the ops room, occasionally bumping into the odd low blast wall or stupidly placed army tent. I'd been told that I could get the latest intelligence on Al Hillah's threat level and what attacks had taken place during the last 24 hours.

I was briefed by a US Army lieutenant, and the picture he painted was that of a town returning to calm after civil unrest. This unrest had been in protest at the escalating levels of violence by insurgents not from Al Hillah who had been brought in from elsewhere in Iraq and further afield to destabilise the place. To me, it seemed to be working, as the lieutenant also informed me that the armed Iraqi guards at the checkpoint leading to the main entrance of Camp Charlie had disappeared from their posts a week earlier and had not returned. Straight away, I thought of the tactics used by the provisional IRA in Armagh to put the shits up the British Forces. They would get whole streets of people to open all their windows, which to a passing foot patrol would spell out that there was a bomb close by and that it was going to go bang, cos everyone had moved their panes to avoid the blast waves. The Poles manning the main gate, having seen their human shield of Iraqi armed guards mysteriously disappear, would now be on edge, not to mention trigger happy, suspecting imminent attack in the form of a suicide bomber.

When approaching bases in Iraq, I'm only ever at ease when it's the British Army facing me – everyone else I treat with extreme caution and the utmost respect for their incompetence. To be fair, suicide bombs are also a lot more prevalent up north (or at least they were at that time). The Poles at Camp Charlie had already been the target of a suicide bomber once before – a septic tank dredger packed with explosives had blown itself, the shit within it and all the unlucky souls at the entrance into stinking oblivion.

There was one piece of information, however, that the lieutenant failed to bring to my attention: that of the mortaring of Camp Charlie that very night. I suppose with all the computers and other technology at the disposal of the Americans, dissemination is still a hard word to spell.

Arriving back at the convoy, I was greeted by the pleasant sight of activity. Bob and Vinny had achieved the nigh-on impossible task of getting all and sundry up and ready to roll. Well, prayers had still to be said and a few cups of tea had to be drunk, but the fact that all the Iraqi transporter drivers were up and their lorries ticking over, making the holding area an eye-stinging health hazard, meant that my plan of leaving the staging area at 0600 and reaching Camp Charlie at 0700 was bang on schedule. The young Iraqi was not too happy about leaving his transporter behind, but I assured him that we'd get him permission to return and recover it. I didn't have the foggiest who would give me this piece of written permission, but I'd have said anything just to get him up in the passenger seat of his mate's transporter and us on our way on time. By a quarter to six, I wanted all the Iraqi drivers sitting behind their big black steering wheels, wearing big cheesy grins under their moustaches, revving the guts out of the engines if they so wished, but ready to roll, and all my convoy pick-ups formed up and ready, each with one Iraqi outside on the back manning a PKM machine gun, because the minute the sergeant gave me the thumbs-up sign, I'd be rolling out of the far checkpoint of Scania, aiming to slip unnoticed towards Camp Charlie through the quiet and desolate early morning streets of Al Hillah.

They were and we did, but not for long. With the first glimpse of the top of the rising sun to our right, one of the transporters slowed and pulled up on the side of the highway as if prompted. Hearing Bob's announcement of the event over the radio, we all came to a halt, the Iraqis deploying out of the vehicles in defence. Time was now precious. The longer we remained on the road, the more chance any insurgents in Al Hillah had to mount an ambush against us. I told Abid One to turn around and drive back to the offending transporter. As we pulled up, I was pleased to hear the engine running. Sitting behind his wheel and beaming with a cheesy smile, the driver said, 'Good, good. No *mushcul* [problem].'

Getting straight on the radio, I gave my orders: 'Right, Vinny, get it all moving. It's sorted here. I'll catch you up.' I wanted the show rolling again as fast as possible, and not wasting the few seconds for us to drive back up front would help get us to Camp Charlie sooner rather than later. Abid One could just put his foot down and overtake the moving convoy to regain our position.

We'd not gone more than a mile when Bob announced, 'Looks like it's all gone Pete Tong again. The same transporter's pulled up.' I couldn't believe it. Enraged, I gave orders for Vinny to get everyone into defensive positions then instructed Abid One to return us to the transporter. Once again, the driver was sitting in his cab revving the arse off of the engine. After getting him to take his foot off the accelerator so we could hear ourselves think, I established through Abid One's still awful English that there was a problem – not what it was, just that there was a problem! 'Fucking hell, problem. You're fucking right there's a problem, and it's him,' I said, pointing straight at the driver sitting up high in his cab. 'Smiling fucking Abdul, that's the fucking problem.' The driver got the message that I was not at all amused, yet continued to wear a pathetic smile, which sent me into even more of a rage.

I actually didn't believe him in the slightest. All the drivers carried mobiles, some even had sat phones, and I felt sure he was setting us up for a hit. Still raging, I pointed first at him then at my Kalashnikov in my right hand and shouted, 'You fucking problem – I leave you here, big *muschul* with America.'

'OK, OK, no *muschul*, slow, slow, me,' he said, still not looking the slightest bit concerned. 'Anta fucking waheed convoy, anta number waheed sierra, fucking roo,' I told him in my still awful Arabic. Translated into English, I had said, 'Get up to the front – you will be the first transporter in the convoy now.' Well, literally translated, I said something more like, 'You fucking one convoy, you number one vehicle, fucking go.' He understood. Leaving me smarting in the black exhaust fumes, he took his slowly moving transporter up to front position.

The two unscheduled halts had blown any chance of us slipping quietly into Al Hillah. The insurgents had probably now had time for a leisurely breakfast before setting out for ambush duty. Just up ahead was the turn-off from the main highway that would take us through a large village and on over to the other north–south highway that ran into Al Hillah. At the start of this crossover road, and also at the other side, we'd have to pass through an Iraqi Police checkpoint. Being ever cynical and paranoid, I believed that the police at this checkpoint were in cahoots with the insurgents, feeding them information on all comings and goings. By the time we turned onto the minor road, it was well past 0700, and the best I could hope for was to arrive safely in about 20 to 30 minutes' time.

The police checkpoint was no more than a dilapidated, sand-filled chicane with a square, single-storey building of cracked and peeling whitewash. Outside, some cheap plastic chairs were littered around. As we drew close, I saw that two of these chairs were occupied by blue-shirted Iraqi policemen. At their feet was a mangy-looking mutt, who paid more attention to us than did the police officers. I wasn't fooled by their blatant lack of interest, though. Every detail of the convoy would have been observed. Hopefully, that was as far as the information would go.

'That's me through the checkpoint.' I acknowledged Bob's radio message with a click-click. Looking in the nearside wing mirror, which had been adjusted to aid my observation, and seeing Vinny and the red beat-up transporter, I told Abid One to speed up to 50 kilometres per hour. The terrain either side of the road featured lots of palm trees, which further on would become large groves of palms, lending this part of Iraq – at one time the site of Babylon – its mystical aura. I wasn't sightseeing, though, as I was too busy looking for signs of ambushes and IEDs.

That stretch of road always made me feel uneasy. I was sure our presence on the main highway would already have been noted by the insurgents, and because it was the only road into Al Hillah it was the ideal spot for attack. Once the ambushers had wreaked their havoc, they would easily be able to escape under the cover of the dense palm trees. Now more or less halfway across the link road, the convoy passed slowly through the village. As always, the local kids ran out, shouting excitedly and waving to us. 'Good, nothing untoward going on here,' I thought. If an attack was imminent, the place would have been scarily deserted.

Bob gave me an update: 'That's me clear of the village.' Click-click.

With Vinny and the red transporter still in my wing mirror, it looked like it would be only ten minutes or so before our safe arrival at Camp Charlie. The police checkpoint at the other side came into view. Beyond this, cars and lorries could clearly be seen travelling fast in both directions on the main road. This was a comforting sight: normal, busy traffic into which we might blend. But my sense of security was misplaced, since we actually stood out in such a scene – slow moving convoys with manned machine guns, albeit crudely fixed onto the backs of pick-ups, weren't going to go unnoticed even in the rush hour.

We passed unhindered through the heavily manned police checkpoint. Vinny then raced forward to block the highway by placing his vehicle across the south-bound carriageway, guns facing the stopped traffic. This enabled me to lead the convoy out and left, heading towards the now visible buildings of Al Hillah. From here on in, attack could come from all corners: a bomb placed at the roadside or several well-armed insurgents firing at us from the mass of buildings right and left. My eyes were everywhere, the tension in the vehicle now acute. I could sense Abid One's apprehension and fear. I could also see it, as he was gripping the steering wheel hard and subconsciously rocking ever so slightly backwards and forwards.

'Abid, whatever happens, you just fucking drive, OK. Fucking drive,' I said, continuing to look hard ahead and trying to maintain a normal, matter-of-fact voice. Cars were passing in the opposite direction, which was a good sign. A rupture in the flow would have suggested trouble up ahead.

With Camp Charlie's high perimeter wall now visible some 200 metres up on the right, we were nearly home and dry. Suddenly, a car appeared from the opposite direction repeatedly flashing its lights. As it slowed, the driver shouted something to Abid One and to Allah, who was manning the gun on the back of the pick-up. My stomach turned and a sudden rush of adrenalin surged to my temples and finger tips. Another Arab man in the car was waving his hands. I could read his unmistakable concern, his gestures clearly saying turn back. Agitated, they were still shouting at us as they pulled away. Brave men, but I fucking hated them for putting me on the spot – 200 metres to go and I was supposed to turn the whole fucking convoy round because someone flashed his lights and gesticulated 'no good, no good'? Having now slowed the convoy right down, my brain was racing, my eyes trying to search out any dangers ahead. Allah was leaning over my side and shouting 'no good, Simon' and Abid One was also telling me 'no good'.

'What's no fucking good? Tell me, for fuck's sake!'

'Man said no good,' Abid pleaded with me.

'Iraq no fucking good, mate. Fucking drive, Allah. *Chouff, chouff*,' I shouted in barely controlled rage at my predicament. How do you turn a large convoy round on a busy each-way road in a town, with the possibility of ambush from hidden gunmen while your artics are trying to perform a series of three-point turns? Nightmare! But to carry on into a potential ambush and be killed, or worse survive and get some of my men killed, was a potentially bigger one. On top of this, I could see Abid One was now shitting it.

'Right, lads, make ready. Only about 200 metres till we're alongside the wall of the camp, but a local has just given me a warning of possible trouble ahead. Eyes up, let's go.' After sending this message over the radio, I armed my Kalashnikov, holding it in both hands ready to let rip. Rolling forward with Vinny reassuringly 30 metres or so behind me, we edged closer to the camp. The sound of gunfire rang out up ahead – two or three bursts of automatic, at least three hundred metres away and not aimed at us. By that point, my vehicle was level with a Polish sentry post on the wall, and I leaned out of the window and shouted up to him, 'Hey, mate, what's happening up ahead?' Only his head and shoulders were visible to me, and I could see that he was scanning in the direction of the gunfire with a pair of binoculars. He looked down at me and said in a heavy Eastern-bloc accent, 'Good, good, no problem.'

Thinking to myself that everything in Iraq was 'good' or 'no good', I got back on the radio: 'Just spoke to one of the Polish guards. Looks like we're clear to run on in. Don't follow the transporters' route in – follow me.'

The entrance to Camp Charlie was now just down on our right, but the transporters would have to go a further 200 metres to where there was a longer break in the pavement.

There was a smaller break before this that was sufficient to let our pick-ups through – ideal. I didn't want us going any further into downtown Al Hillah than was strictly necessary. Turning right and now facing the chicaned entrance to the camp, I jumped out onto the road and gestured at the first transporter to continue on down so he could turn into the approach road. Vinny had followed me round, and when I saw that the first transporter understood and was carrying on I jumped back in the pick-up and announced over the radio, 'Ahmed and Bob, turn where I've turned, leave the transporters to continue.' I was just about to tell Abid One to advance when there was an almighty noise on my right and the rear passenger window exploded, showering fragments of glass everywhere. Instantly tensing up, I pushed the barrel of my AK-47 out of the window and let rip, screaming at Abid One 'Go, go, go!' He did, sending the vehicle racing for the safety of the high blast wall of the chicaned entrance. I could hear Allah firing, and after my initial aimless burst I'd got visual on a fast disappearing 4x4. I managed to get another burst of fire on it before it was obscured by the transporters, now further down the road.

I was beginning to calm down and get a grip on the situation when the back window shattered into tiny pieces. Rounds were slamming into the pick-up from behind. (Unknown to me at that time, Vinny's vehicle was taking the brunt of these rounds, being fired on by insurgents positioned some 200 metres directly behind us.) This accurate fire was also raking the now cowering Poles guarding the main entrance, who, unbelievably, started to pour rounds into my and Vinny's vehicles. It took me a few seconds to realise that we were under fire from the front and rear. With the front windscreen now holed in several places, I opened the door to leap out and take cover. I felt rounds whizzing close by my head in both directions. Without thinking, I dived behind the vehicle where Abid One and Allah were already both cowering down low. Rounds continued to slam into the front of the vehicle from the Poles only 30 metres away. The insurgents behind were also still firing at us. Under intense attack from both front and rear, there was only one course of action: I would have to make a dash for the concrete chicane wall about 20 metres distant. Crouching low and sprinting hard, I fixed the wall with my eyes, knowing that if I made it there I'd live. Doubled up and going hell for leather, I was expecting nothingness any second. I clearly remember thinking that's what it would be like if a round slammed into me and killed me: I would experience 'nothingness'.

Rounds were whizzing passed me – schoo, schoo, crack, crack – and pinging off the tarmac on either side. Anticipating oblivion, I just kept looking at the chicane wall, repeating to myself that if I got there, I'd live. I launched myself at the wall in a dive, hitting the ground hard.

My only thought was a selfish one – I'd made it, I was safe, I was gonna fucking live. Now out of the Poles' fire and out of sight of the insurgents, I just wanted to stay hidden where I was and come out when the firing stopped. But my conscience was already nagging: 'You're in charge, Simon. Your men are caught in crossfire. Or at least they're being shot at by both Poles and insurgents and probably lying dead and wounded, so do something about it.' I simply couldn't remain where I was.

I lifted my head to peer over the chicane at the Poles. They were still firing wildly and looking decidedly scared. My, Vinny's and Ahmed's pick-ups were all stationary with the doors wide open, between me and the Poles. I couldn't see all of my men but some were lying underneath the vehicles. I was sure that we'd taken heavy casualties, possibly even suffered some fatalities. Sensing that the fire from the insurgents had dropped considerably, I started shouting to the Poles,

'Stop firing, stop firing, we're English.' I then raised my hands above my head, stood up and walked towards them. Seeing their guns all now menacingly pointed at me, I kept repeating, 'Don't shoot, we're English.' When I was about ten metres from the first Pole, he motioned me to get down on the floor, still pointing his weapon at me. Now enraged at his behaviour, I shouted, 'There's fucking insurgents out there.' I then pointed back behind me and continued, 'And one of my call signs is stuck out there, so stop pointing your fucking weapon at me and go and get them.' He knew what I was saying, but the fear that was written across his face was clearly paralysing any rational thought.

Envisaging the situation deteriorating and not wanting to remain exposed to any further insurgent attack, I shouted at my vehicle commanders for a sit-rep on casualties. Vinny called back that his driver, Abid Two, had sustained an injury to his eye, and Ahmed shouted over from the shrubs at the side of the camp where he had taken refuge that Fadi had a wound on his arm. Bob was still stuck about 100 metres further out, his vehicle abandoned on the main road with its doors open. He had got himself and his team undercover behind one of the outer concrete blast walls. Ignoring the Poles, I grabbed my handheld radio and asked Bob for a sit-rep.

'We're all OK,' he replied 'but what the fuck's going on? Who's shooting at us from your end?'

'The fucking Polaks.'

'Why?'

'Cos they're wankers. Can you see the insurgents from where you are?'

'No, but they were at the end of the road further into town. I think they've bugged out.'

'Right, cover your driver while he gets the vehicle down here, then we'll cover your move on foot into our position.'

We had by now taken up fire positions facing towards Bob. His driver sprinted out to his vehicle, started it and raced into the cover of the high blast walls at the main entrance to Camp Charlie. I hollered out to Bob, 'OK, Bob, go.' We covered any possible attack from the insurgents as Bob and Yarub sprinted for all they were worth into our position. Throughout all this, the Poles remained passive and hidden.

Now that we were all regrouped, I was able to conduct a more thorough check of the wounded. My and Vinny's vehicles had the appearance of colanders. They also looked like they'd bled to death, with coolant running out from underneath them into two large pools of bluish-green, oily water. My passenger door alone had three rounds through it, both headlights and rear lights were shot to pieces, and little squares of broken glass were scattered all over the seats and floor. Vinny's was in a similar state. Both our tailgates had bullet holes from insurgents' fire from behind us and shot-out headlights from the Poles to our front. But with all the rounds that had hit our vehicles and flown inches past, the miraculous thing was that only two of us were wounded, neither with a bullet hole in them – Abid Two had glass or some other foreign object in his right eye and Fadi gravel rash on his arm. How we'd got off so lightly beggared belief, but we had.

The transporters stuck out on the main road were all untouched, which made me more convinced than ever that the drivers were in on it. My theory was that they had informed their contact the previous night that we would be arriving from Scania, and that the insurgents were actually waiting for us further down, where I'd sent the transporters. Realising we were turning off short, they sent a 4x4 up to do a drive-pass shooting and then hit us from behind as we ran for cover.

The pick-ups were dragged into Camp Charlie by a Polish recovery truck, and the transporters unloaded their cargo inside. Meanwhile, I got on the satellite phone to Armor Group HQ, reporting that we'd been involved in an ambush by insurgents and had taken friendly fire from the Poles at the same time. I itemised the very light injuries and reported the badly shot-up state of our vehicles, one of which wouldn't start. In addition to a replacement vehicle, we would also need two teams, consisting of a total of six private-military contractors in two vehicles, to bolster our numbers for running back up to Baghdad the next day, a Friday.

Friday was the day of prayers at mosques scattered all over Al Hillah, and there would be car loads of men, guns and all, on the roads, making their way to prayer. More importantly, Friday was a day when such groups, gathered en masse and fired up, would be primed and ready to mount opportunist or planned attacks, such as the one that could be awaiting our departure from the Polish base. With only two vehicles roadworthy, I wasn't going to pack everyone in like sardines and risk running back up and through Baghdad like that. And I certainly wasn't going to have the two shot-up pick-ups recovered in the same move. They could stay where they were in Camp Charlie and be recovered in slow time, incognito. I couldn't have emphasised this more to HQ.

After the call, and happy with Armor's confirmation that the two teams and an extra vehicle would be sent down for us the next day, I went in search of the Polish 'if we've just shot you up for no reason, complain to me' officer. Eventually, stumbling across an office with an English-speaking NCO, I set about ripping into the actions of the guards on the main gate. Pulling no punches, I accused them of cowardice, as they had not even covered Bob's withdrawal into the camp. My speech fell not on deaf ears, but on soldiers of another cast. Having served with many Poles in the Legion, it was a bit of a surprise to see them in such a bad light. I'd known some very brave Polish legionnaires. Here, the morale seemed to be on the floor, as if none of them wanted to be in this kind of theatre.

Eventually, an American military liaison officer on the camp turned up. After listening to my side of events, he said he was astounded that the insurgents felt comfortable enough to mount an ambush to all intents and purposes right in front of the base. I wasn't in the least. He then told me I had to ring some British Army major. He passed me the number, and I did just that. I'd be lying if I said it wasn't good to hear a calm and reassuring British Officer's voice in a time of trouble. Stiff upper lip, dear boy, stiff upper lip!

After a brief introduction, the major asked, 'What is the British Army doing in Al Hillah?'

'I don't fucking know, sir.'

'What unit are you?'

'Armor Group.'

'Oh, I was under the impression that it was the British Army involved in a firefight. Are you all OK?'

'Yes, sir. Thanks for your concern.' I then went on to give him a rundown of the events, after which he asked if there was anything he could do for me at his end. 'Yes, sir, there is one thing. You could send me a helicopter to get me out of here!' Laughing, the major wished me and my men good luck, then we said our goodbyes and hung up. I thought, 'I'll take that as a no on the helicopter, then.'

During the phone call, another individual had appeared in the office. He was inordinately gung-ho, having almost every conceivable gadget hooked, taped, welded or tied to his combat-uniformed body. Most striking of all was the upside-down knife on the shoulder strap of his webbing. He introduced himself to me as the Polish regimental sergeant major (RSM) at the camp. Now I knew why so many of his soldiers were wearing camouflaged bandannas on their heads: Hollywood had gone east! Despite his current role as a walking army-surplus store, the RSM proceeded to offer a sincere apology for his men's actions, and/or the lack of them. On my return to Baghdad, I personally submitted a report on the incident to the American military HQ in Saddam's Palace but heard no more of it.

The following morning, a call came in from Armor HQ. They advised me that the additional teams were on their way down and should be with us in around an hour and a half. To prevent another potential blue on blue, I let the Polish guard commander know that they were coming, and prior to the expected time of arrival got everyone ready for a fast and furious run out of Al Hillah. Just as we were expecting them, I heard a burst of automatic gunfire coming from the main-gate area. Worried our guys could be caught up in some trouble, I went over and enquired what was going on. The sergeant, or whatever rank it was he wore, assured me that everything was OK and that his men had just fired warning shots at a civilian car that had come towards them.

As he was speaking, another burst of fire came from one of the guards up on the wall. Following the sergeant out onto the approach, I saw a member of Armor Group. He was standing next to a dark-blue civilian saloon and holding a plastic A4-sized Union Jack above his head. Though he was obviously not a threat to the Poles, their reactions were fucking scared and highly volatile. Furiously, I yelled out, 'Hey, they're from Armor Group. Stop your fucking shooting and let them in!' I still couldn't believe how dangerous these Poles were. Christ, their imaginations had total control of them.

As the Armor Group lads drove in, I got rather confused, because they only had one civilian car and a tow truck. Once inside on the form-up area, I went over to the car, which was crammed full with three expat PMCs and two Iraqis, and asked where my replacement vehicle was and what were they doing with the recovery truck. The reply to my first question was, 'What vehicle?' As for the recovery truck, they said it was for towing the two broken-down vehicles back to Baghdad.

'What fucking broken-down vehicles?' I replied.

'Your fucking broken-down vehicles.'

'Come and have a look at my fucking "broken-down" vehicles.' With that, I marched over to the two bullet-riddled pick-ups in the far corner of the form-up area, the three PMCs following me. '*Voilà.* The two fucking "broken-down" vehicles,' I said. The PMCs stared in disbelief. The reason for their incredulity became clear when they said HQ had told them our convoy had had two vehicles break down and that they were to escort a recovery truck up to us to bring the said vehicles back to Baghdad. I could barely believe my ears, and got straight onto the sat phone. I quickly got through to HQ and was all ready to give them a piece of my mind when I had second thoughts. I bit my lip. I didn't want to make myself look more petulant than I already was. Instead of launching into a tirade of anger, I just said I'd see them on my return but not with the two shot-up vehicles. I emphasised 'shot-up'.

Talking to the three PMCs, I said, 'Right, just fuck the recovery vehicle off. He can make his own way back [the driver of the tow truck was an Iraqi and could blend in]. My two injured can get into your civilian car along with your two Iraqis and go with the recovery vehicle. You three can jump in with us. In fact, two of you can man the guns on the back.'

Hearing this, one of them, a tall skinny bloke who'd not yet spoken, said, 'I'm not going with you. I'm staying with the civilian car. I'm on leave in a few days' time.'

'What's your fucking leave got to do with it?' I replied, looking at him like he was a bad smell. It was clear he was bottling it at the thought of being in a recognisable pick-up in the same streets where they'd been involved in a firefight with local insurgents the day before.

'I'm not going with you,' he repeated.

'Not a problem,' I said. 'You just get back in your civilian car and fuck off.' With that I walked off in disgust, telling my two injured Iraqis to go back with the skinny bloke and the empty tow truck. The other two PMCs, fair play to them, had no qualms about getting out on the exposed backs of the pick-ups to run through the Friday streets of Al Hillah and on to Baghdad.

Back in the capital, the return journey having been thankfully uneventful, I went to see who was responsible for the cock-up. It turned out to be someone I'd not seen before, whose job as far as I could gather was procurement. There we were, out in the shit, right up to our necks, and instead of an operations manager planning and coordinating missions we had someone who bought in material and equipment running the show. Blackadder's quip about prioritising lorry loads of paper clips just about summed it up. When I confronted the procurement bod and asked why no teams had been sent to reinforce us in Al Hillah, his reply was that they'd been late showing up so he had sent the civilian car instead. Where he thought I was meant to put all the personnel from the two shot-up pick-ups, fuck knows. It stank, and the thought uppermost in my head was, 'What if I'd been killed down there? And for this shower!'

I left the procurement bloke standing outside the villa and walked straight into the boss's office. He wasn't there, but his second in command, an ex-Irish Guards officer, was. I told him enough was enough, and that until things improved – including better vehicles and guns for convoy – I wasn't doing another mission.

Life in convoy changed after that. (Ironically, we were reinforced by several more PMCs but not any armoured vehicles or bigger guns – we were given loads of AK-47s and PKMs, but the majority of them didn't work!) We only made the occasional run down to the training school in Al Hillah, and this was either to reinforce them for a few days after they'd sustained an attack, or to supply them with weapons or ammo. We were also used on a daily basis to ferry bods to and from BIAP along the notorious four-mile stretch of road that at one time was tagged the most dangerous stretch of highway on the planet. It was, but I never saw one incident on the road, although I quite often passed by just after or just before one.

Maybe this luck was down to my good mate Jock, who on his departure from Iraq had given me a cutting from a rowan tree all the way from Perthshire. This, he said, was a talisman that had kept him safe and would do the same for me. I had to say, so far it was doing the business. Having a charmed life, I felt I ought to make the most of it. The new routine left a lot of time on our hands, and what better way to spend it than sampling the pleasures of Baghdad's nightlife?

6

OUT ON THE TILES

The social scene in Baghdad is, for its numerous Western visitors, restricted to the Green Zone. Well, not exactly restricted – you can go where you like if your company allows free movement. But for health and safety reasons, it is advisable to stay within the confines of the Green Zone, which actually covers a large part of central Baghdad – I'd say about the size of the City of London, the 'square mile'. It is completely cordoned off by large concrete blast walls and further protected with gun towers manned by heavily armed US soldiers.

The most noticeable building complex inside the Green Zone is Saddam's palace, a vast, extravagantly built piece of real estate, fittingly ostentatious for a man of the late dictator's standing. Beautiful, tranquil-looking lawned gardens with curving walkways lead up to the stately palace building itself. Inside, behind a pair of monstrously large wooden doors a rather disappointing take on a London museum is revealed. Rattling around in the huge, high-ceilinged rooms, the only exhibits now on show are the hordes of military personnel in clean combats working alongside the casually dressed civilians, ID cards around their necks, who together form the HQ staff of the CPA. Although Saddam is not long gone, his palace is now used to run Operation Iraqi Freedom. Deep within the building, further large halls have been partitioned off, creating a labyrinth of corridors, offices and briefing rooms. Massive bunches of taped cabling run along the walls carrying electricity from the outside generators, before splicing off above head height into a warren of offices, where they feed the multitude of humming computers, ultra-fast photocopiers and other hi-tech kit of the military bureaucracy. The corridors are alive with military and civilian personnel, dodging around each another en route to any one of a multitude of departments. With the constant to-ing and fro-ing, there is always the vague but impressive sense that something important is happening.

In the palace gardens to the rear, there is a swimming pool. Where once Saddam and his family enjoyed its cool waters, groups of rowdy American GIs now fool about childishly or lounge around the poolside, enjoying well-earned downtime during their one-year tour of duty in Baghdad's lethal neighbourhoods. Unlike us, the private-military contractors, these GIs were not on massive bucks, and the consumption of alcohol for them was strictly *verboten*. I couldn't help but wonder what the punishment might be if they were caught drinking; to be sent back to the States, even to be put in the nick, hardly seemed a deterrent – more like an incentive, if you ask me. But they all seemed to adhere strictly to the no-alcohol policy.

During my nights out in various establishments in the Green Zone, I only ever saw one or two drinking. One was a master sergeant whom I'd worked with on convoy duty, and I could totally understand why he regularly got pissed. He'd been on the ground with the convoys, and when there weren't enough security firms to do the escorting early on he had once jumped into the cab of one of the Iraqi transporters himself. Then, with his M16 and a handful of rounds in a few magazines, he'd driven off with the Iraqi truckers, leaving the safety of the distribution centre for the dangers of Baghdad and the final destination of Fallujah.

He seemed to take pride in his contempt for his own skin, and during his drinking sessions he would become as pissed as a newt – hardly unnoticeable on the way home. It was hard to believe that none of his superiors knew about his drinking. Why did they overlook it? I guess because heroes, or idiots, like him were short on the ground, and he was a lot more use there in Iraq than in some military pen back home.

Outside the palace grounds, but still within the relative safety of the Green Zone, there were several commercial establishments for the purposes of rest and recreation. These include the American Military PX, a cyber café, a Pizza Hut-style takeaway and two Chinese restaurant-cum-bars, one of them incorporating a massage parlour. There were also several small cafés and rotisseries dotted around the avenues, a rooftop terrace bar in the Olive Security firm's villa complex (invites only) and the most macabre bar I've ever had the pleasure or misfortune to drink in, a morgue (no invite necessary). There was even a street market within the Green Zone, full of stalls run by local Iraqis, selling everything from sim cards for the Iraqna phone company Baghdad network (a must for PMCs to operate around Baghdad) to nunchakus (another must for certain PMCs to operate in Baghdad!). I say there 'was' a street market, because a suicide bomber blew himself up one day, and unselfishly the mobile-phone seller too, I hope, to share in the waiting virgins. After that, the market's customer base swiftly disappeared.

With all these attractions laid on, there was plenty to amuse us after the convoy operations melted down. All right, there wasn't your Wetherspoons or your Pizza Express, but there was beer, food and the occasional massage. And here massage meant what it said and nothing more: a real Chinese massage, from the delicate hands of softly spoken Chinese women, brought in by some canny entrepreneur.

Our days now consisted of mad dashes up the BIAP road to the airport and back, sometimes two or three times a day, and longer runs down to the training school in Al Hillah, plus occasionally we had to take various individuals to some location or other in Baghdad. This routine gave us plenty of downtime, but we didn't squander it all on self-indulgence. By about five in the afternoon, Dave, Bob and I were usually able to schlep off, so we'd all jump into a pick-up, dressed in our running gear of shorts, vests and pumps. Then, with webbing and body armour over the top and our Kalashnikovs loaded, we'd head off into the Green Zone for a few miles' run around the streets. We'd leave Vinny to practise on his saxophone to his heart's content – in between answering text messages from his other half, of course.

Parking on the car park in front of the palace entrance, we'd leave our Kalashnikovs locked in the pick-up, hidden beneath our body armour in the rear footwell. However, feeling naked, we always kept hold of our nine-mil Brownings strapped to our bodies underneath the running vests. There were a few lonely spots within the Green Zone, ideal for any insurgents who'd infiltrated to pump silenced rounds into an unsuspecting jogger.

Returning to the villa after one running session, I logged on to my emails and saw a message from Ralf, a good friend from my Legion days. Was it me, he wanted to know, who had just been running around the Green Zone in Baghdad? Ralf was a German, and having not met up with him since

1990 back in French Guiana, his email came as a pleasant surprise. The fact that he was working as a PMC for another private-security company and living in the Green Zone meant that if ever an excuse was needed for a night out on the tiles, this was a strong candidate. Ralf and I arranged to meet up that same night, in the rear garden of one of the Chinese restaurants.

The large table in the restaurant's garden soon stacked up with beers, and the chairs around it quickly filled with other ex-legionnaires now serving as PMCs. Some faces I didn't recognise, others like the ex-*adjudant unite* of the third company of the parachute regiment were well known to me. A giant of a Yugoslav who'd had no trouble keeping the likes of Sergent Chef J. under control, he was now heading up a team of close-protection specialists in Baghdad.

Having not clapped eyes on Ralf for nigh on 15 years, I was surprised to see how little he'd changed. His fluent English was still spoken with a cockney accent, even though he'd never set foot in England. And things were going well for him. Domiciled in South Africa, he was busily making plans to marry his long-term girlfriend, and he invited me to the wedding, which was scheduled for early 2005.

As the beer and conversation flowed, another sound began to fill the air. It was the rumble of several approaching US helicopters, growing louder as they neared the military hospital located just behind us. Judging by the extended din of the rotor blades as they hovered awaiting their turn to disgorge the wounded, it seemed likely the Americans had been involved in heavy fighting with insurgents somewhere in Baghdad. The aftermath of the crisis was now unfolding right next to us, unseen but in close range of the beer garden, and it made conversation very difficult. The juxtaposition was bizarre in its way: the drama and urgency of injured men – some critically, perhaps – being airlifted to waiting medics and us sitting next door in a twee beer garden enjoying lashings of booze and Chinese snacks.

After a couple of hours sampling the delights of the Chinese beer garden, a few of us, Dave and Ralf included, decided to move on and suffer the delights of the Green Café. This café was situated at the other end of the hospital and was run by a local Iraqi who served cold bottled beer and pizza or roast chicken and chips. The only downside to this watering hole was the awful Arab pop videos that constantly blared out from the TV in the corner. Each time we left the place, we vowed never to return, but because we were a few beers to the wind its charms now beckoned again.

On the night of my arrival in Iraq, Jock and I had ended up in the Green Café, chewing the fat with Sean. And if there was any doubt in my mind about the state of things in Baghdad at that time, the resounding crumps of exploding mortars landing nearby well and truly dispelled them – an exciting eye-opening start to my contract. Tonight there were no mortars landing, just loud vibrating from the TV. Ralf remarked, in his finest German cockney, 'I fink I prefer the facking helicopters.' After gorging on fried chicken and chips, the lively beer-filled evening came to an end, and we swapped mobile numbers with a view to doing it all again one night. Ralf and the others headed back to their various villas in the relatively safe Green Zone, while Dave and I did our quick dash to downtown Baghdad.

It soon became apparent to me and Dave that there was a clique of PMCs on the bar circuit in the Green Zone, and, furthermore, we were fast becoming members! It wasn't long before we were introduced to the morgue bar by Scotty, one of Armor Group's liaison officers with the American military. Scotty was an ex-officer of a Gurkha regiment, but, unlike a lot of British ex-officers, he didn't have his nose up his own arse. Instead, it was firmly wedged in a beer can, preferably half full. Ever the optimist, Scotty was certainly straight out of the public-school mould and cut a dash with his loud and confident rugger-player persona. When I first met him, I tended to be on my back foot. Having spent seven years as a low life in the British Army, I was conditioned to the 'them and us' of its class structure and my humble place as a Brit squaddie therein. Officer cadre and posh voice notwithstanding, Scotty was solidly one of the lads, and there was no side with him. Consequently, we had a whale of a time before he moved on to fresh deserts and oases new in the Middle East.

Anyway, back to the morgue bar. Just before the large roundabout before the palace was an insignificant-looking road that led off to a series of one- and two-storey buildings, tucked away and unremarkable in their run-down Arabesque way. There was nothing to suggest that there was a morgue situated there, nor indeed a drinking den. The old morgue building gave away no clue that it was under new management and, like all those high-street banks, a trendy bar! A bar it most definitely was, but trendy it was not – more a 'leave your hardware in your pick-up and drink' sort of establishment. From what I could gather, it was run by a Canadian EOD (bomb disposal) team that, like all private-security firms on the band wagon, were cashing in on the mess that was Iraq. Not happy with just picking up grenades and rockets and defusing big bombs, they had diversified into the licensed, or rather unlicensed, trade, converting the morgue from a store for stiffs into a welcoming hostelry serving stiff drinks to the thirsty, cash-rich hired guns prowling the Green Zone.

If I hadn't been aware that The Morgue (as it was also referred to in its current incarnation) had once been a cold room for dead bodies, I would probably have guessed it on entering. The large room with white floor-to-ceiling tiles and the sloping run-off were a 'dead' giveaway! As was the chilly, uninviting atmosphere that the clinical walls gave off before the place started to fill up with drinkers. It didn't look as if the Canadian boys had needed much to convert the place – a white-tiled, waist-high slab three-metres long had had a small return added at one end to seal it off with the back wall. A few ashtrays and beer mats had been strategically placed along it and, hey presto, it was a bar counter. Add wall-to-wall beer, a few tables and chairs, a pool table, and a widescreen telly mounted on the wall and you've got a theme pub. Also stuck up on the wall behind the bar were several weapons. Whether these were decommissioned or not was anyone's guess. One was well known to me: a FAMAS (the assault rifle used by the Foreign Legion). Anyway, they added a bit of decoration. *Voilà*, a bar was born. And judging by the crowds of drinkers, a very prosperous one.

It was a commendable makeover job on the part of the EOD lads, not to say a shrewd bit of moonlighting, but the place did still feel macabre. A morgue reinventing itself as a bar is a pretty obscene concept and, in a country where morgues were in such high demand, perverse to say the least. Then again, the beer was always cold. *The* place to be seen, The Morgue was so cool it was hot.

Another of the Green Zone's hot spots was the large five-star hotel, although some of its stars had been packed away, waiting for the 'Freedom' part of the intervention. I only once had a drink there, and seeing people enjoying themselves dancing on the laser-light swept discothèque floor to loud dance music lovingly spun out by the resident DJ seemed horribly out of place. I didn't even manage to finish my beer – scandal.

The nights spent drinking and the days spent driving flat out, dodging death on Baghdad's bloody streets, started to take their toll on me. Reflecting too much on the 'what ifs' and being now totally disillusioned with the Armor Group bosses in Iraq, I was close to jacking. This feeling wasn't helped by something I started to notice around that time – I'm not talking about bodies or blood but something much more prosaic and consequently more compelling. Along with the personnel that we escorted to the airport each day, we would sometimes transport luggage. Among this luggage would be items that had belonged to the PMCs who had been killed. I couldn't help but look at these bags – usually well-used and faded canvas grips, bearing the owner's name on a strip of olive-green masking tape – and imagine my own black grip among them, having been carelessly flung into the back of a pick-up and carted off. At times like that, my mind would go back to when I had gone on leave and the six-feet-five-inch ex-guardsman sitting next to me on the plane had spouted off about opening and shutting his gate in Umm Qasr. Oh, for a gate of my own to open and shut!

Fuck it, I was out of there. It was a hard decision, but I knew Dave was soon to be departing for a job in West Africa, and I didn't want to work with unknowns. And my bottle was not what it used to be. Don't mistake this as me saying I couldn't do my job, but I definitely no longer wanted to do convoy. I had had my time and had got away practically unscathed. Move on. Jock's lucky Rowan might not last for ever. And Jock, no fool, had pulled out long ago.

A new job had just started up in Tikrit with the US Army Corps of Engineers (USACE). Armor Group had a contract to supply 60-plus expat/Gurkha PMCs to guard the base some 15 kilometres from Tikrit and to supply a team of 12 PMCs to escort the EOD personnel to and from Baghdad. These 12 were known as the PSD (private-security detail).

I got to thinking: a base? That must mean at least one gate. I would have to take a slight drop in pay, but my bank manager would, I was sure, understand. And my chances of spending my earnings would rocket. I began to visualise myself far from the madding, murderous crowd, just whiling away the hours on the gate – it would be like playing in goal when all the rough boys are up at the other end of the pitch. However, things were not all money and roses up there: one of the unaccompanied bags that found itself on the daily run to BIAP was that of an ex-Royal Marine, killed by an IED or mine whilst patrolling outside the Tikrit base. I still thought that it was a lot less of a risk than staying in burning Baghdad, though.

My mind made up, I went to see the in-country manager, who at that time was an ex-SAS soldier. I told him that I had had enough of convoy and was volunteering for the job up in Tikrit. He didn't ask me for my reasons: he knew that convoy was a non-starter at that time and not bringing in any hard cash. Also, a lot of the lads coming out fresh to Iraq were after action, and the thought of stagging-on at a base didn't appeal to them, so a volunteer was not to be sniffed at. In fact, his only questions to me were first 'When?', to which my immediate reply was 'asap', and second 'Tomorrow?', to which I answered 'Sounds good'. And that was how I departed convoy in October 2004, some six months after my first day in Iraq.

Saying goodbye to Dave was quite sad, as we both knew that the time we spent on convoy would never be surpassed. Having stared death in the face together, and having been prepared to die for one another, it was now over. There was no false bravado between us. We had quite literally fought for our lives side by side, whilst admitting to one another our fears and faults. For six months, depending entirely on one another, often miles from safety, alone and hopelessly under-armed, we had forged a bond that only these kinds of situations can create.

Early the next day, the PSD came to the convoy villa

to pick me up. I shook hands with Dave, who only had a couple of weeks left in Iraq and told him to keep his head well and truly down for the remainder of his time in the country. He looked me hard in the eye and said, 'Simon, don't get yourself killed, you've got nothing to prove. Keep your wits about you, and take care.' With that, I checked my Kalashnikov and equipment one more time and jumped into the large Ford F350 pick-up that the Tikrit PSD had driven down in. My head was now firmly in 'wits about me' mode. All aboard, off we roared. I hoped Emina would be all right. I had said goodbye to her, but discreetly, as I knew the lads thought there might be something going on between us. There wasn't.

7

TIKRIT NEXT STOP

The project manager for the contract up at Tikrit was an ex-legionnaire known as 'Mado' from the Netherlands. Our paths had never crossed in the Foreign Legion, but we had already met in Iraq. He had previously been deployed up on the Mosul contract. One time when there had been a problem getting a US military flight from Baghdad, he had tagged along with us on a convoy up to Mosul. He was in his mid-30s, bald as a coot and spoke very good English with a comical Dutch accent, which always brought a smile to the lads' faces. He had left the Foreign Legion about four years previously and was definitely keen on climbing the commercial-security ladder.

Like me, he had worked for a few years in Algeria, providing security for the oil industry. Algeria had been fighting home-grown terrorists since the early 1990s and was keen to protect its oil and gas industry. Being the world's fourth-largest producer, gas was Algeria's primary export. To safeguard the foreign workers, and more importantly for the American and other multinational oil companies to qualify for insurance, without which they could not operate, Western private-security firms were brought in. In the early days, these firms supplied armed security-personnel, but later on they worked in more of a consultancy role. The contracts awarded were highly lucrative. And this was where Mado had begun his commercial career, as a security adviser on desert oil rigs. He then moved into a managerial position at his oil company employer's HQ in 'Hassi Massoud', the desert capital of Algeria.

Since Mado was ex-Legion and we were already acquainted, I knew on my arrival in Tikrit that I could be straight up with him. 'Look, Mado,' I said, 'for the moment I've had enough of convoy, and I don't particularly want to go on the road with the PSD team, but I wouldn't mind just staging-on.' Mado didn't mind in the slightest, as most of the lads only wanted to do PSD and not boring guard duty. I had been exactly the same when I had arrived in Iraq, but three ambushes had given me enough excitement – for the time being, at least.

I was moved straight to the Buckmaster Base (named after an EOD specialist killed in Iraq), where my duties involved staging-on at the main gate and overseeing the local armed militia (Rafadan), who physically opened and closed the gate and carried out the vehicle and personnel searches. On occasion, I also had to accompany the EOD team up to another camp two kilometres away. There, we provided them with protection while they collected the volatile ordnance (now littering ASP 2 after the US military's unsuccessful attempt at obliterating the place) and then destroyed it all by controlled explosion at the end of each day.

Buckmaster Base comprised two bases: ASP (ammunition supply point) 1 and ASP 2. These bases had been established many years before during the Saddam Hussein era. (If there was one thing Saddam liked to spend money on, it was armaments, and there were similar sites all over Iraq.) These were vast camps in the semi-desert, with rows of large bunkers covering an area of approximately 20 square kilometres. ASP 1 was the main base, and it was there that our living quarters were situated, along with the EOD teams. Incidentally, the EOD teams were all ex-military, and there were only two serving American military personnel on the base. Our quarters were attached to the side of the main bunker area, which was still intact with over 100 bunkers, each of them Nissen hut-shaped and some 50-metres long and 20-metres high. We were comparatively well looked after, sleeping in two-man Portakabins and sharing a cookhouse and games room – well, it had a pool table and a widescreen TV.

For me, the best part of being there was our isolation. I had no nagging thoughts of a massive bomb suddenly snuffing my life out. Short of a major attack, we could only realistically be hit by mortar fire. Though to hear some people talk, you'd have thought the base was going to be overrun any second. Don't panic, Captain Mainwaring!

The regime up at Tikrit meant I could actually switch off when not on duty, unlike in the convoy villa where I was only a front garden away from downtown Baghdad. The name Ken Bigley should remind every reader of the dangers involved in living in villas in Baghdad. He left his security needs in the hands of local Iraqis, who predictably left their posts, allowing the insurgents to waltz into the villa and kidnap him and his co-workers. I can't understand why he didn't have the likes of us to protect him. What's worse, how could he allow himself to be unarmed and virtually unprotected in a city where shootings, bombings and kidnappings were such regular occurrences? Who advised him? I'm not sure what his work status was; that is, whether he was a freebooter or employed by a company, either directly or on a contract basis, to work in Baghdad. If with a company, I hope his family have received or are seeking a legal explanation as to why that company did not follow a comprehensive risk-assessment review. This would never have left Mr Bigley's safety to poorly paid local guards.

ASP 2, situated two kilometres south-west of Buckmaster ASP 1, resembled Coventry or Dresden during the latter part of the Second World War. For some reason, when the American forces reached this far north they proceeded to blow the ASP to bits. The result was volatile unexploded ordnance scattered amongst the twisted metal frames of the ammo bunkers. This grey inhospitable place was familiar with death, having so far claimed the lives of two Americans, countless Iraqis who raided the ASP when it was abandoned by the US military and most recently an ex-Royal Marine from Plymouth.

For the first few weeks, I worked on a day shift, starting at 0600 and finishing at 1800. I would turn to and get all the relevant intelligence and briefings from the lads on the night shift, then the other two lads on day shift and I would do two cycles of stagging-on at the gate for two hours, doing two hours on mobile patrol and then being on standby for two hours – not bad for £6,000 a month. I kept hearing that song 'I'm In Heaven' in my head! Believe it or not, some lads still dripped about not having enough time off. Six thousand fucking quid in yer pocket every month for a twelve-hour day and not a baddie in sight! Personally, I would have sacked the whingeing, wet-behind-the-ears prima donnas. But professionalism ruled; they had their 'shinffing' (moaning) sessions and life went on.

A much more important issue was that some of the SOPs being practised were highly questionable, most noticeably vis-à-vis the death of the ex-Royal Marine, who had met his maker while on a lunchtime patrol a mere ten metres outside the ASP 2 base. What shocked me most was the lack of awareness among some individuals about the level of threat facing us. And with the insurgency against the US and its coalition partners rapidly growing, PMCs were an indistinguishable part of the alien invading forces, and just as much in the enemy's sights. Having fought for my life in Iraq, I knew that simply because someone held a higher position than me in some office in Baghdad or Tikrit, it did not make them proficient in basic soldiering skills. And if that was the case, they were hardly in a position to order me to carry out drills on the ground. My life is pretty special in my eyes, and no career-hungry ex-officer or other species would ever be given the benefit of the doubt when it came to my own tactical life-or-death operations, whether in Iraq or anywhere else. It mustn't be forgotten that the private-security mob out here wasn't the British Army, or in my case the Foreign Legion, but a mishmash of ex-soldiers, from cooks to Special Forces SAS. Within this varied assembly, there were a lot of egos at work. And a legend in the world of the SAS doesn't necessarily make a good leader of ground troops in a theatre such as Iraq. That said, the ex-SAS officer who took over command of Armor Group Iraq was second to none – on the fucking ball!

At this point, you could be forgiven for thinking, 'What the fuck's his problem? It wasn't him who was killed outside the ASP 2 base. He wasn't even up there at the time!' True, but within two weeks of my arrival at Buckmaster, the head-sheds decided to restart the job at ASP 2 and tasked me with the security of the EOD team whilst they deployed there. There were serious problems to be addressed before I would undertake any such operation. Following the death of the ex-Royal Marine, the job had been immediately brought to a stop and an inquiry was supposed to have taken place into the nature of the incident, determining whether it had been an IED or a mine that had exploded. So, my first question at the briefing the night before redeployment was, 'Was it a mine or an IED?' Instead of an answer, a debate followed, with so-and-so convinced it was a mine and what's-his-name sure it was an IED. My night's sleep had just gone up in smoke, and I could quite literally do likewise the next day!

Although the boss wasn't sporting a strap-on red nose, baggy checked trousers and juggling batons in a wacky car with square wheels and falling-off doors, he was still doing a very good impression of a clown. If it was a mine that had gone off, it had to be assumed that it was one of several. And if it was an IED, where was the observation/firing point? It was as if the job had been stopped for a few weeks only out of respect for the dead man. A worthy enough reason, but without using that period to put in place procedures to stop the same thing from happening again, it was hardly respect.

The second question I asked at the briefing was, 'Why should we patrol ten metres on the outside of the base, when, one, an internal patrol on the inside, right up at the sand berm, is just as effective in showing a visible deterrent, and, two, visibility is not at all improved by the ten metres gained by being on the outside?' I didn't wait for a reply but continued, 'I will not patrol in the open ground on the other side of the berm; however, if base-plate patrolling is deemed necessary, then two more manned vehicles will be needed to boost the patrol at a distance of up to one to three kilometres outside the base.' Base-plate patrols (BPP), if done correctly, would be an effective deterrent from insurgents firing mortars into the base, establishing a firing point or digging in an IED, as they would see frequent, though not predictably timed, heavily armed patrols out in their territory ready to make 'em martyrs. But base plating was not gonna happen at ASP 2, as the budget would not allow for more vehicles and bods, so this bod here wasn't doing it on his 'Jack Jones'. We would just have to play the numbers game if any mortars were lobbed in – not me, not me, any of the others, but not me!

I was also very concerned that we would be deploying first thing in the morning and withdrawing a few hours before last light, leaving ASP 2 absolutely void of any security over night. I believed that this operating procedure was the major factor in allowing the previous fatality to occur, local dickers having observed that there were certain times of night when the base was left unprotected – definitely long enough for the mice to play. On pointing out this major drawback, the response was that we were waiting for reinforcements, after which the site could be manned 24/7. I also pointed out that although the fatal device had been planted outside the base, there was no perimeter fence, only a sand berm, and this meant that devices could be placed inside, lying in wait for the inadequate security personnel on their arrival one quiet morning.

Frankly, it stank of incompetence, and if I were to start the job the following morning, I would be a party to it. Dave's farewell advice was ringing in my ears: 'Simon, don't get yourself killed. You have nothing to prove. Take care.' I was now firmly in Iraq just for the money – and, OK, a little bit of adventure, even, dare I say, a few laughs – but this was 'buckets of ripped-up paper chucked over the audience' stuff! And me in a silly wig, topping the bill while my luck held out. Must try and get some seriously oversized boots!

I was unable to acquire the boots, but against all my better judgement I did enter the ring and go ahead with the job. However, I established an out-of-bounds (OOB) area immediately around the outside of the ASP to a depth of 300 metres to be covered by observation at all times. I think Mado must have wanted to prove a point to me one day when the head-sheds came up on a visit and he drove them right through the OOB area, which he seemed to think was safe, although I knew it wasn't. I was pissing myself laughing as I watched them advance. I imagined Mado giving them a running commentary: 'Oh, and this is where matey copped it with the mine. Or was it an IED? No matter, it was juuuust here!'

In addition to the OOB area, trip flares were positioned around the inside of the ASP, which would be easily seen from Buckmaster if they were set off, alerting us to any nocturnal presence. But dogs and foxes soon began to trigger them on a regular basis, resulting in a bit of a cry-wolf effect. The only real security solution was to occupy the site 24/7, which we managed to achieve some three weeks after my arrival, although it stretched us to the limits at first. On balance, though, I think everyone involved in the job up at ASP 2 was a lot happier with the new SOPs.

However long the days and nights, life itself was sweet. OK, it still wasn't an ideal situation, the night team consisting of just two expat guards, one Gurkha and six very, very nervous Rafadans, but at least we had a permanent eyes-on presence, and over time built on this, doubling the guard and reinforcing the perimeter. The Rafadans remained nervous, but to be fair to them they were mostly just boys of 18. They would spend the night stuck out on the perimeter with an AK-47, a handheld walkie-talkie and not much else.

The new set-up meant that the EOD team could get straight down to business on arrival at ASP 2, rounding up the residual ordnance without having to wait for the daily sweep of the area to look for any hidden surprises. Like us, they were contracted to the US military through security firms and were paid by performance. Having their quotas to meet, any unnecessary hold-ups did not go down well. The completion deadline for this ASP was now some nine months away, before which time the entire site had to be cleared of all ordnance over 30 mm. To do this, the EOD team had split the ASP into eight areas and would walk up a section of ground inch by inch, carefully picking up all ordnance found over 30 mm and piling it up nearby. At the end of each day, the pile would be packed with explosives and blown up. Each of these eight areas would take several weeks to clear. The EOD team worked from just after first light until around 1600, in soaring temperatures in the summer months and on through the chill winter and mud-soaked misery of the rainy season. The mind-numbing tedium of this work was coupled with perpetual danger, handling unstable shells obviously being a nerve-racking activity. They couldn't switch off for a second. Coasting can be a life-saver in other repetitive jobs but would be the opposite for the EOD team, because a second's bad handling could be fatal. All of the guys had horrendous cautionary tales of what had happened to so-and-so and the difficulty he now had in wiping his behind!

I really enjoyed my days up at ASP 2; the EOD team were a good bunch, and the SOPs I put in place were totally relevant to the terrain and manpower available. This was not Algeria – where the shit just wasn't hitting the proverbial fan any more – this was Tikrit, once home of the beloved Saddam, and there was plenty of shit around and many a fan to choose from. So, if you ain't got your shit together, you'll have a *dead* good EOD team.

My main contingency concern was always to get a good grip on the EOD team as soon as any incident kicked off, either containing them *in situ* and awaiting the quick-reaction force (QRF) or withdrawing to pre-planned emergency RVs (ERVs) for exfiltration by the QRF. The golden rule, as ever, was to keep it simple – drill, drill, drill!

After several months of working and good SOPs, we were fortunate to suffer no further incidents at ASP 2. There was, however, an evil, sickening incident involving the workers from the ASP 1. Because ASP 1 had been left intact, the work there was more a case of emptying or stocking the bunkers. An Iraqi workforce of 90 men and boys had been hired to carry out most of the manual labour. They were not from the Tikrit area but lodged in nearby hotels and were bussed in each day. In fact, they were the bane of my life when I was in charge of the main gate in the morning and had to oversee their admittance onto the base – an unruly bunch of smelly rag-heads! But like all of us, they were only trying to make a living.

Early one morning, the two coaches carrying the workers were about three kilometres from the base when they were stopped by two unmarked cars at the 'Y' junction for the road to Buckmaster. The driver of the second coach realised what was going down and bravely refused to stop, swinging his vehicle around and heading back in the other direction. The first coach had no choice but to stop, whereupon it was approached by several armed men from the two unmarked cars. They boarded the coach, shooting the driver dead in his seat. This provoked understandable mass panic, with everyone else on board attempting to scramble to the rear exit. When I later talked to Cal, who was part of the first QRF on site, he told me that the dead bodies were piled on top of each other at the back of the bus. They had not died in the crush but from gunshot wounds, the attackers having systematically fired into 17 of them as they cowered in fear, fathers and sons perishing together. One boy survived, covered by the bloody, brain-spattered body of his father.

The massacre made headline news and destroyed several more close and loving Iraqi families. The coach killings brought work on the ASP to a halt for a few days, a major event for a commercial organisation. The incident also brought home the reality of the situation in Iraq to several of the American base workers. The horse had well and truly bolted, but, as always, the stable door had to be publicly locked, and tents were instantly provided on the base for those Iraqis still brave or desperate enough to work there.

As for me, true to form, all good things come to an end. To be fair to Dan, who was now in charge in Tikrit, I was given a choice – that of saying yes. A position had to be filled up in Kirkuk for five weeks, and he wanted to know if I would do it. 'Of course, Danny, love to. What is it?' We'll get to that.

Mado had now gone off to somewhere in Russia, I believe, and Dan had replaced him. An ex-para, Dan was not the sort of bloke it was advisable to get on the wrong side of – not in the slightest. He brought new life to the contract, allowing individual team leaders to do their jobs. If you worked well, you didn't have him breathing down your neck, but if things started to go pear-shaped, his breath stank. Cal (from the QRF on the coach), an ex-Scots Guard from Australia, was Dan's second in command, and he was totally committed to our contract. For the most part, he dealt with behind-the-scenes problems, never had a bad word for the job in hand and was instrumental in creating a good team spirit among the lads. Not an easy achievement on a contract that wasn't all guns going bang and dead baddies to be bagged and tagged! Then there was the operations manager Chas, an ex-Royal Marine who already had over a year under his belt on various contracts throughout Iraq. He was basically the overseer of all operations, current and forthcoming, originating from Buckmaster. His reputation from work done on the ground preceded him, and his ability to not only talk the job but also walk it left no room for slacking.

The Buckmaster contract was working well and fast turning into a nice little number. With a feeling of having just settled in, I really wanted to say no to Dan and not go to Kirkuk.

On the positive side, however, it was for only five weeks, and it was in Kirkuk. Well, nothing happens in Kirkuk does it? 'Yep, Dan, I'll do it. What was the job again?'

Dan informed me that I would be running a force of 70 Kurds, whose mission was to defend a power station on the outskirts of Kirkuk. To be more precise, I would oversee those 70 Kurds in patrolling the local area up to 15 kilometres around the station and in controlling access to it. He confirmed that it was for five weeks to cover for the expat currently up there who was going on leave over Christmas and New Year. I couldn't understand why he would want to miss Christmas in Kirkuk!

8

KIRKUK FOR CHRISTMAS

The main gate gave the heads-up that the two vehicles sent from Kirkuk were on their way to the parking area. I was in the ops room having a cup of coffee and watching the PSD team's progress towards Baghdad on a VDU screen. Updated every ten minutes, a green dot on a road map showed their position, transmitted from the tracker devices with which all our vehicles on the Tikrit contract had now been fitted. They even had a panic button, which would immediately alert the 24/7 dedicated control centre in Baghdad to their exact location during a contact, although there was some uncertainty as to what a back-up team/QRF could then do. With all and sundry watching the monitors, there was a feel-good factor, I suppose, making deployments a bit less of an isolated experience.

'Oh, shit,' I thought, looking at the two tiny, very dirty, battered white pick-ups sent from Kirkuk to collect me that had just bounced to a stop in the dusty car park in front of the ops room. An old eight-track system would not have looked out of place in them. There was no way that they were fitted with the latest tracking devices. However, the visual state of the vehicles was very much to my liking, but the fact that they were full of smiling Iraqi/Kurdish faces was not! Each man was armed with an AK-47 and five magazines. I was filled with an instant longing to be with the all expat, heavily armed PSD team, in which every man could and would fight, and, if necessary, stand his ground to take care of dead and wounded colleagues. We expats were from many varied backgrounds – the Foreign Legion, Royal Marines, British Army and the New Zealand Army – but as with all front-line troops facing extreme danger and possible death on a daily basis, a strong bond was forged between us. We were not all best buddies, but we were wholly committed to each other on the battlefield. With my past experiences of Iraqis in combat, I had no faith whatsoever in these happily smiling, poorly armed Kurds, yet I was about to deploy with them through Tikrit and along high, lonely roads on the long journey to Kirkuk. I never realised just how much I loved Buckmaster Base and all who sailed in her!

Feeling like the loneliest man on the planet and thinking 'Why me?', I grabbed my pack and grip and slung them into the back of the first pick-up. I couldn't help but notice that both vehicles were ticking over in a disturbingly erratic fashion: just as it seemed as though they were about to stall, they would catch and quicken up, only to slow again and resume the cycle. Any remaining confidence in the vehicles' mechanical state was dispelled by the puffs of black smoke chugging out of the loose, rattling exhaust pipes, increasing and decreasing in synch with the engine's volatile tick-over.

A body emerged – or rather unfolded – from the passenger side of one of the pick-ups, and standing at some six feet ten inches before me was the man I was to take over from for the following five weeks. An Australian, he introduced himself as Mark, and I saw a flash of recognition in his eyes as we shook hands. His face didn't ring any bells with me, though. As far as I knew, the only previous contact we'd had was via a couple of emails when it was confirmed that I was to be his replacement.

He didn't want to hang around that afternoon, as later on he was flying from Kirkuk to Kuwait to start his Christmas leave. The handover was to take place during the deployment from Tikrit to Kirkuk. Mark said he would drive the second vehicle, and I could command it. That way, he said, we could run through the relevant points of the job. I said OK, although I privately thought, 'Fuck the job details. I'm going to concentrate on the mission in hand. Eyes on the road and environs. I want to get to Kirkuk safe, sound, alive and kicking before I discuss the finer points of guarding a power station.' The bigger-picture SOPs are normally straight out of a textbook and hence very rarely relevant or workable. The world they are written in has a cosy predictability. My world was all about immediate SOPs, which, if kept simple, were bread and butter to any soldier worth his salt. Adapt! I'd get it together once I was up there. Besides which, Mark had already given me a good outline of the job in his preliminary emails.

Cal's parting words to me were, 'Hope you've got Green Flag cover!'

'Wouldn't leave home without it,' I lied.

Setting off, Mark straight away asked me if I'd been in the Foreign Legion as I looked like a *sergent* at the time he was going through basic training in Castelnaudary. We quickly established that it was me, but I still had no recollection of him, which wasn't all that strange, as there were three recruit companies and their paths seldom crossed. Luckily, I couldn't remember, say, battering a giant Aussie to within an inch of his life or even having raised my voice to anyone fitting his description, so I could sit back and relax without fear of reprisals from some bitter and twisted, revenge-seeking psycho – phew!

As threatened, Mark went through his working routine during the journey, most of which didn't register or mean much to me. I was preoccupied with scanning the horizon and any passing vehicles. As with every journey by road, however short and in whatever part of Iraq, trouble could come from any direction and at any time. A lapse in concentration could lose you the vital seconds needed to get out of a deadly situation. As we travelled, I instead had my own commentary running constantly in my head: 'Group of vehicles parked up ahead. High ground to the right. People milling around outside a shop up ahead.' And so on. Normally, this would constitute the radio traffic broadcast during a PSD or convoy move, but these two vehicles weren't fitted with radios, each being equipped with a handheld Motorola only. At best, these only worked close up; besides which, only Mark and I spoke English, although Mark did have a reasonable amount of Kurdish – it was pretty impressive hearing him jabber away on the handheld. With no one up to speed on the English side of things and me not speaking their lingo, communication was going to be a bit of a problem.

As we drove on, Mark's monologue on the intricacies of the Kirkuk job for the most part just filled the air. Then he mentioned something that hit me over the head like a hammer. 'You do what?' I asked in astonishment, not believing what he had just said.

Mark, in what I took to be a 'yeah, I know, but it's gotta be done' tone, repeated, 'Around the end of the month – 27th or 28th – you have to go down to Baghdad and pick up the men's wages.'

I had heard him right. I had to know more. 'How much?'
'$30,000.'

'In these vehicles and with six Kurds?'

'Yes.'

'How long've you been doing it?'

'Eight months now.'

'And I'll have to do it too?'

'Er, yeah.'

'Fucking hell, Mark. Seventy Kurds, not to mention the ones you've sacked, know you've been returning on one of two roads every month with $30,000. Fuck me, if it was the UK, you'd have been bumped well and truly over the head by now. Can't it be done by Hercules?'

'Nah, there's no return flight the same day. In fact, it would be a three-day round trip.'

'Why can't one of the office wallahs bring it up?'

'I've always done it.'

That was the end of the conversation. I still couldn't credit it. Nor could I get involved in such a reckless, suicidal errand. Could I? Stupid as it may seem, I was already coming round to the idea – resigned to it, if you like, as if it were my fate. But I also knew I was going to let the office wallahs know my thoughts on the matter. It was strange, but I was still concerned about other people's perceptions of me and the things they might say – 'Yeah, Si up at Kirkuk has refused to do the wages run. Bottler.' – when really it was the sensible thing to decline such an unprofessional operation. Although I saw that this would be the logical response, I suppose there was a game of chicken going on in my head, the old machismo conditioning scrambling my reason. I mean, who in their right mind regularly drives through a lawless, gun-toting country's most dangerous region – the Sunni Triangle – with 70 locals and all their families and acquaintances privy to the fact that $30,000 (many, many, many camels) is heading their way.

Yuletide cheer was fast fading. Not that I'd been planning

on any festivities, but it was definitely fucking humbug for Christmas now. And the only pantomime showing would be 'Ali Simon Bonkers Low and the Seventy Kurds'. Will he take the 30K through the Sunni Triangle? Oh no he won't. Oh yes he will. Oh no he fucking won't! I dared not contemplate the 'behind you' bit.

Mark got his planned flight from the FOB in Kirkuk, and I was left in charge of the Kurdish guard force, many of whom were Sunni, including the head man, but there didn't seem to be any bad feeling between him and the others. The power station was roughly three kilometres from Kirkuk, some four hundred metres off the main Kirkuk to Baqubah road. Parts of the station had been rebuilt to supply electricity to homes and businesses in Kirkuk but work was still in progress. There was a skeleton staff of expat Bechtel Corporation personnel managing a purely local workforce. Armed security for Bechtel was supplied by Armor Group, with a separate security company guarding the Italian firm building the turbines. The armed contractors were all British, around 30 in total, and overall there were more security personnel than builders, painting a pretty clear picture of the difficulties in restoring Iraq's infrastructure. The power station was the forerunner for a massive project scheduled to go ahead in Baqubah, supplying Baghdad with much needed electricity. It was to be a multimillion-dollar scheme, and the staff quarters were already built for the security workers and other personnel. For an American construction company to live and work right in the Sunni Triangle was, to say the least, a challenge, even though Sunnis would be among the beneficiaries of the electricity.

All expat personnel resided on the base, with the local workforce travelling in from their own homes in and around Kirkuk. As with all Bechtel sites, the accommodation was good, each man being assigned his own room with toilet, shower and satellite TV in a series of trailer-type Portakabins. I hoped that I'd soon be watching the *Only Fools and Horses Christmas Special* while getting handsomely paid. If it was on for two hours of my twelve-hour, thirty-day working month, I'd be forty quid better off as Del and Uncle Albert undid that chandelier again. 'This time next year we'll be millionaires, Rodney!' Mind you, they'd have to pay me a lot more to watch fucking *Emmerdale*! But I'd watch *Dad's Army* for free.

The firm supplying security for Bechtel had large Ford Excursions and F350s at their disposal, which they used to take clients to the FOB in Kirkuk for flights out of the country. The other security firm had more incognito vehicles, but they were all in good working order, being regularly serviced by an in-house mechanic, unlike mine. I asked the Bechtel security lot why my vehicles were a heap of shit and serviced by some mate of a mate in a back-street garage in Kirkuk when the Kurds and I had to patrol outside the base for Bechtel. It was pointed out that my contract – signed by Armor Group Iraq not Armor Group PLC, which was responsible for the worldwide Bechtel account – was to control access to the power station and patrol the surrounding countryside for up to 15 kilometres. It further stipulated that Armor Group Iraq would bear the costs of materials and equipment, which meant that the vehicles were not Bechtel's responsibility. On the plus side of things for me, armed contractors working for Armor Group Iraq were on about £1,500 more a month than the armed contractors from Armor Group PLC contracted to Bechtel. There were a lot of unhappy bods on the Armor Group PLC Bechtel contract, as they were exposed to the same risks for a lot less 'spondulees', although they did have the benefit of air-conditioned station wagons.

The Kurdish guard force was split into two twenty-four-hour shifts of thirty-five men each: twenty-four made up the mobile vehicle patrols, while another ten controlled access to the power station. The one remaining man was the local supervisor, who reported for duty daily from 0730 to 1800. Two interpreters were also put at my disposal. The mobile patrols operated 24/7, which explained the crippled state of the vehicles. A two-vehicle patrol would deploy on a predetermined route, leaving the other two to refuel and rest. That, at least, was the theory, but in practice there'd more often than not be a vehicle off the road getting fixed at matey's garage – and at a price. This left just three vehicles rotating, alternating between one- and two-vehicle patrols. If the patrol was close in, a single vehicle would be used. I was now beginning to appreciate the logistical juggling act Mark had been obliged to perform.

Initially, part of my job was to gain a good understanding of the surrounding terrain in order to identify potential staging areas from which insurgents might mount an assault on the power station, either with guns or indirect mortar fire. I would join at least two daytime patrols and at least one during the night, taking care to vary the timings and routes, and I would always change the lying-up positions, even if only by a hundred metres or so. According to the intelligence on the Kirkuk area, it was not trouble free, but insurgent activity in the region was on a far smaller scale to that in Baghdad or Tikrit, and not a patch on its northern neighbour Mosul. One of the reasons for this was that the insurgents were using Kirkuk as a kind of safe haven for themselves and their materials. A few months previously, the power station had been targeted in a direct-fire rocket attack, although no personnel had been injured and only slight structural damage had been incurred. That had been the only insurgent-led attack; the FOB on the other side of Kirkuk, however, was taking mortar fire every day. The general consensus as to why the power station was left largely untouched was that there were too many vested interests in it. If the station was immobilised, Kirkuk would be without electricity, inconveniencing the local big wigs who inevitably had their fat fingers in many greasy pies. Additionally, a hundred local men were being employed whilst construction was under way, thus bringing in hard cash to bolster Kirkuk's economy. The project was, in theory, a model of rebuilding.

After a few days on the job, I got a visit from the local police chief, whose brother was one of my guards. He wore a permanent cheesy smile and clung on to my hand for a few seconds too long after shaking it. I invited him into my office, which consisted of two chairs and one desk. On the desk was a two-tier in–out tray devoid of paperwork. In short, it was my idea of an ideal office. Mark's too, I guess, as it was just how he'd left it.

The police chief was on a fact-finding mission: who I was, how long I'd been in Iraq, etc. My replies were non-committal: I told him I had worked for Armor Group Iraq for just coming on a year, and so on. I also fired a few questions back at him concerning the local security threats, which he repeatedly brushed away with the words that when said by an Iraqi in a responsible position really grip my shit: 'No problem.'

The meeting lasted for about 40 minutes, but my mind had been made up within the first few. I didn't trust or like the man one bit. There are some people I like but don't trust, or trust but don't like, but he was firmly in the 'don't trust, don't like' folder. He didn't strike me as all that clued up, and I got the uneasy feeling he could be aligned with the insurgents. More worryingly, I also figured he knew that at the end of the month I would be collecting a life-changing sum of money, having to pass through roads that only his men controlled. I made a mental note to ensure that his brother was driving the vehicle I would be in so as to muzzle any unnecessary incoming fire. Unless, of course, his brother was shagging his wife, in which case he would profit from a two-birds-with-one-stone hit. And, of course, there was also a chance that I was letting my overworked, vivid imagination run wild and this man was, in fact, one of Iraq's straight coppers, who, with impeccable morals and an unbending hunger to help the Western Coalition finally bring democracy to his country, strived day and night to stamp out the evils of corruption among those in positions of authority. The jury was still out on a very long lunch, though.

I had also begun to muse along a quite different strand, doing a bit of lateral thinking, you might say. Starting out as an innocent daydream, these thoughts were now shaping up into a cunningly formulated plan, a plan that might see me pocketing the $30,000 about to come my way. It would all hinge on the boss's reaction to an email I was preparing to send him. The email concerned the imminent wages run and would basically put on record my doubts and concerns about the mission. I wanted it to read between the lines as 'Are you sure you want this on your conscience if it all goes Pete Tong?' In other words, I was giving him the chance to call it off but not overdoing it enough for him to take me at my word. It was a fine line and had to be played just right. Then, if the job did go pear-shaped, no one could say I hadn't warned them. But that wasn't the only part of the plan. If someone tried to rob me en route, and the odds on that were high, it would be assumed they had got away with the loot. Why? Because that's the way I would make it look. However, the only person getting away with anything would be me, to the tune of a cool $30,000. By my reckoning, I'd more than earned it after the negligence shown by the big boss in Baghdad. My plan was slowly but surely taking shape.

* * *

Mark's SOPs governing access to the power station were well thought out. They were also executed with professionalism by the guard force. Apart from pre-planned convoys delivering material to the plant at any given time, the civilian workforce all arrived within a 30-minute window from 0730 to 0800. They would enter the power station on foot and then be searched. The handful of vehicles permitted into the designated parking space well away from the entrance would also be thoroughly searched.

There were three control points which had to be passed before anyone could enter the power station, after which access was restricted to varying levels according to the workers' different colour-coded badges, which they wore at all times. The first control point consisted of one of the patrol vehicles stationed on the approach road some three hundred metres from the main entrance during the half-hour arrival period. This preliminary checkpoint was to prevent any vehicle-borne bomb from making it as far as the power-station entrance. There seemed no doubt that the premises would be constantly dicked, and this visual SOP would persuade the insurgents to try their luck elsewhere. The second control point was at the main gate itself, the only entrance to the base. All arriving personnel would debus at this point, the majority coming in on three forty-five seater buses, then proceed on foot to the third control point some seventy-five metres inside the compound, although it was still about a hundred metres from all buildings and personnel. At this third control point, they would be met by six of the patrol team on extended line, ready to search each individual worker. And the search technique was very thorough. Head gear was removed and checked, followed by a full-body rub-down, usually provoking good-humoured banter from the workers. Any bags were also opened and thoroughly searched. This whole procedure was well-practised, and no hold-ups or bottlenecks occurred. Throughout the half-hour window, I would casually survey the three control points, my presence keeping the guards in check, especially during the body searches. If they went unsupervised, certain of the more senior white-collar workers could intimidate the security bods into not searching them 100 per cent.

With our resources concentrated on searching the morning influx, and this activity being reinforced with part of the mobile-guard team, it meant that I only had one vehicle out patrolling the other side of the perimeter wall between 0730 and 0800. This made it a vulnerable time for attack, and responses to such an eventuality were constantly at the front of my mind. There were several towers strategically positioned round the inside perimeter, which were manned by Gurkhas under the control of Armor Group Bechtel security, so there was good observation of all approaches. In case of attack, I would pull all my elements in from outside and contain the main entrance, with the patrol elements on standby to reinforce any given point on the perimeter. Whilst surveying the morning arrivals, I would play out attack scenarios in my head, throwing an array of situations at myself, such as being under direct and indirect fire as the workers arrived panicking at the gate, and then getting them sheltered and contained within a safe area to avoid confusion about the source of the attack. Other theoretical situations ranged from radio failure to blue on blue, attacking elements visible and outside, attacking elements visible and inside, attacking elements unseen, and so on. The more scenarios I could imagine, the more it would help if and when the proverbial made it to the fan. The initial reactions to any incident would set the precedent for the outcome. I fully realised the immense responsibility on my shoulders and did not want to have to answer for failing to do what I was being well paid to do: protect the power plant. I could only do so much to deter a well-equipped team of insurgents from mounting an attack, but I could stop that attack from being successful.

I was happy with most of the SOPs and the methods of carrying them out, but all was not entirely as it should have been. The main source of my unease was Abdelkader, the local supervisor of the guard force. Either he had been allowed free rein by Mark, which I very much doubted, or he was seeing how much he could get away with while his boss was away. I'd known early on there would come a point at which I would need to assert my authority with the men, but I was surprised to find the one who required my attention was the person who was supposed to be my right-hand man.

Making your presence felt, or *prise en main* as it's referred to in the Foreign Legion, is, I find, best accomplished when the cards are out on the table, so I waited for the game to get well under way. The daily changeover of the guards took place after the local workforce had cleared all the security checks. In this way, a full complement of guards was assured for the daily searching and control. Even though I was only going to be there for five weeks, I wanted to get to know each of the guards by name, so one morning I set about talking to them on their posts. I had a list of their names with me, and it soon became apparent that not all 34 members of the force were present. This struck me as strange, as I had earlier asked Abdelkader to inform me when the changeover was complete and all was as it should be. I asked the interpreter to tell Abdelkader to RV with me in front of the office. His lack of respect for the chain of command seemed quite clear from the length of time it took him to get there. When he eventually turned up, I played my master card by lulling him into a false sense of authority, first complimenting him on the guards' drills in general, to which he graciously allowed me a nod of his head. At the same time, he raised his thin eyebrows to reveal two glaring, contempt-filled eyes. During and after the interpreter had finished talking, I unflinchingly held Abdelkader's stare, all the while thinking, 'I'll have you, you piece of shit.' 'Eye language' is universal and unmistakable. He read my thoughts and within ten seconds dropped his gaze. Right, to business. The interpreter was going to earn his pay.

'Where are the three missing guards?' I fired out the question while continuing to stare hard at him, though he could not now look me in the face.

'I sent them home because they were sick,' he stammered out feebly.

'You send no one home. I send people home. Clear? Look me in the face.' I turned to the interpreter and ordered him to instruct Abdelkader to look me in the face. He couldn't lift his head to look at me and was now smarting like a chastised kid. I continued, 'From now on, all oncoming guards will check in here every morning and get crossed off this list.' I shook the list under his nose; I wanted to rile him up. 'Failure to do so means to me they are absent and receive no pay for the day. Furthermore, I am the only one who makes decisions concerning the guards. You just supervise that my orders are carried out correctly. Got it?' He was having great difficulty in parting his lips to say yes, so I then gave him an ultimatum. I said that if he did not have the ability to work for me as a supervisor then he could fuck off out the gates, wait a month at home with no pay and then see if he still had a job when Mr Mark returned from leave.

Once this had been translated to him, he looked me in the face and acknowledged that he understood. He was still very much smarting, but I was sure that after a day or so he would come round to my way of thinking. If he didn't, he was history, at least for my time in the job. I wasn't mistaken. He was soon eagerly giving me every detail of the daily running of the guard force, and within a week I had him back controlling guard changeover properly, freeing me up to concentrate on other matters such as updating intelligence. To be fair, Abdelkader was a hard-working and reliable supervisor.

Apart from the satellite patrols, I often had to deploy a couple of minutes ahead of the Bechtel Security vehicles so as to recce the route to the FOB on the other side of Kirkuk, spotting any dangers lying in wait for clients in the 'sore thumb' Ford Excursions. I would position myself in the second of my vehicles with a handheld Motorola on Bechtel's security frequency, radioing constant sit-reps on the roads and flanks up ahead. Quite often, this paid off, and I was able to advise them to either abort or change routes to avoid large traffic and crowds up ahead. Well-known volatile locations included the petrol stations, where large queues of angry locals tended to collect. Sometimes their frustrations led to aggro between themselves and the police, who would think nothing of opening up with firearms.

Once in the FOB, we would go our separate ways, although we would maintain radio communication ready to RV for the return journey. I would use this time to refuel the vehicles at the petrol point. One of the perks for the guards was to fill up their own containers, which were then placed in the back of the pick-ups. The practice was highly illegal, but if I didn't allow it, the guards would spend their time fighting outside the Kirkuk petrol stations rather than guarding the power plant.

On the first occasion, I hadn't checked the suitability of the containers they were using, and, after keeping the US military petrol attendant preoccupied, I was hit by an overpowering smell of petrol as I returned to the vehicles. Petrol was literally pissing out from the tops of flimsy, rag-stuffed plastic containers. 'Shit! What the fuck's gone on here!' I thought. It wasn't as if we could just tip the offending petrol away. I was stuck with two massive, highly volatile, portable petrol bombs. After cursing and balling everyone out for their total incompetence, I came up with a solution: to drive straight to one of the guard's houses in Kirkuk to dump the offending containers. I radioed the Bechtel security team that I was dropping off some supplies bought at the PX for one of the guards at his home, a 20-minute round trip. In reply, they told me to take my time, as they were stopping for lunch at the base.

Driving up to the main gate of the base on our way out, you would have thought that I was driving some seriously cool, head-turning, cruising machine, judging by the astonished looks as we passed by at the regulation ten miles an hour. The last thing I wanted was to be stopped by the US Military Police, who regularly carried out speeding checks on the base. I would have been banged up for petrol trafficking and officially made PNG (*persona non grata*) from all US Military establishments, effectively ending my chances of sticking some serious dosh away. Finally making it out of the base, I relaxed. Now I only had to worry about some switched-on insurgent or sycophantic, coalition-loving Iraqi tossing a lighted cigarette my way. Luckily, the journey to the home of the guard was uneventful, but I wouldn't have liked to be his neighbour. The risk from igniting the noxious petrol fumes was worse given the densely populated neighbourhood.

Just before Christmas, a FOB up in Mosul was the target of a suicide bomber. The big difference this time was that the bomber had strapped the explosives to his body and detonated them in the actual base. The worrying aspects were twofold: first, he must have been known to the base and had daily access; and second, he had managed to pass all of the control points designed to prevent such atrocities.

The pattern had now been set for many more attacks of this nature throughout Iraq. A meeting was immediately called at the power station with all relevant security and construction heads of departments. I was asked if I thought that our own search procedures were up to scratch to prevent the same thing from happening. I maintained that the searching had been more than adequate to detect any unknown suicide bomber trying to gain access to the station but that it would now be necessary to insist that all overcoats, large jumpers and any other clothing bulky enough to conceal strapped explosives be removed and held well away from the person's body on their approach to the search bay. This would require one of the guards to keep back the arriving workers then release them just six at a time to walk forward to the search bay, holding out their removed items of clothing. I conceded that this might not go down too well, but word would quickly spread in town about our ball-breaking methods, again shifting any would-be suicide bomber to the lesser line of resistance – another base. The project manager was 100 per cent behind me, and it was agreed that this procedure would take effect from the following morning.

It definitely did not go down well. The head of the local workforce refused point blank to take off his jacket, and when I in turn refused him entry to the base, he wished that my next shit be a porcupine. He then left, followed by the entire workforce. Nice one, Simon. Here just over a week, and you shut down production. The project manager soon came running, asking where the fuck everyone was. I explained the situation, saying that it was to be expected and that by now all of Kirkuk would be aware of the new regulations. He looked a bit concerned but stood by the ruling, knowing what the deadly consequences would be if we didn't stay ahead of the game.

For the next three mornings, the head of the local workforce returned with his men, each time stubbornly refusing to remove his jacket. Without any fuss, I continued to firmly but politely refuse him entry, even barring him access to see the project manger. On the fourth day, he removed his jacket without even being asked, then advanced to the search bay, where he was duly searched and admitted to the premises. His entire workforce followed in his footsteps. Many of them gave me the thumbs-up, saying 'good, good' as they passed through. To be honest, I felt 'good, good'. I was running a tight ship, and it was now clear that most of the men didn't regard the search procedure as unreasonable.

Throughout my time in Kirkuk, my thoughts were never far away from the impending wages run. A few of the other security contractors I'd spoken to were, like me, astonished it had been going on. Some went so far as to say that there was no way they would ever consider doing it. This was music to my ears, but when you're not personally involved, it's always easy to voice an opinion, as it's not your reputation at stake. I had to be totally honest with myself and could no longer put off the decision. Should I play safe, refuse the mission and to hell with what anyone said about my bottle? If I accepted, was I really going to write my own Baghdad version of Brink's-Mat? If fate was going to string me up, did I want 'lamb' or 'lion' written on my toe label? $30,000 was a lot of money for one day's work – not enough to retire on, true, but a start. And I could buy the boxed set of *Only Fools and Horses* with the loose change – cushty. Christmas was coming; the golden goose was getting fat. Whatever I decided, plans had to be set in motion.

It was now four days before Christmas. For the umpteenth time, I weighed up the pros and cons of the job – the official one and the Brink's-Mat variation. If I refused the mission, the reason I would give to the boss would be simple: the likelihood of an ambush to kill me and steal the money was extremely high, and any pretence of travelling on some fact-finding trip would be ruled out by every Tom, Dick and Abdul knowing where I was headed and what I had on board. It would only need one of the Kurds to tip the wink to some mates, who'd then lie in wait with their weaponry, and they'd all end up extremely well off, with me extremely dead. The other factor on this side of the argument was that I was a mere stand-in for Mark, the Kurds' beloved boss. This made it an ideal time for them to finally do the long-contemplated pay snatch and sort out that ball-breaking temp in the process! There was also the possibility that the local police chief would set up a road block using his uniformed officers. After flagging me down and putting a bullet in my head, they'd make off with the money and claim it was not an IPO job but insurgents dressed as police – a daily occurrence in Iraq.

This was all black and white to me, and given the high probability that one of these scenarios would occur, it was sheer fucking madness to accept the mission. But I also remembered that I'd come to Iraq for money and adventure. More the adventure in the first instance, but now, nearly a year down the line, money was the main incentive. I also knew that if I refused the mission, Iraq was no longer the place for me. In whatever walk of life, there are always people only too willing to put you down the pan, and knowing half of the office wallahs down in Baghdad, I knew that my name would be dirt. That alone meant a lot to me, even though I knew that most of the people dissing me would run a mile at the thought of doing the mission themselves.

Finally, I made up my mind: I would do it! Incredible, really. With all the alarm bells ringing in my head, I was still prepared to put the threat to my reputation before my life. Is that honour or stupidity? Again, the jury was AWOL. But it wasn't just the potential damage to my reputation that had swung it. Now that I was definitely going, I had a terrific sense of excitement from the risk involved. The crack, the buzz: it was all cooking. It would also be a great story to tell my grandchildren – *Mission Impossible* meets *Beau Geste*.

Sitting in my room on the night before the job, I was already getting myself psyched up, and the adrenalin was flowing. Of course, I'd have to get some kids of my own if I wanted to tell my grandchildren, and what would they make of it all? 'Yeah, yeah, Granddad, you were all so violent way back then. Thankfully, America's unrelenting struggle against bad oil-producing countries has enabled us to live in a peaceful ultra-right-wing, evangelical "what did Muslims look like" society. And Granddad, you haven't faced Washington DC five times in prayer today!'

'Shut up and eat your beef jerky.'

The only question that remained was whether or not I would go through with the real Brink's-Mat job – my own $30,000 golden handshake – if there was an ambush on my return to Kirkuk. Well, the plan was already in my head, and it was perfect. All I had to do was press play.

The following morning, I sent an email to my boss in Baghdad – straight to the organ grinder, a habit learned from my previous dealings with the ex-Irish Guards officer. The email laid bare the strong chance of an inside job taking place, referred to the temptations of $30,000 in mobile cash and carefully implied an onus on the boss. I stressed the fact that there were only two roads back to Kirkuk and that a pattern during eight previous runs had been established, with at least seventy locals privy to the details of the mission. No matter how discreetly I left in the early morning, there was only one place I would be going at that time of the month.

The boss didn't manage to read between the lines, but instead congratulated me on my risk assessment and wished me good luck! I'd hoped that he would be shocked at the nature of the mission and come up with a better plan, like sending up a four-vehicle, well-armed team with the dosh, or even sending one of his staff on a military flight via Basra to Kirkuk, where I could discreetly pick him and the wages up – anything to save me from the insurgents and my own temptations. But the mission remained the same and was now sanctioned from on high. Perhaps it was my destiny – as Anthony Quinn says in *Lawrence of Arabia*, 'It is written.'

The blatant lack of concern on HQ's part pissed me off, and I vowed to let them know as much. They had presented me with the final bit of justification I needed for stealing the cash, and I was now in a foot-stamping, arms-crossed, revengeful sulk, thinking, 'It'll serve you right!'

The plan itself was simple. The only real dodgy bit was that I had to survive and escape an ambush. Unfortunately, I could only expect to get away with the money if we were genuinely ambushed, as the five Kurds along for the ride were not in on my scheme. They would unwittingly add to the credibility of the robbery when they told their version of the events – those of them that survived, that is. In addition to my own customary weapon and webbing, I would take along my emergency 'crash bag', which contained all the necessary equipment to bug out if I was in the shit: water, rations, compass, maps, money, change of clothing, ammunition, etc. It also now contained a pack of blank A4 paper. I'd also take a 30-litre day sack, ostensibly for carrying the $30,000, which, like my crash bag, would nestle at my feet in the footwell of the front passenger seat. It would be made apparent to everyone at the villa in Baghdad, and to the Kurds with me, that the money had been placed in this bag. I'd make a point of the office wallahs seeing me ram the cash into it, while uttering some quip about having the most expensive day sack around, ha-ha.

The tricky bit would be swapping the money for the blank A4 paper at an opportune moment. Obviously, this couldn't be done in front of the Kurds, and I'd have to come up with an excuse to leave the driver and gunner sitting in the back while I got out of the car for a minute or two. I decided that the best ploy would be to send out for some food – a customary practice – and then get the Kurds to share it out from the other car. While this was going on, I'd make the switch. I would be in the hands of fate after that, hoping for an attack. The minute we took any incoming rounds, I would sling the sack containing the blank paper out of the window, while turning my full attention to shooting my way out of the ambush. Later, I could justify my actions by saying that the shooting had ceased (which I'd be praying it would have) the minute the sack was slung out of the window, proving that it was an inside job. To add weight to my position, I had stored the email to my boss highlighting the dangers. When news of events reached head office in London, this would document my, as it turned out, correct reservations.

Predicting a search of my personal effects, I had prepared a hiding place for the $30,000 in the power plant till I returned to Tikrit. From there, I would take it to Kuwait, open a bank account and put it all away for a rainy day. The only stage that might present a problem was the military flight from Baghdad to Kuwait. I wasn't worried about the authorities – it wasn't yet standard practice to search luggage – but I was concerned about Armor Group, who might earmark me for a search if they were at all suspicious. I planned to get around this by paying someone on the same rotation to take the money through for me. All this for $30,000! OK, it wasn't the Great Train Robbery, but it was a bloody good drink.

There was one other item I wanted to have on my person for the mission: a defensive hand grenade. This was for two reasons: first, if I should get badly wounded and be taken by insurgents, I could blow my brains out with a painless little tug on the metal pin – not to make a valiant gesture but to avoid falling into the hands of people capable of using power drills and other horrendous and prolonged forms of torture prior to the grand finale of lopping off my head; and second, I would show the grenade to the accompanying Kurds, telling them not to worry in the event of an ambush, as I'd ensure we weren't taken alive – a sort of gypsy's warning not to set anything up. There was only room for one inside-jobber on this haul.

The grenade was easily borrowed from one of the security contractors at the power station, on a use or return basis. Given the choice, I wanted nothing more than to bring it back and pay the guards their wages.

There was no way I was going to leave on the mission with the pick-ups in their current state, as they had given me nothing but trouble. Instead, I would have to hire two fast unmarked cars in Kirkuk. This proved to be no problem whatsoever. A couple of the Kurds assigned to the mission got hold of an Opel Ascona 1.9 and a large American job, common among Iraqis. I wanted these kept well away from the power station until the actual morning of departure, so that no one else would know the type of cars being used.

I had to put my faith in the five Kurds I'd chosen for the mission. One was the supervisor, who was to command the first vehicle – the American pimpmobile, which would be driven by an oldish Kurd, a quiet man who struck me as being OK. In with them would be the interpreter, who I believed to be honest; he was my only means of communication with the others. He could also handle an AK-47, as was apparent when I'd taken the team out to a range to confirm their weapons. My vehicle would be driven by the brother of the police chief, hopefully insuring against a police heist. The back-seat gunner would be Kurdish Mustapha, who had fought with the PKK in the past. I trusted him implicitly, for no other reason than I judged him to be a loyal, honest man. Out of all the guards, he was one I had struck up a good rapport with, and his weapon-handling skills were those of an experienced soldier. I had to have someone sitting directly behind me with a loaded gun, and it had to be Mustapha. However, I was under no illusions. My choice of Kurds for the mission was based on a couple of weeks working with them, and I could only hope my choices were the right ones.

The date crept closer. The day before the mission, I took a detour from my regular patrol and drove out with Abdelkader to inspect the two newly acquired vehicles. Both seemed mechanically sound with good tyres, including the spares, and a working jack with wrenches that fitted the wheel nuts! Both cars were low on petrol, but the drivers assured me they would be filled up later that day. Seeing the vehicles' appearance, I felt happy that we would blend easily into the normal Iraqi traffic, and I was satisfied that I'd now minimised as many of the risks as possible. The rest was down to suck it and see!

That night, I locked myself away in my room and religiously cleaned and oiled my weapons: a 9-mm Browning pistol and my best mate the AK-47, with the two gouges scored into the wooden grip a constant reminder of my narrow escape from the ambush in Samara. I then emptied all my rounds onto the bed (king size, lumpy mattress) and individually wiped every last one of them. I then cleaned the mags and checked the tensions of their springs before slipping them still empty into my black chest webbing. Putting on my body armour, I clipped the chest webbing onto the metal rings I'd sewn on just below the shoulder straps, then fastened the straps of the webbing onto the Velcro patches on the sides of the armour. The webbing was now secured nice and tightly, ever so gently squeezing me, as if giving me a reassuring hug.

I sat down on a wooden chair and began my contact action drills, speaking out loud as I ran through the motions: 'Contact. Ready [weapon cocked]. Point weapon out of window. Automatic fire. [Shout to driver] drive, drive. Keep firing. Weapon stops. Change mag. Unclip drum mag. Let it fall. New mag on. Ready. Fire.' The drum mag fell, cushioned by the two pillows I'd placed on the floor.

I repeated the drill several times over, watching, as it were, from outside myself. Firing a weapon is the easy part; it's the mag changes that need constant work, as they can seem to take an eternity, and it's at such moments that panic can overtake you, reducing a fighting man to a quivering wreck. Drills must be an automatic reflex, and only repetition can produce this. The mag-change drill has to be precise as to which mag is taken and be practised over and over again, every time taking the same mag from the same pouch with the same robotic movements.

I remembered a weapons training session I'd once had with an especially switched-on cookie of an instructor. He began by saying that if a lesson was both simple and dynamic, it would be burned into your memory for ever. He then called a recruit forward, as if to help him demonstrate something. As the recruit approached, the instructor threw a punch hard and fast at his face. The recruit instantly ducked, shielding his face with his hands and jerking out of range of the punch. The instructor shouted, 'That's a fucking reflex. He did it without thinking.' Then, in a quiet, relaxed voice, he said, 'And that, gentlemen, is what will save your lives.' His voice dropped to a whisper: 'Reflex actions.' He didn't pick a brain-dead numpty for his demo, though, which was my misfortune when I later took my first lesson as an instructor with the Legion and proceeded to break the nose of a Russian: 'And that, gentlemen, is one semi-conscious peasant.'

Sweating, I meticulously rebombed every mag, counting each round in. The readiness of every mag was reassuring, as was placing each one carefully into the webbing pouches, triple checking the ease of movement for that first reflex change. I loaded the drum mag straight onto my AK, its safety-catch selector as always on full automatic, only needing to be made ready to give me an extra, sustained burst of firepower in those crucial first seconds of the ambush.

Then I remembered the money. Amid all that fast and furious dry drilling in the silence of my lonely room, I had not rehearsed the physical act of bending forward, grabbing the sack containing the A4 paper and slinging it out of the window. I'd have to stop firing to do that. When the time came, would the will to live allow it, or would the urge to get the fuck out of the killing zone, as bowel-loosening firepower slammed into the flimsy bodywork of the car, put paid to my dreams of a Kuwaiti nest egg? There was no way I'd pause to reach for the day sack during a firefight – not for $30 million, never mind $30,000. Once out of the killing zone, I might.

Satisfied with my weapons drills and equipment state, I put the question away and lay down on the bed to watch a bit of telly. The BBC was reporting on Christmas consumer spending in the UK, miserably down on last year! Perhaps I should do my bit by buying those Del Boy DVDs after all. 'This time next year, Rodney, we'll be . . .' With the dilemma of the dollars drifting in and out of my head, I eventually dropped off to sleep.

Up at sparrow's fart, I made my way to the ops room to book out. The room had a completely different atmosphere in the early morning hours, just a low comforting hum of computers, with the occasional routine radio check breaking the long night's silence. Rich, an ex-legionnaire I'd worked with a few years before in Algeria, was on stag, reading a well-thumbed Wilbur Smith novel. I drank some lukewarm coffee, made small talk and checked that my route out and in was as agreed and marked the day before. I confirmed that I'd ring on my arrival at the HQ villa in Baghdad and again prior to departure. As I was at the door ready to go, I turned and told Rich what happens to the hero in the Wilbur Smith novel.

Walking through the quiet, darkened power station, my mind was firmly on the task ahead, going over each phase, from the pre-departure brief and checks right through to the best and last part, the final approach and radio message confirming my safe arrival back at the power station. At the main gate, Abdelkader, Mustapha and Karim the interpreter were waiting, along with the two duty guards, warming themselves around the holed and rusty half-drum of fire. We shook hands, then I asked them one question: 'Ready?'

'Yes, yes, good, ready,' was the unanimous reply.

It was now 0545 and I wanted to be well on my way just before 0600. Any earlier would be dangerous, arousing the suspicion of both the US military and any dickers at seeing two fast-moving vehicles, fully occupied by males. By 0600, traffic would start to appear on the main north–south highway, building within the hour to a steady stream of trucks and cars. Leaving any later than this would knock our timings back, which, because of the gridlock in Baghdad, would mean a return journey in darkness, heightening the risk of being stopped at illegal checkpoints run by heavily armed, xenophobic militia. If our arrival at the HQ villa was cutting it fine for the return journey, I would kip there for the night.

It was now ten to six. 'Where are the fucking cars?' I asked Karim, trying to sound more annoyed than nervous. 'They are coming, they are coming, Simon,' Karim assured me, though I wasn't sure how he knew this. My question was more to vent the fear building inside me. It was highly likely the vehicles had been stopped in a snap VCP (vehicle checkpoint), which were often mounted by either the local police or US military in and around Kirkuk in the early morning.

'There they are. They're coming, Simon.' Two sets of car headlights were visible on the main highway. Turning right onto the approach road, they slowed, the lead vehicle's lights dipping then brightening as it negotiated the deeply potholed road. The vehicles halted, and the two drivers got out, leaving the engines running and doors open. I tapped my watch several times with my right forefinger then opened my palms, fingers splayed to convey the message, 'Where've you been? You're late!'

'Checkpoint, checkpoint,' they answered in unison.

'OK, OK. Everything OK?' I asked, but Karim was already talking to them, and it sounded like everything was not OK.

'They could not get any petrol,' Karim informed me, shaking his head, an apologetic look on his face.

'What? Fucking hell! Fuck it, I don't believe it. Why the fuck didn't they say last night, for fuck's sake!' My getting more nerved up wasn't solving the problem, so I turned and walked off. It had been nagging me since the day before about the petrol, what with all the difficulties in getting the stuff, but the Kurds had been fairly blasé about it. Really this cock-up was down to me. I raced the options through my mind: abort and go tomorrow – nah couldn't handle the anxiety of another day's thinking about the job; go later after having got some petrol from the FOB – but that would mean going up in the pick-ups as only they could get on the FOB, so I'd have to fill up jerry cans. By the time I'd got back to fill the two cars up, it would definitely mean stopping the night in Baghdad.

'How much petrol is in them both?' I asked, returning to the group. No one answered, so I looked at both petrol gauges. The Ascona registered just over half and the pimpmobile just on half. 'These gauges work?' I asked, pointing at the Ascona's gauge.

Karim translated the question, to which the two drivers chanted, 'Yes, yes, good, good.' Having no confidence in them or the gauges, I got them to take off the petrol caps then shook each vehicle. I could hear a sloshing of petrol in both tanks. Suddenly, Abdelkader piped up: 'OK, Mr Simon, good, good.' In his hand were two long thin bits of wood waiting to be burned on the fire. He dipped one in the Ascona's tank and pulled it out, showing a dark petrol stain a good way up. It was the same for the pimpmobile. I'd like to say he wasn't just a pretty face but . . .

We loaded up, and after a quick rebrief on vehicle spacing and actions in an ambush or IED attack, we left the base. The pimpmobile was first, followed by me, Mustapha and 'my brother's the police chief' in the Ascona. It was now 0620 and still dark. Only a few trucks and cars were on the main highway. I had decided to take a chance on the fuel. Driving through the small towns dotted along the highway, there were often hawkers selling plastic containers of petrol at inflated prices, so, with luck, we could top up on the way. While the cars were being filled, I could stay out of sight, wrapping my shemagh around my face. If we couldn't find a hawker before half the existing fuel was used up, I would abort the mission with sufficient juice to get us back to base.

Once out on the main north–south highway, I relaxed and

focused on the job in hand. The dangers facing me were numerous, but being in an ordinary car, hidden beneath a black-and-white shemagh and dish-dash coat, with two genuine dark skins alongside me was a comfort. Likewise the body armour and webbing concealed under the dish-dash, and the AK resting on my thighs. However, trouble could always arise, especially if we got stuck in traffic in one of the small towns en route, where some sharp-eyed local might spot me as a white man. Alternatively, an American patrol or observation post might pick up on our two cars and get a glimpse of the weapons held in our hands, and with six Iraqi occupants, one of them looking extremely dodgy in a voluminous shemagh, the outcome could be swift and fatal.

I was carrying a plastic A4-size American flag but would only show this when absolutely necessary and then as discreetly as possible. The flag was by no means a guarantor of safety. Military checkpoints were prime targets for attack, and if it was me on sentry duty, a car full of Iraqi-looking men would have my finger on the trigger, little plastic flag or not. The flag might actually make someone more wary, as they weren't hard to come by. I would just have to gauge the Americans' reactions at the time and, if necessary, remove the shemagh entirely.

Baghdad was going to be a nightmare to negotiate. Previously, I had travelled as part of a recognisable coalition force in a convoy of distinctive vehicles that had forced its way through the nose-to-tail traffic with horns blasting and guns out. This time, I would be part of that traffic getting pushed out of the way, obliged, like every one else, to crawl my way slowly through the crowded thoroughfares. I reflected on the romantic, novelistic aspect of it all. Here I was, a lone Englishman with five Kurds, about to drive through the heart of the Sunni Triangle with only the weapons I carried for protection and absolutely no back-up whatsoever. I was under no illusion that if we had to shoot our way out of trouble, any US military nearby would open up on us as well. The minute they saw two civilian cars with weapons blazing, even if the fire wasn't directed at them, they would annihilate us. I was on my own but loving it all the more for that. The setting, the sense of being *in extremis*, the sheer buccaneering beauty of the situation was pure John Buchan. A cocktail of high adventure, shot through with the tantalisingly bitter tang of danger and more than a soupçon of mortality. All quite unnecessary, but then so is climbing mountains. Adding to the Lawrence of Arabia feel, on leaving the power station Mustapha leaned over, tapped me on the shoulder and said in a heavily accented tone, 'Whatever happen, I with you.' I knew he meant it. Nice one, mate. I hope one day you get that Kurdish State.

It was still dark as we came into the first small town. Communication had been lost with the pimpmobile, as it was now too far ahead. I'd soon stopped trying to contact it with the hand-held Motorola and resigned myself to concentrating on what was immediately around me. Although still dark, there was a throng of people on either side of the tree-lined main road that cut through the town. Cars were pulling on and off this road, some with lights, some without. Police were parked up in their blue-and-white pick-ups, large guns mounted on the back. Their balaclava-covered faces swivelled as we passed by, giving me an uneasy feeling. There was no sign of petrol hawkers. They must be doing all right and having a lie-in.

Further along the road, close to what I imagined was the town centre, more people lined the dark pavements in front of concrete, glass-fronted shops, which were unlike the wooden shacks on the outskirts. Clearly, this was the local Bluewater. We passed another group of gun-toting policemen parked haphazardly at the junction, their pick-ups facing different directions and their guns manned. Three or four of them were standing around holding Kalashnikovs. All of them had their faces covered with black balaclavas; the eeriness of the dark, muted tableau was made more menacing as their turning heads followed our movements. All romance had now drained away, replaced by a current of unease swirling up in my stomach. Among those balaclavas and dish-dashes, I'd have given anything to see some US troops.

Some hundred metres ahead on the right was an untidy line of several cars, two and three abreast. Surrounding the cars were groups of Iraqi men. I calmed myself down, repeating in my head how well we blended in and that we looked just like all the other Iraqi vehicles trundling about. If anyone took particular notice of us as we passed, I'd order my driver to stick his foot down as soon as we were out of sight and put some distance behind them and us, then hope they didn't have sat phones or any other efficient comms to give the heads-up to insurgents or bandits further along the route. Perhaps the huddle was innocent and I was letting my imagination get the upper hand. To stay effective and sane I had to balance due caution with a 'fuck-it, let's breeze on' attitude.

Getting closer, it became apparent that the huddle was the queue for the town's petrol station. We passed the mass of bodies unnoticed. I was just loosening my stomach muscles when a sudden lurch of the vehicle caused them to tighten again. My driver had taken an abrupt right and swung us onto the petrol-station forecourt, stopping just short of the pumps. The clusters of bodies in the queue turned and stared directly at us.

'Fucking hell. What the fucking hell are you doing, you fucking wanker!' I said in a high-pitched, teeth-clenched voice. My left hand crossed instinctively over my AK, grabbing hold of the cocking lever ready to shoot my way out. On the forecourt was one of the blue-and-white police pick-ups with some armed policemen standing around. Everyone had now stopped their filling up and was looking at us, struggling after the initial surprise of our arrival to find adequate expressions for someone who has just jumped a three-day queue. 'Would you Adam and Eve it!' said their faces. And who could blame them with me in the front passenger seat encased in a black-and-white shemagh with only a slit for my eyes and us waltzing to the front of the line. An imperious, 'Fill her up, will you, my good man?' would top it off nicely.

One of the balaclava-wearing policemen slowly approached. I could sense Mustapha's tension as he too adjusted his position on the back seat, getting ready to react. My driver, who in response to my foul-mouthed fury at his actions had simply said 'petrol, petrol', was now getting out of the car to meet the advancing policeman. They exchanged a few words, after which the policeman came over to my window. Only his sharp black eyes were visible through the holes of his balaclava. As he looked at me, I sensed he was smiling. Still shrouded in my shemagh, I discreetly showed my American DOD (department of defence) ID card. He glanced at it then turned away and waved his arms at a car at one of the petrol pumps. It moved off, and with the space clear he beckoned us over to fill up. Hopefully, they'd now all think I was Yasser Arafat! But somehow I very much doubted it.

My eyes were constantly scanning the surroundings. All attention was still focused on us, but the groups were now talking amongst themselves. I was trying to see if anyone was using a sat phone or mobile. If so, I had to assume we were about to be either checked out or ambushed after leaving the station. My driver paid the attendant, who added the dinar notes to his fat roll of money. Nodding my thanks to the police, we reversed up, turned around and left the forecourt, turning right in the direction of Khalis. Neither Mustapha nor I had seen anyone on a phone, but we accelerated hard when we'd cleared the town on the other side, keeping the speed up for a good 15 minutes.

The Motorola started to crackle into life for a few seconds, then went quiet; this was followed by carrier crackling. I figured it was probably the others in the pimpmobile, who I hoped we were now catching up. A little later, we re-established radio contact with them and found out that they had managed to get petrol from some hawkers. Back on track, with both vehicles refuelled and the sun now rising on our left-hand side, I was once again enjoying the mission. Putting distance between Kirkuk and the town's last petrol station meant we were finally losing ourselves in the busy civilian traffic.

The sunrise is rarely clear in Iraq, the change from night to day usually being diffused through a blanket of cloud. That morning was no exception, with the darkness melting slowly into pale grey before eventually breaking open to reveal a cold, blue, cloudless sky. Travelling fast along the single-lane raised highway with the landscape unfolding before us, it was easy to forget the dangers that were present.

We were approaching a winding high road that led up to a pass. After the pass the road would then wind its way through steep-sided terrain down to the lower ground and on in the direction of northern Baghdad. Before reaching the capital, though, we would have to travel through the Sunni town of Khalis with its perilous hinterland, the pass over the high hills being notorious for bandits. Bandits and insurgents held the same menace for me. I would be a good catch to sell on. At least the pimpmobile up ahead would be able to give us good warning of any checkpoints or figures waiting on either side of the high ground.

As we neared the summit of the pass, the radio buzzed into life: 'Simon, American checkpoint ahead.'

'OK, mate. Let them see your flag. Go slow.'

Up ahead was an American military Humvee just off the highway, equipped with a 12.7-mm gun pointing our way. Getting closer, I could see another one further on facing the other way and a third stationed on the high ground above. My fear was that the troops might panic if they saw our weapons.

We slowed to a crawl, a plastic flag showing in each of our vehicles. A hand appeared from the window of the closest Humvee to wave us through and then gestured for us to lower the flags. It was comforting to see some US forces. I hoped they might now signal our presence to others on the route.

On the other side of the pass, I could see why this remote area, with its high ground on either side, was ideal for the old bandit game. The blind, twisting bends were perfect for lying in wait, with cover from positions up high totally dominating the isolated road.

Forty minutes later, we reached the predominantly Sunni town of Khalis, a hotbed of insurgency. Rolling up to the army checkpoint, an Iraqi soldier leaned into the car and bade me to open up my shemagh. As he registered my pale skin, I discreetly flashed my DOD card. He then stood back and motioned us through with a sweep of his arm. Entering the town, the military base was on our left, running parallel to the main road some 50 metres back. Two hundred metres further on we passed the approach to the main entrance of the base, chicaned with several concrete barriers. The road then took us through the market place crammed with stalls, shops and garages, selling everything from live tethered goats, their pungent odour impossible to ignore, to bottles of 7UP and old, oily engines displayed proudly on dirty, frayed tarpaulins. Throngs of mostly men and boys milled about, while groups of traditionally attired men in long white-and-grey dish-dashes sat and stood around, deep in debate. Some held strings of beads, which they deftly swung and manipulated with their finger tips, while others held hands as if in the Amsterdam of the Middle East. Gesticulating traders worked tirelessly to entice the streams of uninterested passers-by. Amid all the noise and activity, we passed unnoticed. It felt good to be invisible, no head turning, no hate-fuelled eyes locking on to us.

Passing out of the centre of town, we came to a large fork in the road, where a signpost indicated Baqubah to the left and Baghdad to the right. We took the right fork, in effect a continuation of the road we were already on. Coming into Baghdad on this road would take us through some of the capital's most heavily populated districts with their crowded streets and frustrating traffic jams. For us, the jams were also dangerous. But to have taken the alternative route from Kirkuk to Baghdad would have first meant a journey over to Tikrit then on down the main highway, skirting Samara, Balad and Taji. From there, we would have transferred onto the expressway on Baghdad's northern fringes, and it would have been plain sailing right the way in to our HQ villas. But given the speed of the insurgents' bush telegraph, the chance of being compromised in Tikrit, with its one-lane bridge, was a risk too high.

The traffic in north-west Baghdad was heavy but moving. We rolled steadily past the two- and three-storey sandy-coloured buildings and villas which lined the street. From this main thoroughfare, smaller streets and lanes spliced off, the spindly alleys threading like dense-woven fibres deep into the hidden heart of Baghdad.

My main concern was that when we inevitably ground to a

complete halt, I'd stick out like a pork pie at a kosher picnic. I could keep the shemagh over my face with just my sunglasses visible, but what was a practical fashion statement in the heat and dust of the desert took on a much more sinister aspect in Baghdad. Seeing me dressed like Roy Orbison playing Omar Sharif, the local militia would materialise from the back alleys and pull me over for a quiet word in my 'shell-like'. 'What's with the shades, man? Sheikh the other one, pal, it's got bells on!' Beneath the tea-towel disguise, they'd find, to their depraved delight, one more body for a fetching orange jumpsuit. 'Suits you, sir.' In such a scenario, I'd have to fight my way out on foot, try to reach a free-moving road and commandeer a vehicle. Alternatively, there was the hand grenade.

For this reason, on reaching northern Baghdad, I removed the sunglasses and arranged the shemagh to sit on my head, with a long swathe dropping down the right-hand side of my face, covering it as far as possible. The only problem was that this drastically reduced my right-hand field of view, which in these crowded streets, not patrolled by the US military, was a more immediate drawback. The need for all-round observation outweighed the disguise factor, and I pushed the shemagh back off my face. In truth, I'd missed a trick with my facial appearance: growing a beard and moustache, even darkening the complexion of my hands and face, would have camouflaged me. If there was a next time, I'd be sure to get a makeover before deploying. 'Nah, love, that shade's just a teensy-weensy bit too dark. It'll clash with me AK, yeah. Tell you what, though, that new Midnight Café Surprise looks promising . . .'

We didn't have to wait long before the slow-moving queue of traffic became a static one. We were now wedged in tight within a seemingly endless line of horn-tooting vehicles, with pedestrians walking past on either side within arm's length.

Bored drivers and passengers were now becoming inquisitive about what was around them. I did my best to keep my face hidden while trying not to look too cloak and dagger. My eyes were on high alert, weighing up approaching pedestrians, scanning the shop fronts and alleyways for danger signs and trying as casually as possible to observe the occupants of the cars caught up around us.

My anxiety escalated as all the negatives of the situation began tripping off 'in-it-up-to-my-neck' scenarios, with me starring in the lead role. I was stuck in traffic with a handful of untested Kurds, far from any US presence, surrounded by hordes of civilian Iraqis, who if not participating in an imminent fight to kill or capture me, would watch the ensuing melee with docile pleasure, and I had no communication with any outside elements.

Hidden by my dark-brown dish-dash, I laid the AK across my thighs and grasped my 9-mm Browning firmly in my hands. It had one up the spout but with the hammer forward, acting as safety, my thumb poised to draw it back and let loose the 13 hollow-point rounds. The Browning was easier to manoeuvre from a covert position when taking on a close target, although I could also bring the AK-47 quickly into play if required. I was on max alert with no time or thought for anything but my immediate surroundings.

We had now been stationary for well over five nerve-grinding minutes. The more impatient drivers continually beeped their car horns, accompanied by tinny Arab pop music from a small radio hung outside a corner shop. There were pedestrians everywhere, strolling up and down, standing in groups talking, or weaving in and out of the cars. One of them trailed his hand across our bonnet as he crossed the road. I had a strong impulse to dart my head about, watching every possible angle, but this would immediately elicit curiosity. All I could do was hiss like a ventriloquist at Mustapha, '*Chouff, chouff.* Look, look.'

'Yes, yes, OK. Good, good,' Mustapha replied as he endeavoured to appear casual in his observations. There was no communication with the pimpmobile, for even picking up the radio would immediately reveal our presence. The only transmission now would be to inform the other vehicle of compromise or imminent contact with insurgents.

Just ahead on the right-hand pavement, a fat, middle-aged, pot-bellied Arab was sitting beside a flaming chicken rotisserie, his eyes roaming idly over the stalled traffic. The pleasant, sweet smell of the roasting chicken wafted to my nostrils. Through the corner of my eye, I'd been paying particular attention to this fat Arab, whose gaze had so far not rested on our vehicle. As we slowly passed his level, I watched him in the right-hand wing mirror, purposely positioned to see directly behind me. Throughout my observations, I ran response actions through my head. As we crept past, the Arab's face registered no change. I would have been extremely worried if he had got out a mobile phone.

With fat man safely behind us, I turned my attentions to up front, left and right, glancing now and then in the wing mirror, and, in what I hoped was a casual manner, over my left shoulder. Mustapha was also taking things extremely seriously, staying alert and constantly scanning the surroundings. Presumably, those in the pimpmobile, now four cars in front of us, were not experiencing the same kind of anxiety, being three bona fide Arabs in a run-of-the-mill car. They had only to keep their weapons out of sight and maintain a low profile.

After stopping and starting for what seemed a lifetime, we eventually picked up speed to around 30 miles per hour, at which point I relaxed a bit. I wondered how the fuck Mark had done this eight times, and in the white pick-ups. On its own, a pick-up would blend in perfectly, but two together was risky.

Recognising some landmarks up ahead, I realised we'd soon be passing a notorious point in our journey: the heavily fortified entrance to the Green Zone known as 'Assassins Gate'. The name alone made me shudder – although, on occasion, I was close to doing worse than that when I was in its vicinity, assassins having on several occasions blown themselves and their explosive packed cars up as near to the gate as possible. The entrance was situated just off a manic junction, with vehicles passing in all directions and cars queuing to be searched for admittance to the Green Zone. There were police everywhere, parked and standing about, as well as civilians queuing, milling around, hawking or trying to make money by some other means. As an initial point of control, elements of the Iraqi Army manned the approach to the gate, the first line of defence against suicide bombers. A further 50 metres on, the first American troops were stationed in front of the actual entrance to the Green Zone.

After distancing ourselves from the Assassins Gate, we immediately hit heavy traffic caused by the convergence of several large roads up ahead and a knock-on from the permanent closure of certain arterial routes. On this occasion, we would have to join the queue – a bit different from bulldozing our way through as a heavily armed PSD team. I was now going to find out what life was like for your common-or-garden-variety Iraqi motorist around here.

Glancing in the wing mirror, I noticed that cars further back were pulling off the road, forcing pedestrians to smartly sidestep. It soon became apparent why. A large American 4x4 was fast looming up behind, with its horn blasting aggressively, headlights flashing and two small blue LED lights in its dashboard going like the clappers. It scattered all in its path, us included. We pushed our way onto the pavement, along with all the other civilian cars. My overriding concern was to keep our weapons out of sight, since the private-military contractors sitting high up in the 4x4 would be able to see down into our vehicle. And there was no way we could show the plastic Stars and Stripes, as this would compromise us with the other traffic.

Abdelkader and the others in the pimpmobile had got themselves out of the way. Being intensely aware of what the consequences would be if the charging PMCs saw three armed Arabs, they too would be hiding their weapons. The leading 4x4 quickly passed by. It was dangerously close to us, a dark blur of blue metal bang up against the passenger side windows as it overtook. Speeding along behind, a second 4x4 managed to hog even more space, forcing the already dispersed civilian vehicles to cower. Two more identical vehicles followed then a fifth, all in quick and hostile succession, guns poking menacingly at the array of vehicles and pedestrians caught in the slipstream. As the last 4x4 went by, a large gun levelled itself in our direction from the open tailgate, the gunner in a black helmet and large goggles staring at us like some eyeless alien. The untidy conglomeration of slewed cars immediately began jostling to rejoin the road, filling the lesion left by the 4x4s.

After this first-hand experience of being shoved out of the way by foreigners brandishing guns in obscenely large vehicles, I could only wonder at the level of outrage and impotence the Iraqis must feel suffering such treatment several times a day. Instead of inflicting the insult, I had now been on the receiving end. However, I knew that in the interests of saving my skin, I'd be dishing it out again before long, despite the fact that this kind of SOP might further alienate the law-abiding (if there were any laws left to abide by) Iraqi civilian population.

∗∗

We arrived at the HQ villas just before midday. There was now a high concrete blast wall blocking off the main road nearby. Not before time. Sitting outside the front of the villas on the same old plastic chair was the same old unarmed guard, paid to sit there and occasionally to be a gofer. Sending Abdelkader in the pimpmobile to buy some fried chicken and chips from a nearby stall, I took off the dish-dash and shemagh and left them on the car seat. On my way into the offices, I bumped straight into the boss. We shook hands, and he asked me how the journey had been. I replied that it had gone fine so far, but that I wasn't happy with the mission as an SOP in itself and definitely wouldn't do it again, citing alternative ways in which the money could be moved. In true boss style, he listened but didn't make a big thing of it, just remarking that it would have to be looked into and that it was nice seeing me but he had to dash. He then wished me a safe return and was gone. I felt that my comments on this situation, and the other bad practices that had been in place since before his arrival and appointment as in-country boss, had been taken on board as something to be dealt with. (I am not able to say whether the modus operandi was changed, because after returning to Tikrit I was no longer privy to that information.)

I phoned the ops room at Kirkuk to tell them I'd arrived safely, then climbed the stairs to the wages office. Thankfully, the head of local wages was there, so there was no time lost. Just before Christmas, I had emailed him the guards' timesheets. When working with Dave on convoy, he had impressed on me the need to mark down meticulously every absence of every guard and the explanation for it. This would cut down on unnecessary days off, because as soon as the guards saw it was 'no ticky, no washy' they'd stop any malingering. And if a dispute arose, the reason for the unpaid day would be documented in black and white.

I wonder if old Lawrence had this trouble: 'I know you've got a migraine, Hassan, but we really do need to blow up this train before lunch in order to bring down the Ottoman Empire.'

Thanks to my emails, the wages had already been prepared for each guard, so all I had to do was check the amounts and cross them off the list. Satisfied, I stuffed the cash into my day sack and closed it tight. 'The most expensive sack around!' I said, slipping my arm through the drawstring. Everyone laughed politely. I didn't want to hang around, so I said my goodbyes then phoned the ops room at Kirkuk informing them of my imminent departure from Baghdad, giving an ETA of approximately 2000.

Back outside, the Kurds were all standing around the pimpmobile eating. Abdelkader shouted to me and held up my portion of chicken and chips. Opening the door of the empty Ascona, I did the necessary to secure the money then joined the others to eat.

We had spent just over an hour at the villas, and it was not yet 1330, but we were already back on the road, $30,000 heavier. Depending on what happened on the way, we could be back well before the ETA, as early as 1830 even. Before leaving, my driver had pointed out that it would be wise to put some petrol in both the cars. I was fairly confident that it would be easy to come by, petrol hawkers being a common sight on the main roads leading out of Baghdad. I therefore decided not to stop till we were on the fast bit of road heading back out towards Baqubah and Khalis.

We were soon at the mercy of the crowded Baghdad streets once again. I was not at all familiar with the district through which we had come earlier and would now be exiting the city. However, one area I definitely did not want to pass through again, having previously had dealings there, was Sada City. Built by the old regime and named by Saddam after himself, Sada had become a ghetto for the Shiite Muslims now enjoying comparative freedom from persecution. These Shiites had embraced the charismatic leader Muqtada al-Sadr and formed a brigade in his militia, the Mahdi Army. I'd had a glimpse of members of this militia whilst on convoy. Sometimes at the Abu Ghraib distribution centre, or at the Police Academy on the other side of town, waiting while materials or vehicles were grouped, counted and loaded up would take longer than expected. When this happened, we got paid to just sit around. Often on such days, staff would have to flit between the two sites, so we would be tasked to escort the one US military soldier responsible for the materials between Abu Ghraib and the Police Academy. Sada City was situated off a main road along this route. One day, as we were nearing the turn-off for Sada, we saw that the cars just ahead of us were stopping, doing a U-turn and then driving off at speed. Up front, Dave at first assumed that there must be a US road block ahead. It wasn't till his panicking driver pointed out several shemagh-wearing gunmen brandishing RPGs and screaming 'Mahdi Army, Mahdi Army' that he realised otherwise and shouted over the radio, 'Illegal checkpoint ahead. Turn around. Turn around now. Go, go!' Being a lot further back, I didn't feel as threatened as Dave, who must have been within 100 metres of the action as he smartly chucked a U-turn under the noses of the gunmen. Unbelievably, they all just watched as our four silver Pajeros, obviously occupied by private-security contractors, hightailed it away, one from within spitting distance of them. We couldn't figure out why they hadn't engaged us. We never used that route again.

The Baghdad traffic was now horrendous, forcing us several times to turn around and try parallel roads that turned out to be equally jammed. Each time we deviated, I said, 'No Sada City.'

'No problem, no problem.'

'No, it's not no fucking problem, it's NO Sada City!' My driver really pissed me off with his no problems!

I couldn't follow the map, being too preoccupied with the possible dangers all around, but I had checked the overhead and roadside signs for orientation and hadn't so far seen any mention of Sada City, so hopefully everyone was on message. After an incredible two and a half hours, we finally made it to the outskirts of Baghdad and the two-lane road for Baqubah and Khalis. There was no problem getting petrol; hawkers were in abundance, and without any fuss we pulled over and filled the cars up. I was now a bit concerned about the time, but if all ran smoothly from then on in, it looked like our ETA would be around 1900.

The traffic was now nipping along, and with the momentum and the open road I began to relax again. The next real point of concern for me was Khalis, much more so than on our way through it that morning. It wasn't somewhere I'd been familiar with before the mission, but when I had read the relevant intelligence on the areas I would have to pass through it had caught my eye on numerous occasions. Heading towards it at that moment, Khalis was looming large, a threatening presence in my thoughts. Picturing the morning scene, I calculated that all we had to do was pass the market place, hopefully now empty, drive along the road parallel to the base and then clear the Iraqi Army checkpoint. After that, it was out onto the open road and up through the high pass.

On arriving in Khalis, the Baqubah junction was moving freely, but further on towards the market place the traffic slowed considerably, and by the time we reached it we were down to a snail's pace. Ahead was total gridlock. Fear gripped me, my insides churned and an instant rush of adrenalin coursed through my hands, stomach and finger tips. I armed my AK in readiness, the ominous metallic clatter punctuating the looming sense of danger. Now smack bang in the middle of the market place, a mass of cars blocked any escape route if we were compromised or, worse still, plunged into a firefight.

The market was quieter than it had been that morning, with groups of very sinister-looking, shemagh-wearing Arabs standing around. None seemed to be armed, but their presence in numbers was worrying enough. The smell of woodsmoke from the early evening fires mingled with the nauseous exhaust fumes of the backed-up traffic. I slowly pulled the shemagh well down over my face. We were now firmly boxed in by the cars behind. I did a quick assessment of the situation. If we were compromised and attacked, there was nowhere for the car to go, and the only option would be for us to try to make it up to the entrance to the base on foot, but that was still about 300 metres ahead – it would be every man for himself. If the insurgents or crowd didn't kill us, I felt sure that the Iraqis or US military up at the entrance would. First of all they would hear a ferocious gun battle, followed by the sight of armed men running towards their positions. If it was the British Army up there, I'd rate our chances – their reactions are a lot more disciplined than that of the nervous and often unaccountable Americans.

The cause of the gridlock was unclear, although the crowd's attention was focused on something up ahead. Even if I'd wanted to do an about-turn, which I didn't, there was now no option, with cars blocked in solidly on either side of us. The exhaust fumes were making the memory of that morning's goat odour a fond one. I vowed not to complain about the M25 if I ever found myself on it again.

'Mustapha, *chouff*, good,' I said unnecessarily.

'Yes, yes, Simon. Good, good,' he replied nervously, surveying the throng of people and drivers around us.

The crowd in the market place was now swelling even

more. My fear was of being pointed out by someone and the mob getting frenzied, all wanting a piece of me. Images of the two signallers in Northern Ireland in the late 1980s came to mind. They were savagely beaten to death by a bloodthirsty mob, and I've never been able to watch more than the initial rush of the crowd towards the vehicle. 'Viewers may find the following images upsetting.' Why the fuck didn't the poor blokes empty their weapons into the bastards? This savage and shaming episode reached its unnatural conclusion on a piece of wasteland as the stripped and broken bodies received the last rites from a priest. There were no priests in Iraq but wasteland in abundance.

I was ready and willing to shoot and kill all attackers, armed or unarmed. The particular dread now gripping me was a primordial one. I was in terror of the barbarism that lurks in the soul of every man beneath the thin veneer of civilisation: death by a thousand cuts; seeing my own limbs and innards wrenched out whilst still conscious. I thought of the weighty grenade veiled beneath my dish-dash and secured onto my chest webbing – its use oblivion. Before it came to that, I would fight: the more panic my shots caused, the better my chances of survival.

In all likelihood, it was an IED by the entrance to the base that was causing the hold-up, with troops being deployed on the road. With everyone's attention focused forward, I continued to scan the cars and the crowd for anyone paying attention to me or my vehicle. The shemagh over most of my face was a bit suss and might itself invite curiosity, but my blue-eyed, white face and blondish-grey hair would be impossible to miss and had to remain covered. The pimpmobile was only a couple of cars away, but it wasn't under suspicion as long as the weapons were out of sight. I wasn't banking on its occupants coming to our aid if all hell did break loose, though.

The next hour had to be the most frightening of my life. Unable to take action or predict how long we would be stuck there, the claustrophobia was torturous and the nightmare that could follow one wrong glance was becoming ever more palpable. When the traffic finally did start to move, I felt so elated that the prospect of an ambush ahead seemed almost trivial. Just to be in motion and away from the smell and stifling proximity of the crowd and its latent horrors was a blessed relief.

With daylight still in our favour and Khalis now in the rear-view mirror, I felt as though the worst was over. It wasn't until we began the drive up towards the lonely pass that fear returned. All I could do was sit tight, observe and keep thinking actions on: pouring firepower out of the window, keeping the driver driving, where I would head to on foot if we were immobilised, etc. Climbing steeply, I expected all hell to break loose at every bend. I kept telling myself that we hadn't been compromised, so the only danger was from bandits – it wouldn't be a planned ambush waiting for us. But with only the occasional car coming down the other way, all looked to be clear. I was sure that if there were bandits up ahead, at least one of the approaching cars would have tipped us off with arms waving frantically out of the window, the Iraqi version of UK motorists flashing their headlights to warn others about speed traps. The pimpmobile was about 400 metres further on, comms between us were good and visibility, though fading into early evening dusk, was still sufficient to observe and clear the rocky high ground on either side of us. They were therefore in a position to give us prior warning of any dangers or checkpoints, illegal or not. It was their turn to sweat it out a little.

We made it through the pass without incident. We were on the last stage of our journey, through the few remaining villages and towns on the other side and then on to Kirkuk.

It was just after 1900, and I reckoned we had another hour and a half at least to go – but before that darkness would fall. From that point on, I was more concerned about an inside job taking place and started keeping more of a covert eye on the attitude of Ali the driver, as I had convinced myself that if anyone was going to pull a stunt, either blatantly or with a moody road block, it would be him and his police-chief brother.

The roads were fairly empty, and we were making very good ground, doing around 90 miles per hour. Entering the town in which we'd made the impromptu petrol stop that morning, we were greeted with the pleasant smell of woodsmoke and roasting meat from several little food stalls and shacks along the edge of the main road. A few cars were driving up and down, and it was mainly men who were milling around the open emporiums, but there were also a few black-shrouded women and their barefoot kids. It was a much less ominous scene than that of a few hours before, and the atmosphere, warmth and plenitude of a colourful Middle Eastern town going about its early evening routine was now almost enjoyable. A few policemen were in evidence, but they were no longer hidden behind black balaclavas and seemed more relaxed, with not one of them even glancing in our direction.

We were now only half an hour away from the power station, and for the first time I allowed myself the luxury of believing I was gonna get there unharmed. Ali had up until that point given me no cause for alarm with his behaviour. However, I was not expecting what happened next. Mustapha took out his mobile phone, dialled a number and started blabbering away in Kurdish. 'Mustapha!' I thought. 'What's going down here?' Next, Ali got involved in the conversation. I desperately wanted to reach round and grab the mobile phone from Mustapha, but I knew that if I did, my trust in him and his loyalty to me would end in an instant, although perhaps it was already too late for that. 'Well,' I thought, 'if this is it, then the fucking wankers are fucking dead too.' It was now completely dark, and if Mustapha wasn't calling his missus to tell her to put the chips on, he was telling his accomplices of our imminent arrival at their ambush point, which would be in the next five minutes, as I could now see the lights of Kirkuk in the distance. Mustapha continued talking into his phone. Along with the fear, a wave of hurt and sorrow flooded over me. I couldn't help it. 'Mustapha, I trusted you, mate, and this is how you repay me.' With fingers gripping my AK and a lump in my throat, I prepared for the worst . . .

Mark was all smiles on his return from his extended leave. He'd had five weeks off, with Christmas and New Year thrown in – largesse on a scale unheard of in my game! There must have been a double-barrelled name somewhere with a family snapshot on their big important desk and a big important secret that Mark knew too much about. But I could afford to be magnanimous. I was just glad to have seen in the New Year, period. Two thousand and five, I'm still alive, cha, cha, cha!

Those last moments on the road back to Kirkuk had been intense. As Mustapha had continued his phone call, I'd weighed up two alternative translations: 'Hi, love, it's me. Awful traffic. Home soon. Love you too,' and 'The unclean blaspheming infidel is in the Ascona with the backshish [wonga], and we're just approaching your position.' Hoping for the first, but fearing the second, I had gestured resolutely at him to end the call and get back to observing. He had sounded displeased and shot me an annoyed glance as he hung up. I thought, 'That's it. I'm going to have to kill him before he kills me.' Then my radio had started to buzz, and

I had heard the guards at the power station. Even in the dark, I knew the stretch of road and that in a few hundred metres we'd be at the potholed approach. I got on the radio and with more joy than ever before expressed over the airwaves said, 'Hello, ops, this is Simon in your location, figures five [minutes].' However, the next message I sent a few minutes after that trumped it: 'Now back in your location.' Mustapha, having forgiven me for interrupting his chat with her indoors, gave me a genuine smile. Top man. And guess what? The cookhouse was still open. Result!

It was ironic, but after the wages run was done and dusted I really developed a liking for Kirkuk, partly, I suppose, because the threat of the impending dodgy mission was no longer a factor. The guards were, on the whole, a good bunch. You always get a handful of wasters, but the majority worked long and hard, and were, most importantly, conscientious. For my part, I was left very much to my own devices by the Bechtel management. With the comparative freedom and the good living accommodation, it was a comfortable regime. Kirkuk had nowhere near the level of bombings and shootings as elsewhere in northern Iraq, and it was a good way to pass the first five weeks of a nine-week tour of duty. Then again, it only takes one round from a rusty old gun or a sliver of shrapnel to end yer days on the planet. But there were a lot more rusty guns and shrapnel elsewhere.

If I had been asked to stay on in Kirkuk rather than return to Tikrit, it would have been a tough call to make. If the wages run had come into the equation, Kirkuk would have most definitely been told to shove it. In the event, I was not asked to stay. There had been talk of a second in command for Mark, but I wouldn't have been comfortable in that role, so Kirkuk remained a one-expat posting.

When Mark returned, I didn't hang around, leaving the following day for Tikrit in the Ascona with the pimpmobile up front. Morale at Buckmaster was on an all-time high, as the week before a QRF led by Chas had successfully captured five armed insurgents who had been terrorising and killing our local workers travelling on the approach road from Tikrit. They had documented the capture with several photos, some showing the weapons and vehicles used by the insurgents. The best ones, however, were of the insurgents themselves, the abject fear radiating from their eyes and faces. One had even wet himself.

There was no such glamorous action for me, just back to staging-on at ASP 1 and 2. I only had four weeks of it to hack until my next leave, but the days at Buckmaster passed rather slowly, and I started toying with the idea of getting back on the road. It wasn't long before I was asking for a spell on the PSD team. This was a lot more dangerous, involving regular trips to Baghdad, but having now lain low for a while I knew that thrills and spills were what it was really all about for me.

The big difference with the PSD team in Tikrit was the total lack of Iraqis. Instead, it was all experienced ex-soldiers from some of the best armies in the world, and the SOPs and drills, regularly and meticulously practised, were of the highest standard, honed through regular application in live situations. I managed to get a place on the team starting after my next leave.

Only one scary thing happened to me while I was on leave. Back in the UK, I had to make some decisions about money. There was no hot nest egg in Kuwait, but my wages alone were now stacking up to a substantial sum. On my first leave, with the wings of the angel of death in my head, I'd gone on a spending spree. Thanks to the Hilton and the fine dining, the drinking and the 'larging' it in general, I had managed to get through ten grand. Despite this financial abandon, the grim reaper had not yet called my name. Now bursting with rude health, I'd gone all Mr Thrift. Popping into London with nothing special in mind, I nipped into the bank to check out my savings accounts. How naive can you get?

As a young lad, it had always been impressed upon me that I should put away my pennies, and I would look forward to Saturday visits to the large, dingy post office in Camberwell Green to deposit some of my pocket money. It was a great pleasure to watch the clerk take my battered Post Office savings book and, with the speed of a piston, hammer the rubber stamp on the ink pad twice, then hammer it onto the open page once. Bang, bang! Bang! Under closer scrutiny, the clerk's flamboyant dexterity didn't always come up to scratch – some of the stamps in my book were way wide of the black circle. This mattered not a jot when a new page in the book was reached, a milestone of my saving achievement. The heady prospect of actually filling a book and starting a second was a veritable rite of passage. The day you got that new book, you queued up a boy and walked out a Post Office adolescent. And if you can keep on saving while all about are buying T-Rex LPs, much more than this, you'll be a man, my son.

Later on, working at my Saturday job in the Camberwell Green mirror shop, I reflected (sorry) that grown-up wages must be saved the grown-up way, and I opened an account with the all-new Abbey National Building Society. My first withdrawal of five pounds was spent on a much too large pair of hobnailed army boots from Winners Surplus on the Walworth Road. That was the 1970s, when interest rates were treated with respect, bankrupts were ashamed of themselves and credit was called by its proper name – the 'never, never'.

No one saves up for stuff now, they just get a loan. Anyway, old habits die hard, so I went into the bank and transferred my earnings into an instant saver bonus something or other at 2¾ per cent. Checking my balance on the ATM some five minutes later, I was baffled to see myself fifteen thousand pounds richer, this sum having been credited on top of my deposit. Upon enquiry, this loan was found to carry a generous APR of just 17 per cent – generous to the bank, to be precise. What a result. I hadn't asked about a loan, but they'd kindly given me one anyway. It was the best-laid ambush I'd ever been in. Once regrouped, I counter-attacked. Actually, I approached the counter politely but firmly and cancelled the loan, paying back the money. Someone told me this was called 'inertia selling'. Oh.

9

THE VORTEX

I returned from leave refreshed and keen to get out on the roads with the PSD team. The team was domiciled in a row of Portakabins and numbered around 12 to 16 personnel, depending on who was on leave and what jobs were to be done. There were veterans of the British Army, Royal Marines and the New Zealand Army, with me and two others, Pete and Mac, making up the Foreign Legion contingent. There had been a fourth ex-legionnaire called Davey, but he had jumped ship to go to Afghanistan. That really pissed a lot of the lads off, as some of them had been trying to get out there for ages. Along comes Davey, fairly new to the Tikrit job but having worked for Armor for several years, and he pulls strings with the London office and disappears.

The PSD missions consisted mainly of runs to Speicher and Danger, the two FOBs in and around Tikrit. These jobs mainly consisted of dropping off and collecting mail, and taking expats for medical consultation or flights out from FOB Speicher. This FOB was named after a US airman downed in the first Gulf War in the 1990s. The Americans believe that Speicher was held alive in Tikrit right up until the invasion of 2003. They even have photos of what is believed to be his name scratched in a wall of the former Iraqi base, now FOB Speicher.

The PSD team also conducted regular patrols in the vast prairie-type terrain up to about 15 kilometres around Buckmaster, mounting snap VCPs and showing a general presence to hinder and deter any terrorist activities, and made routine trips to Baghdad with personnel going on and returning from leave. There wasn't the excitement of escorting high-profile individuals on VIP contract; nevertheless, the same notoriously deadly roads to and through Baghdad had to be negotiated, sometimes as often as five times a week, and these trips didn't always go unpunished.

The PSD vehicles consisted of three white 'up-armoured' Ford F350s and two 4x4 Ford Excursions. These were unmistakably American, such cars being used solely by the foreign private-security companies – nothing remotely similar was driven by Iraqis. As such, we were the sorest of thumbs, and the insurgents had little trouble identifying us for who we were. Regrettably, the US military were not so competent at recognition, even though these vehicles were supplied and owned by the United States Army Corps of Engineers. There was even a little sticker on the dashboard with a bar code and the words 'Property of the Defence Department', presumably so they could claim back the wreck once they'd shot it up in error – or perhaps not in error. We were all aware of blue-on-blue contacts – so-called friendly fire – but on one occasion the US military opened fire on us whilst clearly in recognisable friendly vehicles and more alarmingly posing no threat whatsoever to them at the time. I am aware of several other incidents of this nature, but the following was the only one at which I was present.

On a PSD convoy, the two armoured Ford Excursions

would be at the centre of the formation, with the clients escorted within. Our appearance was, you might say, obtrusive, with orange dayglo panels and A4-sized coloured flags at hand for showing in the windscreens. Large antennas protruded from each vehicle, and the last F350 had a gunner out on the back facing rearwards to close the march. The convoy might stretch for between 150 and 200 metres, depending on the road conditions. Every man wore a black helmet, apart, that is, from John, a slight but dangerous Irishman already a veteran of several gun battles with insurgents who had managed to nick a rather Gucci green affair! In short, you couldn't miss us rolling along, lairy as a carnival. And to give the insurgents credit, they were able to clearly identify us from quite a distance. Therefore, you'd assume that a gunner on a US Humvee only 100 metres up ahead of us could as well.

Our drills, be it for a contact or a flat tyre, covered every possible variation our collective tiny minds could dream up. This would avoid any misunderstandings when the rhythm of life suddenly went off the Richter scale, every man knowing his place and role in the given emergency. Naturally, the more dynamic of the drills were those preparing us for contact with enemy forces. In a training session, these drills would first be practised in slow time, a procedure known as a 'walk through, talk through'. Each phase of the action would be broken down, from the initial shots being fired, through to the final re-org and headcount, the whole thing performed at a snail's pace with a running commentary from the trainer. 'Right. That's good. Your vehicle stops this side of the immobilised vehicle, the opposite side to the incoming . . . You, you lay down covering fire . . . You, you extradite the wounded from the immobilised vehicle . . .' The drill would then accelerate with each repetition, until the speed and urgency was up to real-time, often to the extent of injuries being sustained, even though there was no actual firing.

This happened to me on one of our PSD drills. Not being quick enough to grab hold in the back of an accelerating pick-up, I fell hard onto the metal floor, with my right knee taking the brunt. The pain was severe and for a few seconds incapacitating. Lesson learned. On my next visit to a PX, I invested in a pair of knee protectors which I wore whenever I was out on the road, much to the amusement of my comrades.

Once drills had been honed to perfection in dry training, we would then use live rounds, again in slow time first, building up to the tenor of the real thing. The only thing missing was a few smelly, rotten-toothed insurgents. The scenarios we drilled for ranged from the first F350 taking a direct hit from a roadside IED to one in which all vehicles were hit and immobilised by rocket and small-arms fire. We also drilled for our reactions on seeing an American military vehicle patrol ahead. Training was continuous and on-going, partly to induct the new members regularly joining the team and also to instil procedures in everyone until they were second nature.

For once, I think all of us really enjoyed our training, which came without the bullshit you have to put up with in a regular army. Knowing the situation in Iraq, we could be pretty much certain that we weren't just 'square bashing' or playing at soldiers and that all our rehearsals would, sooner or later, culminate in a live show. Everyone trained hard and serious on the PSD team, and a strong bond formed between us. I hasten to add that this was with none of your embarrassing American-style 'bro' hugs, though some of the Kiwis bordered on the *Band of Brothers* stuff. Overall, though, our comradeship was a typically taciturn, British thing – a quiet knowledge of absolute kinship which required no crude verbalising.

My place on the PSD team was inside the lead vehicle, sitting on the rear bench seat. In this position, I could cover both sides and, if need be, fire through the gun ports on either rear side door. My weapon was a Minimi 5.56-mm machine gun with 200 belted rounds in a hard plastic magazine. I carried an additional five of these magazines, three in a small day sack permanently on my back and two more in a canvas satchel slung over my neck and shoulder. This gave a total of 1,200 belted rounds, which if I had to debus would be on my person, giving me and the team considerable firepower. The vehicle was driven by Phil, a portly Glaswegian and ex-RCT who was in the process of saving up sufficient spondulees to escape to Turkey with his missus. I pointed out to him that he could just sit tight in Glasgow and Turkey would come to him when they joined the EU. Daz, in the front passenger seat, was also from Glasgow, and the PSD team commander. Formerly with a Scottish regiment, Daz was a calm and capable leader.

The vehicle itself was armoured, with bullet-proof glass fitted on the inside of the windscreen and windows and armour plating bolted to the insides of the doors. Strapped on the outside of the cab roof was a Kevlar sheet, capable of stopping the small-arms fire that often rained down on us when we passed under bridges. The heavy armour continually rattled in transit, but the added protection was very comforting, and the added weight only slightly affected the vehicle's performance, the big nasty lump of an engine sending the burdened beast flying up the road whenever the accelerator needed to be floored.

One day, having negotiated the packed roads out of Baghdad, with their crawling cars and streams of pedestrians adding to the risk of attack either by bombs or small-arms fire from bridges, side streets and wasteland, we moved onto the faster stretch of tarmac between Taji, to the north of Baghdad, and Balad. The convoy stretched some 200 metres back, the one client cocooned in the dark-blue armoured Ford Excursion sandwiched between the second and third pick-ups. Doing a nifty 120 kilometres per hour, we were carving easily through the light traffic. Sitting on the back seat, I was busy scanning left and right at the now familiar topography. On the left, about 100 metres away, a railway track ran parallel to the road. Behind this track, the undulating ground with its many blind spots offered ample provision for mounting a shoot or initiating an IED at passing convoys. The railway line would also hinder any follow-up, making escape a surer bet for any attacker. Off to the right were strips of cultivated land, interspersed with small, square, clay-built and rendered, single-storey smallholdings, the occupants bent over working the soil in twos and threes.

Phil was concentrating hard on the road ahead, lining up the vehicle to pass the slower-moving Iraqi traffic. Every so often, I would glance behind through the rear windscreen and check on the others' progress. The chatter coming over the radio into my earpiece, worn by every one of us, except the client in the Excursion, was, as usual, drawing attention to any potential dangers: 'One pax on high ground, three hundred metres my three o'clock . . . Car stopped on opposite carriageway, two hundred metres up front . . . Three pax outside small building, five hundred metres two o'clock . . .'

Then Daz announced, 'American army patrol, 400 metres up ahead.' In front were at least two Humvees, travelling in the same direction as us but a lot slower, probably at about 60 kilometres per hour. Phil came immediately off the accelerator, and Daz held up the plastic A4 Stars and Stripes along with the orange dayglo flash panel, both in clear visibility of the rear Humvee, that identified us as private-military contractors. We were now about 100 metres behind them; Daz left the flag and dayglo flash pressed against the windscreen. The American soldier standing and facing rear on the last Humvee acknowledged our presence by gesturing for us to remain at this distance. This we did, keeping the same speed as the army patrol for the best part of five minutes.

Just before we reached the first row of shops and stalls that mark the beginning of Balad, another US Army patrol appeared, this one from the other direction and travelling slower because of the Abrahams tank that it had with it. Not wishing to leave anything to chance with the Americans, our flags and dayglo flashes were also displayed for this group to see. They thundered remorselessly by, the tank engine roaring, its huge tracks grinding the tarmac as the road shuddered.

We were maintaining the 100-metres distance behind the Humvees ahead of us, and everything seemed to be hunky-dory. It was just as we were entering the town of Balad itself that things took a rather different turn. Without any warning, the US soldier on the last Humvee raised his M16 and aimed it at our vehicle. We then heard a sharp clang on the inner bullet-proof windscreen. In the same split second, the Humvee sped off, following the patrol in a right turn. Phil slammed on the anchors, and Daz jumped out of the vehicle. Facing the fast-accelerating Humvee, he raised his arms in disbelief, shouting, 'What the fuck was that for?' What else could anyone say!

We could not believe what had just taken place. Having clearly identified ourselves and been acknowledged, and having then followed on for five minutes, an American soldier had taken a well-aimed shot at our driver. And he could only have been shooting to kill. Close inspection of the windscreen left no doubt on the matter, or the fact that without the bullet-proof glass Phil would certainly have stopped the bullet. And since the man who fired would have no way of knowing that the vehicle was protected in this way, this action was tantamount to attempted murder. Furthermore, the way the Humvee sped away suggested that it was a premeditated action, a calculated decision to kill a military contractor for sport – 'Just for the goddam hell of it, man.' Not wanting to hang around the area, we recorded the time and location of the incident and headed back to Buckmaster.

During our usual post-deployment debrief, a formal complaint was raised with the US military to ascertain the unit concerned and exactly who fired the shot and why. We were assured by a representative of the American Corps of Engineers that the culprit would be brought to book. Two weeks later, there was still nothing forthcoming, and, as far as I'm aware, no action was ever taken.

This incident was more shocking than taking any number of rounds from insurgents. Not only had an American soldier deliberately aimed and fired at friendly forces, he had done so not knowing if a fellow countryman might be in his sights. Maybe I am naive, but would a British soldier shoot to kill another Brit fighting on the same side? Nah, I don't think so. That one round made every subsequent encounter with American forces on the highways a tense time for me, diverting my attention from its proper priority, attack from insurgents. And American forces on the roads were a fairly common occurrence.

However, I still expected the insurgents to hit us whenever an opportunity arose, and, to be honest, I had admiration for some of their daring operations. One such attack occurred on the crazy downtown expressways of Baghdad.

Once again, I was on the back seat of the lead vehicle. Cradling my Minimi, I prepared for an attack. We were entering Baghdad from the north and had just passed Taji. The atmosphere intensified from then on, with every man on the PSD team scanning rooftops, bridges and rubbish-strewn wastelands along the Baghdad streets for signs of trouble. The usual mayhem reigned: clapped-out Iraqi cars weaving in and out of the lanes; horns constantly blasting; American military patrols steaming through any which way and stopping other cars, including ours, in their bullying advance. These enforced stops were nervous interludes to the journey, our three large pick-ups and two 4x4 Excursions drawing the eyes of Iraqis standing along the roadside. Private-military contractors were now as commonplace as US military patrols, but that didn't mean white-faced, heavily armed men in civvies, driving large foreign vehicles were gonna be offered tea, toast and a picnic table when they took a break on the highway. Insurgents were never far away, and we were like a red rag to them.

On that particular day, we were en route for the Armor Group villas in downtown Baghdad, first having to negotiate the highways that run through inner Baghdad. These highways were linked by a series of concrete spaghetti junctions, with expressways and run-offs circling up to other expressways coming off at a tangent, criss-crossing under and over each other. The looping 3-D networks were ideal for ambushers. If you were caught on one of these expressways, there was nowhere to hide and no possibility of turning on the insurgents on higher ground. All you could do was floor the accelerator and pour rounds down or up on the insurgents and hope lady luck was still cracking a smile.

We called one of these intersections the 'Vortex' and for good reason. Ambushes in this snake's nest of roads were commonplace. Insurgent gunmen high up and well hidden behind the low concrete wall of the overpass could easily dominate the complex of turnoffs and ramps. They would be informed of approaching PMC convoys or PSDs by their dickers on the Baghdad approach roads. The insurgents had then only to wait till the PMCs crossed the point of no return, unable to break off left or right. If stopped, there would be nowhere to go and nowhere to take cover – a classic turkey shoot, with the insurgents firing down from on high at the fleeing or trapped PMCs.

'Vortex up ahead, 200 metres,' Jason announced over the radio. Jason was Daz's second in command and was PSD commander during Daz's leave. He too was from a Scottish regiment and was another cool and competent leader of men, sure of himself and his actions, having been a company sergeant major. This was reflected in his team. There's nothing worse for morale than not having confidence in the boss, but Jason's composure and his Scottish infantry background were enough for me to put my trust in his judgements.

Jason's radio message was acknowledged by all call signs double clicking. All eyes were now focused on and around the fast-approaching Vortex. We were looking for cars stopped for no apparent reason, a glint of metal, a head or hand from behind the low walls of the overpass, anything that suggested a waiting, watching presence. So far, so good, just like every other time we'd passed through.

Approaching the Vortex from the direction of Taji, the road climbs up, revealing the east–west expressway below, the one leading to Abu Ghraib and used by me almost daily back in the days of convoy. Either side of us were the circular off-ramps leading down to the expressway. Continuing straight on, we started moving down towards this road, which would then take us onto the BIAP road. We were now channelled in on either side by large concrete walls and were effectively in a 'U-tube'. The south to north side of the expressway was above us, with the overpass running left to right. No place to run, no place to hide. On we raced.

Being the lead vehicle, we were within 30 metres or so from the end of the U-tube and in sight of the three lanes of expressway ahead when we heard the crack of gunfire. It seemed clear that the fire was being directed at us, showering deadly rain from above and hitting the tarmac just in front of the vehicle. The insurgents had held their fire until they were certain that we were caught in the U-tube, forcing us to run the gauntlet through the hail of bullets.

'Contact above, contact above,' Jason yelled into the radio as he hit the panic button on the tracker system. Phil floored the accelerator, and the powerful lump of an engine propelled us fast down the concrete tube and through the barrage of rounds punching into the tarmac just ahead. I forced the barrel of my Minimi through the gun port on the right-hand rear passenger door, trying to get as sharp an upward angle as the cramped space in the armoured vehicle would allow. I let off several bursts of rounds. I knew I wasn't hitting anything, but it was either carry on shooting or pray. I chose to fire the Minimi *and* pray – pray that the rounds slamming down were not of sufficient calibre to penetrate the Kevlar sheeting bolted to the pick-up roof.

As we sped onto the clear expressway, I stopped firing. There were villas on either side of us now. I looked back towards the remainder of the PSD. Unable to stick my weapon through the thick bullet-proof glass of the rear window, I could only will them through. I thought, 'I'm safe. I've made it through, and I love this bullet-proofed tin can.' But I also felt utterly useless as I watched the others who were still ensnared and under fire. The whole thing only lasted a few seconds, as the PSD was fairly tightly closed up. The last pick-up came through fast, driven by Rob W. His vehicle was only up-armoured, with a bullet-proof windscreen and a couple of sheets of thick metal bolted onto the doors the only added protection. Having no side windows and with a rear gunner out on the back, this vehicle commanded by Ivan 'the Red' (Man U supporter) was our gunship. As it exited the down ramp, all guns were blazing. Ivan the Red and Maru 'the All Black' (a monster of a Maori), were both hanging halfway out of their windows, their AK-47s spewing bullets up at the insurgents on the overpass. Adding to this barrage was young Micky out on the back letting loose with his Minimi as if hell had come to breakfast. I could see their rounds impacting on the concrete wall of the overpass, large clouds of concrete dust kicking up and filling the surrounding air. The insurgents, under such a hail of deadly accurate bullets, were either lying dead and wounded on the other side or beating a hasty retreat.

The ambush, from the first rounds impacting around us and our returning fire to our emergence from the open-top tunnel, had lasted just 45 seconds. Yet in that time the lads on the gunship had managed to fire off some 500 rounds, the majority of them well aimed. Throughout all of this, we had stayed in formation and maintained calm, coherent radio comms with each other. Once reorganised, we had aborted the mission to the villas and instead limped towards Camp Victory, as all our vehicles had taken hits and were in need of repair at the workshop there. The damage was mainly shot-up tyres and, since it was unsafe to stop, damage to the wheel rims from scratching our way along the BIAP road, sparks flying like in some police-chase video, although we were only going about 20 miles an hour. En route, we passed a static American military patrol who escorted us the rest of the way.

The best part of the ambush was that we hadn't sustained any serious injuries, and once in the safety of the camp we could get out and congratulate each other. The mood was jubilant – buzzing. For some of the lads, it was actually the first time in a long military career that they had been able to fire off rounds at an enemy. Micky had had a lucky escape, the gouge marks on the armour of his improvised gun emplacement on the pick-up bearing witness to this fact, and Maru picked out a round lodged in the roof just above his door. Ivan the Red had also had a close shave, with a round entering the dash right in front of him and ricocheting off onto his thigh leaving him a large bluish-black bruise as a souvenir. And for me, although I didn't get much of the action, it was brilliant to have been part of a well-disciplined team that responded quickly and with such deadly firepower, everyone prepared to cover and react for one another, under control. The long hours of training had been put into practice, resulting in us all coming through but with a good chance that the enemy hadn't. What the insurgents hadn't bargained for was the sheer volume of firepower we poured on them, most of it from just one of our pick-ups. One thing was for sure, they had been the ones cowering, with their tails firmly between their legs, and I hoped they were now shitting it thinking about their next ambush. Team PSD had fought fire with fire and turned the tables on them. It felt good. With the vehicles taken in for repair, we held a debriefing, going through every phase of the ambush in minute detail. Straight away, we were looking at ways of bettering our SOPs and chances in the next ambush.

EPILOGUE

For some, there were plenty more ambushes waiting. Daz, Ivan the Red, and Rob W. were all to be hit by IEDs. Daz not only received serious leg wounds when he was blown up by a roadside bomb but also nearly bled to death at the scene. The last I heard, he was out of hospital and convalescing at home but was still in severe pain. And Nams, another team member we picked up from leave on that run down to Baghdad, got himself killed in an IED attack in the city a year later – a quiet, unassuming man but ever the South Sea warrior.

The grievances Dave and I had had on convoy all came to a head around six months after the team was started, and to be fair to Armor Group they now have in place all that we pushed for – too late for me or Dave, but that's always the way. Jobs get started, shortcomings are found and through sometimes bitter wrangling and tantrums appropriate requirements are met. A lot of our particular problems had revolved round the company hierarchy in Baghdad. I realised later that the more worrying reports and complaints that

Dave and I were putting in were not getting back to Armor Group London. Instead of getting an operation worthy of the conflict facing us in Iraq up and running, the head-sheds in Baghdad were on a swan, pulling in serious money and doing jack shit for it. They all eventually moved on, but a lot of damage had been done by then, which took the new boss and his hand-picked team a lot of time and effort to put right. In the end, they got an operation worthy of Armor Group standards up and running. One big asset for Armor Group throughout was Lucy back in London. She would always ask after you, keep up with your fortunes and mishaps, and without fail visit any wounded operatives in hospital.

After the Vortex, there were no more ambushes in the insurgents' in tray for me. With 15 months of service in Iraq, I was now the proud owner of a fat bank account and many a yarn. And having an overwhelming sense of the beautiful gift that life is I saw the fucking light at last and got out while I could. The bigger 'vortex' remains, sucking in others as it did me, dragging them into the deadly maelstrom that is the war in Iraq. I could join the chorus of 'Fucking hell, Tony, you made one helluva mistake!' but I'd be called a hypocrite. Wrong as the invasion was – with no weapons of mass destruction and the taste of political deceit stronger than ever – it had given me, a former professional soldier, the chance of high adventure. To tote big guns for big bucks with big risks as a mercenary had been a long-harboured dream, and with all my strong reservations about the war I'd willingly taken part. To this day, I feel privileged. Selfish, but that's the truth.

Now my only involvement with Iraq is, like the majority of the world's, a detached one, sitting warm, comfortable and well-fed in front of my telly, watching some anonymous footage (no Western reporters have ventured onto the war-torn streets of Baghdad/Iraq for many a moon; they just front a brief description of the day's bloody events standing safely in the Green Zone with an Arabesque backdrop) of distraught Iraqi civilians, head-slapping and filling the camera lens with their faces, demanding 'why?' The mortaring of a market in Sarajevo killing 40-odd brought swift international condemnation and retribution, but Iraq is a different beast, and its continual atrocities are now 'slow news'. The answer to 'why?' changed from 'weapons of mass destruction' to 'Saddam was a nasty bastard!' I hope the Iraqi people still living give us credit for that.

And I bet Robert Mugabe is quaking in his flip-flops, for surely it won't be long before George and Tony get round to his regime. There's an army of PMCs out there up for it.

WHERE ARE THEY NOW?

After the incident in Calvi with the *caporal*, Geds passed '*report chef de corps*' later that week, receiving 15 days in the nick. For a *sous officier*, this is either spent at home or in the mess – wherever he's living at that time. The real punishment is the black mark on your P file (personnel file), as it can effectively ruin your chances of promotion. However, this was not the case for Geds, as he was promoted some seven months later to *adjudant chef* (WO1). On hearing the news, I asked him if he wanted me to come down to Corsica so we could have a drunken brawl or two and get him up another rank. For some reason, he wasn't too keen on the idea.

The last conversation I had with Scotty, my officer drinking buddy who introduced me to the delights of The Morgue, was when he rang me in Plymouth. He told me to get my arse down to Barcelona where he and Dave were on a mission to drink the San Miguel brewery dry. I regretted not going, but, hey, there'll be other times. At the time of writing, I've still not met up with Dave, but we're often in touch by phone and email.

As for the others, after ten months in Iraq and having gotten convoy up and running, Jock left for Africa, where he remains to this day. Vinny is no longer in Iraq, and, who knows, maybe in between text messages he's making a living playing the saxophone. Bob, last I heard, was still in Iraq, although at the time of enquiring he was having a quiet holiday in Magaluf! Ralf has left Iraq; unfortunately, I didn't make it for his wedding, and I'm not sure he did either! Dan, Cal, Chas and several of the lads are still in the country, though no longer in Tikrit. Ivan the Red has just returned to Iraq after a long spell recovering after being blown up – some call it dedication or is it due to the price of a season ticket nowadays! And Emina still does a bit of cleaning in between watching telly.

George and Tony are still clinging on – or should that be 'are still cling-ons'? At least the Star Trek crew knew there *was* a final frontier – the Star-Spangled Banner crew lumber myopically on through time and space, not wanting to succeed, just wanting to be right. And for Blair, sorry seems to be the hardest word – someone should tell him that, like sympathy, it's in the dictionary between shit and syphilis.

Carrière has not resurfaced, but I bumped into Winstone in GT Motorcycles in Plymouth one Saturday in 1999. We were both looking for a bike, and he was a serving Royal Marine at the time. Saito's body, as far as I'm aware, has never been recovered. The Green Café got hit by an IED, blowing the television, several drinkers and the owner up. Sadly, only the television could be replaced.

A word about the Brink's-Mat plan, which obviously I couldn't execute as no one tried to rob me on the way back up to Kirkuk. (Never an ambush around when you want one, is there?) But if they had, would I have chucked the bag of A4 paper out of the window and pocketed the $30,000? It would have been difficult, because I left the A4 paper in my room before departing for Baghdad to collect the money – on purpose, I hasten to add.

As for me, I (presumptuously) reckon that there's another book in me yet. Dave did set me up with a good job in Algeria, but, due to family matters, I unfortunately couldn't take it. Looking back, those six months on the convoys will always rank for me as among the most exciting and frightening of my life. If you're reading this, Dave, we'll get some beers in soon, mate. Convoys are us!

GLOSSARY

actions on – the what-ifs and contingency plans that run through a person's head during a mission

adjudant unite – company sergeant major

artic – articulated lorry

ASP – ammunition supply point

BIAP – Baghdad International Airport

BPP – base-plate patrols

blue on blue – friendly fire

bod – person

bomb-bursting – scattering quickly; moving off fast and with no clearly defined path

VBIED – vehicle-borne improvised explosive device

capitaine – captain

caporal – corporal

caporal chef – master corporal (no equivalent rank in British Army)

chef de corps – commanding officer

chef de group – section commander

chef de section – platoon commander

CAT – counter-attack team

CEA – *Compagnie d'Eclairage et d'Appui*; support company

chaff – heat flares fired from planes to head off heat-seeking missiles; these flares burn at a very high temperature once fired

CPA – Coalition Provisional Authority

CO – commanding officer

comms – communications

confirm weapons – to check that they fire and the sights are accurate (zeroed)

CSM – company sergeant major

cross load – to transfer personnel and/or material from one vehicle to another, quite often in the heat of battle, although it can equally apply when unloading from a broken-down vehicle not in a contact situation

dead ground – ground lost to observation due to undulating terrain

debussing – alighting from a vehicle

dicker – someone who discreetly watches/notes troop movements/timings/habits for use against them later in the form of attack

dicking – the act of a dicker

dissing – to show disrespect

DOD – department of defence

double-tapping – to fire two aimed rounds in quick succession

DZ – drop zone

ERV – emergency RV

EOD – bomb disposal

ETA – estimated time of arrival

exfiltration – the pre-planned withdrawal phase of an operation (infiltration being the pre-planned move in)

fill yer boots – to leave

first field dressing – bandage with ties for gunshot and other large wounds; NATO standard issue

first parade – checks undertaken by a vehicle's driver daily and/or prior to departure on missions, including lights, oil, water, tyres, toolkit, fuel, etc.

FOB – forward operational base

GI – US infantry soldier

go firm – occupy, secure and defend a strategic point/building/ location

IED – improvised explosive device

IPO – Iraqi Police Officer

int-rep – intelligence report

jacked – to have given up, thrown in the towel

KOSB – King's Own Scottish Borderers

lamping – catching/killing game with the use of a lamp

Legio Patria Nostra – The Legion is My Country; Foreign Legion motto

NCO – non-commissioned officer

oppo – battle partner, buddy, mucker, mate, *binome* (Foreign Legion)

ops room – operations room

OOB – out-of-bounds area

oulou – a large expanse of open land/desert/savannah/moorland/ wilderness

P file – personnel file

PAM – personnel/armament/material

pax – individuals

PKK – Kurdish guerilla organisation

PKM – type of machine gun

play the grey man – intentionally keep a low profile

PM – *Police Militaire*; French military police

PMC – private-military contractors

PSD – private-security detail

PX – NAAFI

QRF – quick-reaction force

RCT – Royal Corps of Transport (now amalgamated into the Royal Logistics Corps)

recce – reconnaissance mission

regs – regulations

REMF – rear-echelon mother fuckers

rebombed – reloaded

re-enactment case – someone who spends their weekends dressed up in bygone military uniforms and drives/admires the military transport of the past, often re-enacting battle scenes

RSM – regimental sergeant major

RV – rendezvous

RVs – rendezvous points

re-org – reorganisation

RPG – rocket-propelled grenade

sergent – sergeant

sergent chef – colour sergeant

shell-like – ear

side – pretence

sit-rep – situation report

smudges – slang term for oil paintings

SNCO – senior non-commissioned officer

sous officier – SNCO

sparrow's fart – early morning, before even the dawn chorus gets its act together

SOP – standard operating procedure

SAM – surface-to-air missile

TRM 4000 – France's equivalent to a Bedford four-tonne army truck

turn to – start work

one up the spout – a round (bullet) loaded into the chamber of a gun

up-armoured – to modify a vehicle with armour plating after acquisition

USACE – US Army Corps of Engineers

VAB – *vehicle avant blinde*; armoured troop-carrying vehicle, mounted with 12.7-mm gun

VCP – vehicle checkpoint

VDU – visual display unit

VLRA – large open-top Land Rover-type vehicle

WO1 – warrant officer